Perfect Motherhood

Perfect Motherhood

SCIENCE AND
CHILDREARING IN AMERICA

RIMA D. APPLE

Rutgers University Press

New Brunswick, New Jersey, and London

Library of Congress Cataloging-in-Publication Data

Apple, Rima D. (Rima Dombrow), 1944-
    Perfect motherhood : science and childrearing in America / Rima D. Apple.
      p. cm.
    Includes bibliographical references and index.
    ISBN-13: 978-0-8135-3793-1 (hardcover : alk. paper)
    ISBN-13: 978-0-8135-3843-3 (pbk. : alk. paper)
  1. Mothers—United States—History.   2. Motherhood—United States—History.
3. Physician and patient—United States—History.   I. Title.

HQ759.A58 2006
306.874'30973—dc22

                                        2005024943

A British Cataloging-in-Publication record for this book is available from the British Library.

Manufactured in the United States of America

To Alyssa Lee Cotton and Alexander Seth Apple,
who remind me every day that the more things change,
the more they stay the same

CONTENTS

ILLUSTRATIONS

ACKNOWLEDGMENTS

Perfect Motherhood has had a long gestation. During this extended period, I have been supported and encouraged by many friends and colleagues who joined me in my excitement about the history of motherhood in the United States and who often volunteered nuggets from their own experiences and the experiences of their friends and families. Invariably, when I mentioned my project at meetings, parties, dinners, basketball games, almost any social occasion, friends and even strangers would regale me with very personal stories, stories that enhanced my insights into the development of mothering practices and values in this country over the past century and more. Women would detail how they raised their children and how this differed from their mother's practices. Men, too, would often chime in with their observations about mothers. The glee with which people discussed the topic demonstrated the significance of the history of motherhood in our culture and continued to motivate me in writing this book. I am grateful for these accounts and am sorry that I cannot personally thank each informant. Colleagues were particularly generous with their time and expertise. Robert Bud, Harold Cook, Janet Golden, Gerda Lerner, Pamela Mack, Hilary Marland, Janet McCalman, Marion Nestle, Susan Reverby, Naomi Rogers, Michael Sokal, Nancy Tomes, John Warner, and Jani Westcott shared my enthusiasm countless times. I especially thank Angie Apple and Julie Worzala for their perceptive analyses of their own practices and those of their cohort.

My research was substantially enhanced through the efforts of many archivists. Most particularly, Susan Rishworth (formerly of the archives of the American College of Obstetricians and Gynecologists) and Toby Appel, Bumstead Librarian for Medical History, Yale University, made me welcome in their libraries and facilitated my work there. Joanne Passet's diligent search of periodicals and of the Wisconsin Historical Society Archives and her insights into women's history have added immeasurably to this study.

This project could not have been completed without the financial support of a National Library of Medicine Publication Grant, a Rockefeller Archive Center Grant-in-Aid, a Wellcome Research Travel Grant (Burroughs Wellcome Fund), University of Wisconsin–Madison Vilas Associateship, and an ACOG-Ortho Fellowship in the History of American Obstetrics and Gynecology (American College of Obstetricians and Gynecologists), which enabled me to conduct research in archives throughout the United States and in England. During the long gestation of this project, fellowships at the University of Melbourne and the Wellcome Institute for the History of Medicine (London) provided me the luxury of time with stimulating colleagues that afforded opportunities to develop my analysis. I am grateful for their assistance. Funding for my sabbatical from the University of Wisconsin–Madison Graduate School provided me with the time to complete the manuscript.

As with previous books, two people deserve extra special tribute: Michael Apple and Diane Mary Chase Worzala. Each has endured endless discussions about mothers in the past and in the present and each has never turned a deaf ear to yet another iteration of my analysis. Michael has always been there, with suggestions, with support. Diane has read every word of this book, some of them many, many times, and always given me the critical feedback that every writer needs and wants.

Two others warrant special note: Alyssa Lee Cotton and Alexander Seth Apple. As grandchildren, they keep me close to the issues of mothering and remind me daily about the everyday realities of nurturing and loving, of mothering children. I dedicate this book to them.

Perfect Motherhood

Introduction

REDEFINING MOTHERHOOD

*P*arenting today is virtually synonymous with worry. We want to ensure that our children are healthy—physically, mentally, and emotionally. In our worry, we keenly feel our shortcomings, our inability to know what is best for our children. When is it right to toilet train? Will early toilet training scar the child psychologically? How can we encourage a fussy child to eat? Should the child be allowed to decide which foods to eat? How significant is thumb sucking? How can we protect our child from disease and injury? Should we let our child cry herself to sleep? We are not alone with our worries. Nor are we without recourse. Health-care practitioners, psychologists, and other health professionals and social scientists are ready to advise us on how to provide the best parenting possible in today's world. Bookstores are flooded with titles such as *Nurturing Your Newborn: Young Parents' Guide to Baby's First Month*; *The Complete Parenting Book: Practical Help from Leading Experts*; *Becoming a Mother: From Birth to Six Months*; *Worried All the Time: Overparenting in an Age of Anxiety and How to Stop It*; and the ever popular *Dr. Spock's Baby and Child Care*. There are magazines devoted to giving us advice on childrearing, as well as numerous columns in newspapers and commentators on radio and television. Type "parenting" into Google on the internet and you get over 19 million hits; type in "child care" and you get over 70 million; with "mothering," you get about 948,000; with "motherhood," 2,550,000. While many of these sites offer suggestions from other parents based on their own experiences, many more sites—professional, personal, and commercial—employ the "latest" scientific and medical research findings to validate their claims for solutions to the problems of childrearing.

Scientific and medical advice is the hallmark of contemporary child-care practices. But this "scientific motherhood" is a relatively new phenomenon. For millennia, parents—and by parents here I mean *mothers*—were believed to know instinctually and with common sense how to raise their children, with the help of extended family and involved relations serving as role models. This practice gradually began to change in the mid-nineteenth century; and then with the advancements of the twentieth century—the so-called "century of the child"—this pattern was overthrown altogether. Instinct and tradition in childrearing were replaced by all-important medical and scientific advice. Parents, particularly mothers, clearly required the knowledge of experts in order to raise their families healthfully and appropriately, in order to be good mothers. Evidently parents agreed, as we have seen the sales of parenting literature and enrollment in parenting classes continue to expand throughout the century.

Scientific motherhood refined and redefined what it means to be a good mother, a proper mother. Throughout our history, motherhood has been considered a primary, if not *the* primary, role of women, a time-honored tradition in U.S. society, and most women did become mothers. But the foundation of appropriate mothering has shifted over the decades from a natural, inborn ability to care for children akin to maternal love into a skill that requires extensive training. The image of the educated mother now comes to the fore, the mother who utilizes modern science and medicine to inform her child-care practices, the mother who heeds the advice of experts. As one 1938 advertisement promised: "Add science to love and be 'a perfect mother.'"[1] Women increasingly allowed and even encouraged scientific and medical experts to intervene in their daily lives, to such an extent that even everyday childrearing tasks, such as bathing and dressing, became medicalized.

Perfect Motherhood traces the evolution of scientific motherhood, which is how we have defined motherhood in the United States since the mid-nineteenth century. It is a story with many actors: mothers, doctors, scientists, educators, social commentators. It is not a history of women's oppression, though in some eras mothers were considered to be less independent actors and more handmaidens of medical and scientific advisors. It is not the story of the power of maternal love, though women's emotional commitment to their children is certainly at its heart. It is not a story of continual medical progress, though with time medical and scientific research did disclose more healthful child-care practices. It is a story of women's search for the best child-care practices. It reveals women coping with the trials and tribulations of the daily grind of childrearing, as well as the trauma of illness. It documents the ways in which women accepted, rejected, and reshaped medical and scientific pronouncements in order to ensure the health and well-being of their children. *Perfect Motherhood* demonstrates mothers actively engaged in the transformation of women's roles and the development of modern motherhood in the United States.

*I*n the early nineteenth century, physicians in the U.S. were not the significant factors in health care that they are today, and they were virtually absent from child care. Most medical care was in fact given in the home, and it was the mother—not a doctor—who was the principal care giver. As the historian Charles Rosenberg notes: "The home was important in maintaining health as well as in treating disease. In generations unaware of the germ theory and of the nature and causation of disease generally, the maintenance of health was seen in aggregate—nonspecific—terms. Every aspect of life demanded scrutiny and control. Diet, exercise, air quality, and sleep all could, over time, bring about sickness or preserve health."[2] In seeing to her family's good health, a mother used what she had at hand. Sometimes it was a home medical book written by a physician. There were many available in this country, often reprints of books published in England, such as William Buchan's *Domestic Medicine*, though few of these manuals focused on child care. Perhaps she had some herbal remedies recommended by her mother or a neighbor. If she lived in an urban area, she could buy drugs suggested and prepared by a pharmacist. Most conditions were handled at home, as doctors were called in only for the very ill.

One such child-care manual available to women in the nineteenth century is *The Maternal Physician; A Treatise on the Nurture and Management of Infants, from the Birth until Two Years Old*, originally published in New York in 1811, with a second edition following out of Philadelphia in 1818. This was a ground-breaking publication: the first book on child care written and printed in the United States, and the first medical manual written and published in this country by a woman—the author being identified at the time as "an American matron."[3] Only recently have we learned that the author was Mary Hunt Palmer Tyler, who was well educated and from a politically involved family. She took seriously the ideal of "republican motherhood," that the mother's primary role in society was the nurturing and education of model citizens for the new country.[4]

When Tyler wrote the book, she was thirty-five years old and the mother of eight. Her motivation for writing was the child illness and death that surrounded her, which she blamed on uneducated, unaware mothers. She saw the robust health of her own children and believed that she had the wisdom that other women lacked. Thus she sought to educate other mothers from her extensive personal knowledge by writing a book that coupled the work of the "most approved medical authors" with her "sixteen years' experience in the nursery."[5] True, she would direct mothers to physicians "if your infants are really ill." Yet, on the whole Tyler insisted that a mother knew her child best and cared for her better than anyone else, even a physician. For her, like most women of the period, the mother was the primary care giver in the family.

Other maternal advice books of the period, typically written by men, paid less attention to the physical care of children and more to their "moral upbringing," a tradition dating back to the colonial period in this country.[6] Authors of these manuals gave women primacy in the home but considered that most mothers were in need of instruction if they were going to perform their duties well. In 1833, John S. C. Abbott wrote the widely read *The Mother at Home; or, The Principles of Maternal Duty*. He was most clear on this point, informing his readers that there were many books available for the concerned mother and warning that "many an anxious mother has committed errors to the serious injury of her children, which she might have avoided had she consulted the sources of information which are within reach of all."[7] Injury for Abbott encompassed more than the physical; it also included moral health.

By the 1840s, a different sort of book described a new ideal of motherhood; it was comparable to *The Maternal Physician* with its focus on the physical and health aspects of family life, yet comparable to *The Mother at Home* with its insistence on the need for expert advice in domestic tasks. In 1841, educator Catharine Beecher published *Treatise on Domestic Economy*, which was reprinted virtually every year until 1856. Beecher's biographer, Kathryn Kish Sklar, describes this book as "a scientific but personal guide to improved health and well-being."[8] For Beecher, woman reigned supreme in the domestic sphere, but she could and should learn from the rapidly developing technology and wondrous scientific discoveries of the period. Unlike Tyler, Beecher did not claim personal expertise in all the areas she wrote about, ranging from household maintenance and childrearing, to gardening, cooking, cleaning, and health care. She acknowledged the medical and scientific sources she used and implied that any woman could learn from them. In 1869, Beecher joined with her sister, author Harriet Beecher Stowe, to write *The American Woman's Home*, a household manual that attained similar popularity in the turbulent years following the Civil War, when women were faced with rapid advances in technology and increasingly available new consumer goods, such as canned foods, sewing machines, and wringer dryers.[9]

Both of these books were general housekeeping manuals, which included chapters on child care and childrearing, and both reveled in the authority of science. Beecher and Stowe did not expect that women would become scientists or doctors; they did, however, believe that women should embrace contemporary science and medicine and use them to inform all of their domestic tasks. With an understanding of the processes of physiology, chemistry, and biology, women could perform their domestic tasks as rational, logical professionals. Stowe, too, saw that scientific advice was intertwined with domestic advice in her women's magazine *Hearth and Home*. Discussing the menu for a dinner party, "Mrs. Kate Hunnibee" explained:

> I hesitated for a while between roast beef and baked chicken, but finally decided upon the poultry. According to some authorities, chicken is a little more nutritious than beef, while others claim for beef more heaviness; but chicken digests an hour sooner than beef, and is therefore not so heavy a diet, and I want Tom Slicer's wit and Fannie Blake's fine fancy to be no whit blurred by the good cheer on my mahogany. Cranberry sauce hasn't a bit of *food* in it save the sugar, but it helps the rest assimilate, and is the most delightful of tarts. The same may be said of apples and raisins. As for turnips, they are nearly all water, but their flavor is pleasant. The potato, macaroni, bread, butter, and tapioca will supply starch or carbon to make good the waste by respiration.[10]

"Hunnibee" was not a laboratory scientist, but she used contemporary understandings of nutrition and physiology to create a dinner party that was healthful and aesthetically pleasing.

In these publications Beecher and Stowe did not portray themselves as the source of all knowledge. For instance, in the section on child care in *The American Woman's Home*, the authors explicitly "fill[ed] this chapter chiefly with extracts from various medical writers. . . . Some are quoted verbatim, and some are abridged, from the most approved writers on this subject."[11] Moreover, they proudly noted that "some of the most distinguished physicians of New-York who have examined this chapter give their full approval of the advice given."[12] The ideal of the good mother, well informed on scientific and medical matters pertaining to her family's health, was firmly established.

Though the broad outlines of scientific motherhood were defined in the mid-nineteenth century, the ideal was not static. With continuous scientific discoveries and medical breakthroughs, the role of mother was subtly and consistently altered. Moreover, changing family size, growing industrialization and urbanization, and emerging technological innovation all served to transform life in the United States in the nineteenth and twentieth centuries, and maternal functions within it.

Among the significant factors affecting women's maternal roles were demographic shifts in the U.S. population that fostered a different view of motherhood and changed mothering practices. Just look, for instance, at family size. In 1800, the average number of children born to a white woman surviving to menopause was 7.04. By the turn of the twentieth century, this number had dropped to 3.56. By the end of the twentieth century, the average number of children per family was 1.86. This decline resulted from several interrelated and interacting forces. The United States moved from a primarily agricultural, rural country, to one based on an urban, industrial, and service-based economy, and consequently, children became more expensive. In the earlier period, children were an asset, working on the farm; they represented an economic benefit to the family. In the later period, it was expensive to maintain children in an urban environment, where mandatory education and cultural values kept them out of the workforce; in economic terms, they cost the family. The fertility decline also followed from increased availability of effective birth control and from growing numbers of women attaining education and entering the job market. In the same years, more women remained single and other women married later in life, which meant that individual women spent less time in childrearing. In addition, with smaller families, girls and women had less experience with younger siblings before they started their own families. With different family structures and other changes in the United States over time, many women found themselves raising families in situations quite unlike their mothers' eras, making the expertise of grandmothers less applicable.[13]

Since proponents of scientific motherhood based their advocacy on the critical role of contemporary science and medicine in successful mothering, the content of their advice changed with contemporary scientific and medical developments.[14] In the nineteenth century, much of the focus was on elements in the environment that could be controlled, namely, nutrition, cleanliness, good air. With the advent of the bacteriological revolution in the last three decades of the nineteenth century, attention switched to protection from infectious diseases, with increasing emphasis on fighting germs; at the same time, advisors used the new advances in nutrition to counsel mothers on the most healthful diets for their children, from infant foods and mother's milk substitutes, to the dangers of sugar and candy. In the first half of the twentieth century, with declining infant mortality and morbidity rates and with the development of immunizations, antibiotics, and the like, counselors' advice went beyond the physical health of children. They also discussed concerns for the behavior and the emotional and psychological health of the child, presenting a world of anxiety very different from that of previous generations. Now, doctors, psychologists, and other scientists created tables and standards of weight, height, and chronological milestones such as age of standing, of crawling, of talking, of reading, against which mothers could judge if their children were "normal."[15] But, regardless of the content of their advice, the books, magazines, newspaper columns, radio and television programs all agreed that mothers needed the help of medically and scientifically trained experts to raise their children.

The introduction of "modern" technological conveniences significantly transformed women's domestic tasks in the nineteenth and twentieth centuries. These changes served to distance women from the knowledge of previous generations. Take, for example, the impact of electricity. Once a home was "electrified," all sorts of domestic technology, encompassing vacuum cleaners, refrigerators, electric stoves, washing machines, electric wringers, and, later, dryers, slowly appeared in homes throughout the country. As with any new technology, the spread of electrification was uneven; electricity was first available in the more affluent late-nineteenth-century urban neighborhoods, only slowly entering rural areas, many as late as the 1930s and 1940s with the establishment of the Rural Electrification Agency. Something as common and simple as electric lighting was now available to the household at the flick of a switch. No longer did someone in the household, usually the housewife, need to carefully clean and trim the wicks of oil or kerosene lamps, to cautiously fill the lamps and then warily light them, all the while watching to avoid the possibility of a fire. This is not to say that household electricity simplified all domestic duties and made them easier. As historian Ruth Schwartz Cowan and others have shown, new was not necessarily easier.[16] It was, however, different, and different enough so that instructions handed down from generation to generation, from mother to daughter, were insufficient to cope with the realities of modern life. This reinforced the idea that women needed information from outside traditional female networks in order to succeed in the contemporary world. In the same way, women were encouraged to look beyond mothers, sisters, neighbors, and friends for direction in the modern ways of child care and childrearing.

Over time, developments in science, medicine, technology, education, and U.S. culture also changed the specific advice on child care, such as when to toilet train and how to bathe the infant. However, *Perfect Motherhood* is less interested in the details of this advice and the specifics of mothering practices than in the critical relationship between mothers and experts. Experts were typically, but not always, health-care practitioners. They were scientists, psychologists, teachers, public-health officers, and nurses. A myriad of counselors donned the mantle of science and medicine. Their label is not as important as their status and the rationale for their expertise: that contemporary science and medicine held the answers to healthful, appropriate child care.

Shifts in this relationship tell us much about the changing position of women in U.S. society over the past 150 years. Illustrated in the work of Catharine Beecher and Harriet Beecher Stowe, mid-nineteenth-century mothers were admonished to look to contemporary science and medicine for assistance in housekeeping and childrearing. According to this ideal, mothers were not expected to become experts in their own right, but rather to study relevant materials to aid them in making decisions about the health and welfare of their families. Beecher, Stowe, and their followers believed that intelligent women could and should evaluate for themselves the knowledge that was emerging around them in the period. They envisioned active women, typically middle-class women, women with agency, searching for the best means of raising their families. It was not just lay women who championed this engaged maternal role; physician-authored manuals, which were appearing in greater numbers in the second half of the nineteenth century, also typically spoke to an active, involved mother. During this era, few physicians focused on pediatric practice and fewer still considered themselves pediatric specialists.[17] Mothers were more likely to consult a home medical or child-care book than a physician when they sought out scientific and medical advice. The tradition of female networks of support remained vital during this period. However, the high rates of child mortality and morbidity motivated many mothers to find hope in the latest discoveries of modern science and medicine.

As education and literacy spread through the country in the nineteenth and twentieth centuries, the literature on child care and childrearing grew, with advice consistently informed by contemporary science and medicine.[18] The tone of this counsel slowly shifted. No longer were women depicted as capable of reading and evaluating this information for themselves. Now they are told that they need to follow the directions of experts. In other words, mothers were pictured as passive learners, taking their directions from experts. The expert was usually a male physician since at this time there were relatively few women physicians. It is in this period that we see the emergence of the patriarchal autocratic physician who insists that female patients must heed his every instruction. Along with gender relations, there was also an element of class relations in the spread of scientific motherhood. Slowly over these decades, women increasingly brought their children to physicians. Middle-class mothers with financial wherewithal and access took their children to private physicians; working-class mothers were more likely to attend clinics staffed by public-health physicians and nurses. In either case, the image of the "good" mother, the "proper" mother, was a woman who sought out experts for advice on childrearing and who followed the advice she was given.[19]

By the mid-twentieth century the position of the authoritarian physician was diminishing. The "natural childbirth" movement, as well as the women's movement, the civil rights movement, and the antiwar movement emboldened women to reject the patriarchal medical practitioner and to found organizations such as La Leche League and the Boston Women's Health Book Collective, whose objectives and methods were reminiscent of those advocated by Beecher and Stowe. This generation of women insisted that they were not passive learners sitting at the feet of scientific and medical experts. While upholding the critical role of contemporary science and medicine in the shaping of healthful and appropriate child care, they also insisted that they could and should investigate and evaluate such information for themselves. They affirmed their active position in decisions about their families' health.

In this scenario, women should not be seen as "victims" of a medicalized model that enabled medical and scientific experts to manipulate mothers and that encouraged the imposition of medical and scientific expertise on women in their everyday lives. In some instances we could interpret mothers' actions through a lens of victimization, but to do so ignores the very real material and emotional conditions under which women decided how to take care of their children.[20] We must look beyond any clearly articulated rejection of scientific motherhood, or the eager embrace of its practices, in order to examine how women selected what they chose to apply in their daily lives and to understand the beliefs and values that shaped everyday life.

My discussions of the specifics of child care, say, feeding or bathing, are used to illustrate the increasing acceptance of the crucial role of science and medicine and the shifting power relationships between mothers and experts. I focus primarily on infant-care advice because it is with infants that new mothers, especially inexperienced mothers, are most impressionable. The habits that they develop in the early months, or even early weeks, often continue through the child's later years. Physicians were cognizant of this connection. By the twentieth century, medical practitioners consciously cultivated mothers of young children, mindful that a grateful mother of an infant would continue to look to them for medical care and advice in later years and with other family members, and would tell her friends about her experiences. Early in the century, Dr. W. Nicholas Lackey, practicing in Gallatin, Tennessee, explained that work with infants was a vital element of general medical practice, especially in the rural areas of the United States, noting that "for a young man beginning his professional career a knowledge of pediatric work will create a reputation and give a foothold in establishing a practice as soon as anything I know. For one woman whose baby's life he has saved will give him more advertisements in the community than a full page ad in his county paper."[21] But it was not just the economic argument from physicians, or even physicians' admonitions alone, that changed motherhood in the United States. Mothers themselves often embraced these changes in what they believed was the best interest of their children.

As *Perfect Motherhood* documents, these changes did not affect all women at the same time or at the same pace. The dominant ideology of motherhood, scientific motherhood, can be identified in the written records of professionals and in popular culture. But the history of motherhood in the United States is much more than this abstraction. It is the lived experiences of women, experiences that were shaped in reaction to and interacting with the dominant ideology that was present in their society and their culture. Scientific motherhood is a world view; it does not define mothers' options, but does frame them. Due to accidents of geography, financial ability, literacy rates, unique racial and ethnic traditions, and the like, some groups had access to experts and to expertise earlier than others. Some women were in a position to avail themselves of the benefits of modern science and medicine immediately, while others were too distant, too disadvantaged, or too uninterested to profit from them. Some resisted changes longer than others; some embraced changes without any delay. What is clear, however, is the trajectory of scientific motherhood over the past 150 years: mothers increasingly and willingly accepted the crucial role of contemporary science and medicine in child care and childrearing. They came to expect that medical and scientific experts and expertise should intervene in their daily lives, helping them in all areas of child care, from mundane tasks to critical illness.[22]

CHAPTER 1

"Follow the lead of physicians"

MOTHERHOOD IN THE LATE NINETEENTH CENTURY

*N*arcissa Prentiss Whitman lived in the Oregon territory with her missionary husband. In October 1844, she became the adoptive mother of seven children orphaned when their parents died on the Oregon Trail. The children ranged in age from thirteen years to five months. The infant, Henrietta Naomi Sager, was particularly ill: "arriv[ing] here in the hands of an old filthy woman, sick, emaciated and but just alive . . . had suffered for the want of proper nourishment until she was nearly starved . . . a poor distressed little object, not larger than a babe three weeks old." Whitman's husband was reluctant to accept the infant because of her health, but Whitman insisted. Over the next year, Whitman carefully nurtured Henrietta, washing her in tepid water every day and feeding her milk, often diluted with water to make it more digestible. By May 1846, the child was "strong, healthy, fleshy, heavy, runs any where she is permitted."

Whitman confided to her sister that "I used to think mother was the best hand to take care of babies I ever saw, but I believe, or we have the vanity to think, we have improved upon her plan." One improvement was the addition of the children's daily bath, which she commended to her sister, also explaining that she carefully controlled the children's diet. Such caution, she concluded, "saves many a doctor bill." When the children complained of a headache or a stomach ache, Whitman rarely used medicines or called a physician. She and her husband believed that such problems resulted from eating too much. Instead of dosing the children, she sent them to bed without supper and "they are sure to get up very soon feeling as well as ever." Whitman rarely specified the source of her ideas about infant and child care except to say that many came from her mother, whom she praised effusively.

Letters written by Whitman and other mothers like her portray a writer who is an independent, self-directed care giver, and who is dismissive of medical practitioners, particularly those who were too quick to prescribe drugs.[1]

The blare of medical and scientific counsel written by male medical and scientific professionals has obscured voices of women such as Whitman, but it does not mean that mothers were silent or that they passively deferred to this medically sanctioned counsel. Mothers balanced positive and negative personal experiences with advice from a multitude of sources. Some mothers were like Mary Palmer Tyler: they exuded great confidence in their own abilities, regardless of the advice of others, and they instructed others based on their experiences. Some followed the direction of Catharine Beecher, reading widely and basing their practices on contemporary science. Others preferred routines determined by family, ethnic, and racial custom. Over the nineteenth century and into the twentieth, however, a new consensus slowly emerged from this conglomeration of maternal practices: increasingly women turned to health-care practitioners for advice on all aspects of infant and child care, physical and emotional.[2]

After the publication of *The Maternal Physician* and the *Treatise on Domestic Economy*, physicians, typically male physicians, dominated the field of published child-care advice. Typical of physician-authored books was Dr. John D. West's popular *Maidenhood and Motherhood; or, Ten Phases of Woman's Life*, published in 1888.[3] His directions for infant bathing illustrate the basic tenets of nineteenth-century scientific motherhood. There are two and a half pages of detailed commentary on the importance of bathing. Before his description of bathing an infant in "tepid" water, he informed the reader: "The skin is extremely delicate, sensitive, and easily injured. Moreover, from it there is a constant exudation of waste matter in the form of perspiration. This perspired fluid holds in solution atoms of worn-out animal matter and saline substances. There is, also, a discharge, through the pores of the cuticle, of an oil substance, the purpose of which is to keep the skin-surface soft and pliable, as well as to protect it from injury." West noted that infant bathing was a controversial topic: some "authorities" recommend the use of soap; others reject it. After presenting the reasons, pro and con, West concluded: "A middle course is still better. The saline particles are readily soluble in water alone; so far as their removal is concerned, soap is unnecessary. When, however, the accumulation of the oil substance is such that its removal is desirable, soap is necessary. This form of secretion is insoluble in water, but readily so in soap."[4] In these few pages, the doctor turned a common, everyday maternal task into a medical procedure and, in doing so, he

FIGURE 1.1. Baby's bath. *Source:* Mary R. Melendy, M.D., *Perfect Womanhood for Maidens—Wives—Mothers* (K. T. Boland, 1901), 224.

engaged the intellect of the mother. In effect, he was asking her to understand the theory behind his infant bathing instructions, and expecting that she would agree with him. Whether mothers studied or even cared about the theory is less critical than the fact that West's rhetoric demonstrates physicians' expectations. Doctors assumed that mothers would not follow medical instruction blindly; they needed to see a rationale behind it, even if they did not study it.

As the example of infant bathing shows, physicians were among the most vocal proponents of scientific motherhood. Though doctors were not the first, nor the only, champions of scientific motherhood, their pronouncements became the foundation of the ideology. Their publications, especially those addressed to mothers, reflected both the tenets of scientific motherhood and the environment in which they were written; they provide a window for studying the idealization of motherhood over time. As Dr. John Brisben Walker queried in his article "Motherhood as a Profession" in the magazine *Cosmopolitan* in 1898: "Why should not the members of that profession [motherhood] which embraces so large a number of the human race be forced

FIGURE 1.2. Night-drawers with closed feet. "The night-dress of children who have ceased to wear baby clothes consists of a merino shirt, of thickness varying with the season, and of night-drawers which are of Canton flannel in winter and muslin in summer." *Source:* J. P. Crozer Griffith, M.D., *The Care of the Baby,* 2nd ed. (Philadelphia: W. B. Saunders, 1899), 107.

to recognize that in taking charge of human lives they must do so knowingly and must adapt themselves by a study of the scientific principles affecting the requirements of their life works?"[5] Regardless of whether their audience was medical or nonmedical, physician-authored books, pamphlets, and articles consistently and adamantly insisted that mothers left alone were incapable of raising their children healthfully.

From the mid-nineteenth century onwards, doctors published increasing numbers of child-care manuals to promote their child-care advice, popularizing the belief that women needed professional medically and scientifically based instruction. Developments in printing technology made these publications less and less expensive through the century, cheaper to produce and cheaper to buy. Moreover, with the spread of public education in the United States, there was an increasing audience for these books, which covered everything from infant feeding and bathing to clothes, diapers, and furniture, to behavioral issues, such as thumb sucking, bed wetting, and habit formation. In essence, these physicians were medicalizing mundane and common tasks of women's daily child care. Many of these books were widely reviewed in medical journals, general women's magazines, and child-care magazines, the number of which was also rapidly expanding in the second half of the nineteenth century. By the end of the century the general literate audience was quite familiar with physician-authored magazine columns that provided mothers with descriptions of physician-directed child care. The practice of regularly scheduled medical examinations for well children did not develop until the mid-twentieth century, even for better-off and middle-class families; in the meantime, these magazines offered women a way to benefit from the expertise of physicians by encouraging distraught mothers to send in questions that the doctors answered in subsequent columns.

Both books and magazines assumed that their readers were middle-class mothers with the resources to carry out the instructions they received. Other literature directed toward working-class and immigrant mothers echoed the call for the medical supervision of children. Abraham Jacobi, considered the father of American pediatrics, developed his popular "Rules of the management of infants during the summer months," which was widely distributed to mothers in poorer areas of New York City from the late 1860s through the 1880s. In this he reminded mothers to trust doctors and not neighbor women because "they do not know better than you do yourself."[6] All these publications based their advice on contemporary medical and scientific knowledge and, at the same time, extolled the role of the medical practitioner in infant and child care.

This literature often elided medicine and medical practice with emerging science; doctors were pictured as the epitome of modern science and modern science was the road to good health.[7] Take, for example, germs.[8] From the discovery of these micro-organisms and their role in disease causation in the late nineteenth century, physicians admonished mothers to protect their children from germs. Parents were heartened in the 1890s with the development of the diphtheria anti-toxin and later the diphtheria toxin-anti-toxin, immunization for that fearful disease, which took the lives of many, many children each year But the germ theory could also lead to advice on more prosaic matters; physicians often explained that mothers should not kiss their children because diseases such as diphtheria, tuberculosis, and syphilis could be spread by kissing.[9]

Infant feeding was another area in which doctors claimed scientific expertise. High infant mortality and morbidity statistics were causally and dramatically linked with problems of infant nutrition. A more complex understanding of the physiology of nutrition and the action of newly discovered micronutrients began to appear in books and the popular press in the nineteenth century. These pronouncements supported doctors' contentions that they had special knowledge, knowledge that could insure the health and well-being of infants.[10] Mothers were warned of the dangers of feeding their infants without medical supervision and advised that "haphazard infant feeding by mothers and nurses should be entirely done away with." Instead mothers "must learn that they are ordinarily in no position to decide for themselves upon so important a question, and they should gladly follow the lead of physicians who are making constant efforts to put these matters on a safe and scientific basis. . . . Too much stress cannot be laid upon the necessity in infant feeding for mothers to consult physicians."[11]

The details of physician advice changed with emerging scientific and medical developments as well as commercial innovations, such as disposable diapers and artificial infant foods. Scientific research in the early twentieth century slowly led to an understanding and subsequent treatment of nutritional deficiency diseases, such as rickets and scurvy, conditions which had haunted parents of the earlier period. Developments such as these in bacteriology, nutrition, and physiology heightened public awareness of the potential, if not always the reality, of the benefits of modern science and medicine.[12]

Through much of the nineteenth century, physician-authors, like much of their culture, idealized womanhood and especially motherhood. Some physicians in the early period even acknowledged that they too, like mothers, learned from experiences in child care, perhaps answering critics like *The Maternal Physician*. Dr. Stephen Tracy in his 1853 *The Mother and Her Offspring* praises the young mother for understanding the responsibilities of motherhood and for accepting that she knows very little about how to carry them out successfully. He notes: "Young married women are usually fully aware that many of the duties and responsibilities incident to their new social relations are of the *first* importance, and are also oftentimes painfully conscious of the most entire ignorance in regard to many important subjects connected with them."[13] Don't worry, he comforts her; with his book she will be successful because his "aim is to give such instruction to mothers as shall enable them, by proper and judicious management, to *secure* to themselves and their offspring the greatest possible exemption from pain and disease, and the possession of the most robust and vigorous health of which their respective constitutions will admit."[14] Why his book? Of course he is a physician, but more than that: "In the preparation of the work, the knowledge obtained by fifteen years of parental experience and the care of six children, has not been useless."[15]

Dr. Jerome Walker too informed the mother of her shortcomings but then reassured her. His advice was disguised as a novel, *The First Baby: His Trials and the Trials of His Parents* (1881), in which he warned readers: "My friend, experience in the ways and management of children is the guide to proper care, but it is not expected that parents with their first children will have much of this commodity, yet with 'common sense,' it can be acquired."[16] Girls and boys, women and men, were not taught the basics of physiology and hygiene and consequently "there are many young people who marry, as utterly ignorant of the proper care of a baby." It is for them that he wrote his book, the result of his experiences as a father and as a physician in private practice and institutions.[17] For Tracy and Walker, as for Tyler decades earlier, experience was an important teacher, but now it is experience filtered through the lens of the medical practitioner.

Nineteenth-century manuals assumed that mothers needed scientific and medical advice for healthful childrearing, but it was advice at a distance, advice women could read about and follow. The physical presence of a physician was not necessary in these scenarios, except in cases of illness. With a sick baby the picture changed. With ill children, the mother and the physician played different but complementary roles and the mother was cautioned not to overstep her position. As Dr. Edward Parker warned in *The Handbook for Mothers: A Guide in the Care of Young Children* (1880): "My intention has been . . . to give to the mother just that information which she needs as a mother, and not that which will make her believe that she can do without the services of a physician when her child is sick. A smattering of medical knowledge, is an especially dangerous thing."[18] Yes, mothers needed to be educated in mothercraft, but not too much. Too much education, these physicians feared, could lead a woman to think that she did not need a doctor, which could be physically unhealthy for the child and financially unhealthy for the physician.

From the late nineteenth century onward, doctors earnestly guided mothers into the medical arena, arguing that women needed to be taught the importance of the medical direction in child care and, moreover, blaming mothers for the high rates of infant and child morbidity and mortality. They painted stark pictures of the disasters that mothers would experience if they relied on their own wits rather than medical advice. One physician warned in 1887: "How many mothers undertake the responsible management of children without previous instruction, or without forethought; they undertake it as though it may be learned either by intuition, by instinct, or by affection. This consequence is that frequently they are in a sea of trouble and uncertainty, tossing about without rule or compass; until, too often, their hopes and treasures are shipwrecked and lost."[19] There was hope, of course, when the mother was educated to seek the counsel of physicians. And educated to understand the directions that her doctor gave her.

Over the years, physicians' views of mothers underwent dramatic shifts that justified to them an increasingly authoritarian attitude and greater intervention into everyday life by the early twentieth century. By the end of the century, physicians were generally expressing greater concern about mothers' abilities to take care of their children in an appropriate and healthful way. Their anxiety translated into a denigration of women's knowledge and competence and a concomitant elevation of the physician's role in child care as doctors took on the cloak of authority reinforced by the growing power of the medical profession. The widely published Dr. J. P. Crozer Griffith announced: "It seems often to be taken for granted that the young mother will understand by a sort of intuition the care which her baby requires as though it needed no more than a new born animal of some lower order of life. The fact is such a little animal, slight though its needs are when compared with those of a baby, has a parent which by instinct is far better able to care for it than the human mother for her child."[20] Despite this denunciation of maternal knowledge, Griffith did not dismiss mothers' abilities out of hand. Mothers should use his book, he explained, to recognize their limitations. Careful reading of his *Care of the Baby* would enable a mother to "understand what she can do without medical advice and how she shall do it; when she shall call a physician to her aid, and what she shall do before he comes."[21]

Writers anticipated that mothers would use their books and articles to answer common problems, calling on the physician only in cases of illness. This expectation was most evident before the concept of well-baby visits and schedules of immunization, which became common in the twentieth century. Accordingly, the doctor's column in *Home Science* in 1904 admitted that though sometimes the observation of the family doctor was needed, other times "mothers may be so situated that it is difficult for them to get to their family physician, or the matter may seem to them too trifling for his attention."[22] The columnist noted the "family physician," a general practitioner.

Another rationale for physician-authored literature was the particular knowledge of the specialist. Almost invariably, those writing for the general public, whether or not they took on the label of pediatrician, claimed special knowledge based on intimate experience with children. Though pediatrics emerged as a medical specialty in the 1880s, relatively few physicians took this title. Instead, the vast number of doctors treating children were general practitioners, not pediatricians. If the mother wanted advice from an expert, though an expert who would not observe her child directly, she could utilize one of the many published sources.

Mothers learned to depend on physicians and health-care providers. Slowly, they abandoned traditional methods and family models for scientific and medical expertise and adopted the "modern" practices so highly touted by contemporary counselors. Over the nineteenth century, mothers' everyday tasks increasingly reflected the ideology of scientific motherhood and maternal practices mirrored the advice of experts. In order to learn what women were thinking and doing in the privacy of their own homes, we need to look beyond the advice literature.[23] We need to find the words of mothers themselves, words found in contemporary magazines, such as *Babyhood* and *Ladies' Home Journal,* and in personal writings, such as diaries and letters.

Throughout much of the century, the rate of literacy among women in the United States rose with the expansion of the public education system. In 1870, less than half of the school-aged population, those between the ages of five and nineteen, were enrolled in educational institutions, 48.4 percent. The rate differed dramatically by race and by sex. In that year, 52.7 percent of "white" females and only 10 percent of girls of the "Negro and other races" attended school. The statistics show a fluctuating rate over the next several decades, but by 1910, the figure had grown to 61.3 percent for white females and 46.6 percent for the others. Similarly, in 1870, only 2 percent of the U.S. population 17 years of age graduated from high school; by 1910, this number stood at 8.6 percent. Even more telling is the precipitous decline in the illiteracy rates in these same years.[24] In 1870, one-fifth of the U.S. population was counted as illiterate: among "White," 11.5 percent; among "Negro and other," 79.9 percent. By 1910, the figures were cut by more than half to 7.7 percent among the overall U.S. population, to 5.0 percent for "White"; to 30.5 percent for "Negro and other."[25] We do not have these figures broken down by sex, but since in this period girls graduated from high school in significantly greater numbers than boys, we can safely assume that the illiteracy figures are reasonable for women as well as the total population.

Literate women experiencing motherhood have left us evidence of their hopes and fears, and of their mothering practices in private diaries and letters. At the same time, the number of women's magazines expanded, providing a forum in which women could exchange ideas beyond their geographical communities. Many mothers felt inspired to share their experiences in these arenas, writing to the growing numbers of magazines available to them. We must be careful about generalizing from these sources. The women's voices

FIGURE 1.3. Cover of *Babyhood*, 1885.

we hear are a cross-section of mothers in the country, with some critical limitations. The writers are, obviously, literate women and, even with the expansion of public education, not all women were literate. Literacy was highest among Euro-American women of the middle and upper classes. Beyond the question of literacy, many women in the period lacked access to advice books and magazines; many more lacked access to medical practitioners. For instance, huge distances and the existence of few local physicians limited opportunities for mothers in rural areas and on the frontiers of the country. Even in growing urban areas, mothers without financial resources, immigrant mothers who spoke a different language, working-class mothers balancing work and family responsibilities, African American mothers facing slavery and racial discrimination, all coped with different limitations. Mothers' experiences drawn from magazines, diaries, and letters do not exemplify all mothers in the nineteenth century, but rather illustrate the range of conditions and responses of mothers in the time period.

In using the letters and articles published by mothers in contemporary magazines, there is another caution that should be kept in mind.[26] Editors undoubtedly exerted significant control over what was printed in their magazines. We do not know what proportion of submitted letters was published. We do not know to what extent, if at all, editors rewrote letters before they were published. It is even possible that some of the letters were written by the editors themselves. Only when we can identify the writer can we know with any certainty about any individual letter. However, the similarity across journals and across private and public writings indicates that the letters and articles are representative. Women were proud of their role as mother; and they believed they retained a pivotal role in family, particularly child, health matters. It is also clear that over the period they more and more frequently looked to medical authorities for direction in these areas. By the early years of the twentieth century, mothers accepted and expected the counsel of health-care practitioners when their children were healthy as well as when they were ill, and medical and scientific experts increasingly intervened in the domestic, everyday affairs of families.

Mothers wrote as lyrically about their role in the family as the prescriptive advice books and magazine articles of the nineteenth century. In the popular journal *Babyhood* in 1886, Lucy White Palmer expressed the sentiment of many when she defined motherhood as "the crown and glory of a woman's life." This lyricism gently covered an undertone of worry and fear because with that honor came the "pain and care which so often seem to be woman's peculiar burden." Nonetheless, Palmer considered motherhood "the highest honor and noblest profession possible to woman," despite all the hardships, including "so much less sleep, so much more anxiety; [*sic*] so much less time for the graces of life, so much more careful counting of the pennies."[27] Others added to this dire list the alarming infant and child mortality rate, which was an ever present reality in the nineteenth century—a harsh reality for which the mother was critically responsible—she was responsible for her children's physical welfare as well as their future moral and mental development. Still, as Ada E. Hazell reminded readers of the *Ladies' Home Journal* a few years later, the "true mother" will be amply repaid for her efforts.[28] The life of a caring, dedicated mother was not easy, but the result—a healthy, happy child—was well worth the effort.

In contrast to the proponents of scientific motherhood, some women believed that motherhood brought with it the intuitive knowledge needed to protect the child. As late as 1888 in *Ladies' Home Journal,* "Jack's Wife" claimed that motherhood endowed a woman with a "sixth sense which God vouchsafes *because of the babe.*" In her eyes, this powerful gift vanquishes "known poor judgement in other matters" and makes the mother the superior care giver for her child.[29] Despite the ardor with which she expressed her views, "Jack's Wife" represented a minority opinion among mothers as this idea of innate maternal knowledge slowly lost favor through the century.

More often as the century progressed, mothers decried the hazards of undisciplined mother love and advanced the need to train women for their role as mother. Many, such as Lucy White Palmer, defined motherhood as a profession. Echoing calls taken for granted in medical and scientific advice literature, mothers themselves asserted that women needed direction and training from recognized experts in infant and child care. "Frau Bertha," a frequent correspondent in the columns of *Babyhood* in the 1880s, pitied the fond, but inexperienced and anxious mother. Such a mother was in urgent need of advice, but how shall she judge between bad and good advice? asked Frau Bertha. Her answer, "By constant reading and study of such literature as bears on the mother's profession." Drawing a comparison with medicine, she explained: "Profession it is, the noblest open to women. We would, none of us, think of employing a physician who did not keep himself posted in all the scientific research of his school. Morally and physically can we dare do less than we demand from our medical adviser?"[30]

What did "the profession of motherhood" mean to women in the nineteenth century? In the first place, it was a rejection of the idea that women, as women, had unique and instinctive knowledge of things maternal, "Jack's Wife" notwithstanding. Some even claimed that an untrained mother was a danger to her child. Secondly, the professionalization of motherhood was defined as actively learning from others, from experts. Helen Watterson Moody, writing in the *Ladies' Home Journal* in 1899, equated motherhood with "enlightened knowledge conscientiously acquired and carefully digested."[31] By the turn of the century, mothers encouraged other caring and thoughtful mothers to look outside their homes, outside their own experiences, for authoritative direction in child care. Whether mothers used the distinctive phrase "profession of motherhood" or preferred "trained motherhood" or "modern motherhood" or "scientific motherhood," their phraseology advanced the belief that women need assistance in raising their families healthfully and they expected that this assistance would be in the form of medical and scientific expertise.

While women's comments about maternal practices, their promotion of the profession of motherhood, and most specifically their growing acceptance of medical and scientific authority mirrored much of the advice literature of the period, mothers' writings differed from advice books and articles in one very significant aspect. The manuals and articles commonly posited one standard of mothering practices. They expected that conscientious mothers would read the published advice and diligently follow its recommendations. Moreover, in instances of critical health problems where medical assistance was required, these publications assumed physicians were readily available. Of course, the reality of mothers' lives was rarely that simple and maternal practices were much more heterogeneous. The extent to which mothers used medical and scientific advice varied depending on an individual's circumstances and was shaped by her location; financial conditions; family, ethnic, and racial identity; and the like. Thus, the growing reliance on professional health-care advisors did not proceed uniformly over the century or across the country. For many decades, advice continued to come from many sources, medical practitioners being only one.

Physicians and others who published child-care advice often railed against such other sources as interfering neighbors, friends, and relatives. They warned that the advice of such laypersons was at best misleading and at worst harmful. But these nonprofessional advisors appear often in the historical record, offering both solicited and unsolicited advice. On the Kansas frontier, Rosie Ise found herself with an overabundance of breast milk. A neighbor suggested that she heat a bottle and hold the opening to her breast. As the bottle cooled, the vacuum would draw out the surplus milk. In following the recommendation, unfortunately, Ise applied too hot a bottle to her breast and consequently burned her nipples and was unable to continue nursing her child. As her child grew weaker, she desperately appealed to neighbors for help. In this case, despite the numerous suggestions from neighbors, the child died.[32]

Rather than rejecting nonprofessional guidance out of hand, mothers often appreciated this advice, especially when it coincided with that of medical advisors. Millicent Washburn Shinn, close observer of her niece Ruth, was pleased to report that "our baby did not suffer from thirst, for grandma, nurse, and the good doctor had all entered early warning that 'babies need water,' and that many a baby was treated for colic, insomnia, nervousness, and natural depravity, when all the poor little fellow wanted was a spoonful of cool water."[33] Some mothers were grateful for neighborly suggestions and other women resisted. "H." of Brooklyn, New York, complained to *Babyhood* that her friends insisted that "nearly all of my Baby's ill-feelings are caused by 'worms,' and say, give her salt, pumpkin-seeds, and, worst of all, that awful castor-oil," a remedy often suggested by physicians. Her mother had never used castor oil with three babies, and she refused to subject her daughter to the medicine.[34] Neighbors, grandma, nurse, physician: clearly there was no consensus on who held the authority in infant and child care.

Another common source of information was a nurse. Typically in the nineteenth century, upper-class and middle-class women birthed at home and stayed in bed for two weeks or more following a birth.[35] During this lying-in period, the infant was cared for by a woman hired especially for this purpose, the monthly nurse. These women were rarely formally trained nurses. Nurse training was only beginning in the late nineteenth century in the United States, and nurse registration does not appear until the twentieth century. A knowledgeable monthly nurse was a boon and a practical expert, while an unskilled one, a nightmare. "S." had six children who experienced severe colic. With the seventh infant, she had a nurse who introduced her to the use of glycerine; she mixed "one teaspoonful into three of warm water administered enough to keep the little new baby from all worrying and crying." "S." was delighted to report that with this treatment "the baby seemed soothed and comforted."[36] This was the sort of knowledge that a capable nurse provided.

Not every mother was pleased with her nurse. In 1871, Harriet Blaine of Philadelphia wrote in desperation from her post-partum bed: "The only other room occupant is a dreadful trial to me. I call her everything I can think of—Goody, a Witch, a Crone, an Old Hag, a Circe, a Fateful Sister; in fact, she is only a nurse, but if you will transpose the *n* into a *c* you will hit her character much better. I have had seven children, but I never longed before with all my heart to be well enough to wait on myself."[37] Others complained that under the nurse's care, infants became colicky or were overfed or underfed; basically the nurse was incompetent. "A true lover of babies," of New Bedford, Massachusetts, faced just such a situation. She was chagrined to learn that her first nurse maintained that "breathing fresh air gave babies the colic."[38] Though these and other mothers faced problems with their nurses, many new mothers were sorry if they could not afford nurses to help in the first few weeks.[39] They felt inadequate and looked to nurses and others to teach them about child care.

These mothers' experiences indicate that not only was there no one authoritative source for information on child care in the nineteenth century, but also that women could and did choose from a variety of sources depending on their apparent success and as their circumstances changed. Ise reached out to many neighbors and friends for advice in a time of need. Whitman looked to her own mother's practices as a model, which she modified according to her experience. Julia Carpenter Gage, in the Dakota territory, utilized a similar range for help with her son James Lucien, born in 1888. Because Jamie was sickly, Gage went through a raft of different foods that were suggested by her nurse, a wet nurse, and at least three doctors, whom she visited by train.[40] The 1850s journal of Mary Ann Owen Sims, of Arkansas, documents a similar variety of practices: sometimes a medical practitioner, sometimes remedies from her pantry, such as calomel.[41]

These personal sources—friends, relatives, nurses, even physicians—were not unique to the nineteenth century; they were a continuation of long-standing traditional avenues for maternal instruction. However, at this time and within this hodge-podge of advice, a new perspective appeared: calls for scientific, trained motherhood, which insisted that women learn healthful, modern child-care practices from contemporary experts. Increasingly, women were expected and did expect to look beyond their personal situation to seek information from a wider variety of sources, especially science-based sources. At the same time, medical and scientific investigations brought news of the unseen world of microbes and the wondrous effects of newly developed vaccines on physical health and of the significance of microscopic nutrients in a healthful diet, news that inspired the public to look to scientists and physicians for solutions to the problems of illness. Concerned, caring mothers looked particularly to medical practitioners for direction in child care.

The reformer Elizabeth Cady Stanton was perhaps the most well known of these nineteenth-century maternal proponents of scientific motherhood. She considered it shocking how little motherhood education women received: "If we buy a plant of a horticulturist we ask him many questions as to its needs, whether it thrives best in sunshine or shade, whether it needs much or little water, what degrees of heat or cold; but when we hold in our arms for the first time, a being of infinite possibilities, in whose wisdom may rest the destiny of a nation, we take it for granted that the laws governing its life, health, and happiness are intuitively understood, that there is nothing new to be learned in regard to it."[42] Stanton revealed in her autobiography that she was nervous and concerned upon the birth of her first child because all around her she saw pale and sickly children. "Having gone through the ordeal of bearing a child, I was determined, if possible to keep him, so I read everything I could find on the subject," she recalled, only to be confused and further worried. She felt fortunate, however, for "one powerful ray of light [that] illuminated the darkness; it was the work of Andrew Combe on 'Infancy.'"[43]

It is not surprising that Stanton recommended a book for women seek-ing enlightenment. Literate women throughout the century had sought ma-ternal guidance from books.[44] As we have seen, both medical practitioners and laypersons produced numerous publications in the nineteenth century. Without sales statistics, which are lacking for the period, we can only esti-mate their popularity. We do see frequent mention of these books in women's writings, especially letters and articles in contemporary magazines. These ref-erences document a general familiarity with published advice. Yet, books were but one source available in the nineteenth century for the inquisitive mother. And, by the end of the century, women turned increasingly to other forms of maternal education.

Mothers' clubs were one such forum for maternal education. In the first half of the nineteenth century, these groups had tended to focus on children's moral and religious education, discussing pedagogical articles in religious and early mothers' magazines. For example, Elizabeth Smith noted in her diary for 24 February 1841, "In the afternoon attended the Maternal meeting the subject discussed an interesting one self denial in our children."[45] Over the century, the structure and scope of these grass-roots organizations changed, moving from concerns with mortality and religious training to the ideals of scientific motherhood. For one thing, the meetings centered on presentations either by professionals, such as physicians, or by experienced mothers. For another, the topics focused more on the pragmatics of child care, particularly physical care.

In a sense, mothers' clubs represent a bridge between traditional infor-mation sources, sister-sister advice, and the modern expert, advice from medi-cal practitioners. L. McD. of Des Moines, Iowa, was particularly impressed with the exchange of tried and true ideas at the meeting of one club in the Midwest: "One lady spoke of a home-made medicine chest, while another described an improvised bathtub and a third one gave an interesting account of the home-made toys, including some simple scientific apparatus, that she and her husband always made it a point to provide their children."[46] The meet-ings of the Lowell House Mothers' Club were typical of the turn of the cen-tury. They included a lecture on 13 January 1903 by a Dr. Teele, who spoke on the diet of children and was asked by another member of the club about the cure for constipation. Declaring that the condition resulted from a lack of bowel muscle tone, she recommended soap suppositories for children and a diet rich in grapes, figs, and apples for adults. A few months later, on 10 March, the speaker was Mrs. Charlie Morris, another member, who stressed the importance of fresh air, cleanliness, and regularity in feeding. She also recommended a cure for colic: the mother should place a hot-water bottle filled with warm water on her lap, lay the baby stomach down on the hot-water bottle and rub its back; "in a few minutes," she reported, "the child is relieved."[47]

Beyond these face-to-face forums, general women's magazines and journals specializing in infant and child care, as well as home-health columns in other periodicals, reaffirmed and extended the ideology of scientific motherhood. Like the mothers' clubs, over time these publications served to replace traditional sisterly advice. Mothers wrote lengthy, detailed letters and articles in which they explained their problems and described their practices and they reached out to find answers to their questions and to provide answers to others. Such detail provides us with unique insights into the lives of women of the period. Mrs. J. M. Mulligan's story, published in one of the many nineteenth-century magazines geared to agricultural communities around the country, demonstrates how mothers unburdened themselves in magazines.

As she related: Baby L was born on 19 July 1889. The baby was healthy but cried much of the time. Friends and neighbors, as well as a nurse and a physician, offered suggestions, including paregoric (an opium derivative), "however this drug was seldom resorted to, on account of its effect on the nerves, causing the child to start and moan in his sleep." Other attempts to calm the infant involved a variety of potions encompassing items from traditional domestic medicine as well as those found in contemporary pharmacies, such as "toddy, catnip (an infusion of the flowers), syrup of rhubarb and magnesia, charcoal and loaf-sugar, asafetida and paregoric, anise and calamus." Nothing calmed the infant nor resulted in more than two hours' sleep; "not one night of unbroken rest had come to the household on account of the dreadful colic, or whatever it is that causes so many little ones to cry during the first months of their existence." The family also tried several manufactured foods and various cow's milk or cream mixtures with and without sugar. Finally, after weeks of trial and error, the family attempted pure cow's milk: first the milk from a cow with a young calf, but the child still suffered; then the morning milk from a more mature cow, on which the child thrived.[48]

Mulligan stated unambiguously her purpose for submitting this article to *American Agriculturist*: "Such a record would doubtless prove helpful to many mothers." Just as women talked with neighbors and friends about their experiences in order to help mothers on a personal basis, and as they presented their experiences in mothers' clubs to help mothers on a communal basis, so too did women publish their experiences to help mothers beyond their immediate communities.

Over the years, mothers continued to communicate with each other through magazines, considered trusted sources of both sisterly and professional information. In gratitude they reported their successes. "Mamma" of Hudson, New York, had felt nervous and inexpert with her child; then she was delighted to discover *Babyhood*: "I would like to tell you with what joy I hailed the first number of *Babyhood* that was put into my hands about a year ago, and how eagerly I have read every article since. I knew so little of the care of children that I trembled for my little girl when she came to us, lest she should often suffer while I gained experience."[49] The ideology of scientific motherhood was so widely known by the mid-1880s that this woman took it for granted that instruction was essential if she were to be a competent mother; she explicitly acknowledged that she needed expert direction in order to raise her child healthfully.

Given the explosion in published child-care advice in the period, the problem was identifying the best advice and separating it from "foolish fears and superstitions," as Stanton had discovered. Mothers were well aware of the difficulty, as a series of letters in *Babyhood* relates. "A grateful reader" decried the dangers of "a little knowledge" and also saw the hazards of its opposite, an overabundance of contradictory advice. She called for "the wider circulation of really scientific journals such as *Babyhood*." However, she warned of "not forgetting to read *Babyhood* so diligently ourselves that we may be humble in our own conceit and not degenerate in our old age into amateur doctors." Readers of *Babyhood* must, she declared, become missionaries and spread the word about scientific child care, but be careful not to usurp the role of physician.[50] In the next several issues of the journal, readers as diverse as "A country physician" and R.C.F. of National City, California, supported "A grateful reader's" call for greater appreciation of scientific magazines like *Babyhood*.[51] A. P. Carter was so impressed with *Babyhood* that she bundled up back issues and sent them on to mothers in isolated areas of the United States in the South and West. She enthusiastically reported that they were "joyously" welcomed and lent to others as well.[52] Other mothers wrote about saving back issues of journals for future reference.[53] "A grateful reader," A. P. Carter, and other subscribers acted on the basic components of scientific motherhood: they applauded the application of science in child care and facilitated its dissemination.

The columns and articles in these journals served several different, complementary purposes. Through them mothers sought more detailed instructions than were available from other sources. Mothers expected the periodical literature to substitute for unavailable physicians or supply a second opinion. Magazines also provided a forum through which women could widen their communities for collecting and dispensing sisterly advice.

Many mothers confused about incomplete and contradictory advice wrote and expected that their trusted magazines would provide the required vital clarification. Their queries frequently related to practical matters. "A new reader" from Penn Yan, New York, was well aware of the importance of using pasteurized milk in bottle-feeding her seven-month-old daughter. Less clear on how to insure that the heating procedure was adequate, she asked *Babyhood* in 1896, "In testing with a thermometer is it necessary to test the milk in the bottles or the water around the bottles? Will the milk be nearly the same temperature?" She timidly added, "This seems a stupid question, but I do not understand whether 167° for pasteurizing means the water or the milk in the bottles."[54] Similarly, F.B.S. of Atlanta, Georgia, felt confident that *Babyhood* would answer her queries because "your valuable magazine has done much toward teaching me the necessity of watching the minutest details in the care of children, so I am sure you will gladly answer my numerous questions." She explained that for the last two months, her daughter had been fed Horlick's Malted Milk, a popular artificial infant feeding product. Now, as the child approached her first birthday, the mother recognized the need to add more substantial food to her diet and was considering a mixture of cow's milk and oatmeal. In addition to questions about the appropriate combination of ingredients, F.B.S. wondered what schedule she should use with a one-year-old. She valued the advice of Dr. Holt, a prominent physician of the period, but was puzzled by what she read in this instance.

> I notice that Dr. Holt gives five as the proper number of meals a day for one year, but does not approve night feeding after 9 months. Now my baby's present meals are at 6 and 10 a.m. and at 2, 6 and 11 p.m. If I leave off the night feeding she would have only the four meals— 32 oz.—too little for her age? What do you advise? And if I do not leave off the night feeding now, when should it be left off, and how would it be best to arrange the meals so as to get in the requisite amount of food?[55]

In each case the journal supplied a detailed, reasoned answer.

Conscientious reading of the advice in magazines does not mean that mothers ignored physicians. Some sought out professional medical advice for sick children but not for well ones. E.V.D. of Brooklyn, New York, had used sterilized milk for her first child, but then she read an article in *Babyhood* on pasteurization and used that process because she realized "now that pasteurized milk is thought superior." But, she wondered, at what age should she discontinue the procedure? She also requested information about milk formulas for her second child. As she explained to the journal, "I do not know the quantity of milk, etc., for an average child, for my first, having scarlet fever and measles before she was two, was fed as a sick child directed by my physician."[56] In other words, in this turn-of-the-century transition period, E.V.D. recognized that physicians held important knowledge in cases of illness. However, there were other reputable sources of scientific advice for the well child. She respected the information published in *Babyhood*, which she considered a scientific journal.

Other mothers looked to these journals either when their own physician was unavailable or when several physicians gave conflicting advice.[57] Though mothers questioned physicians, they were not rejecting the tenets of scientific motherhood. True, they were unhappy with the results of their own physicians' counsel, but the columnists of journals such as *Babyhood*, *American Motherhood*, and *Ladies' Home Journal* were, by the late nineteenth and early twentieth centuries, medical practitioners as well. Clearly, dissatisfaction with one or even several physicians did not lead these mothers to deny the importance of medical direction. Rather, in turning to physician-columnists, mothers were enlarging their universe of medically related resources for information on child care.

It is important to note that mothers used these journals for more than questioning their physicians' advice or clarifying perplexing directions. They also dispensed advice to other mothers, creating a virtual community of maternal support. In effect, the journals enabled women to replace sisterly correspondence networks and neighborhood chats with a broader circle that reached well beyond family and friends. Of course, books could serve a similar purpose. Some women, following in the path of Mary Palmer Tyler, did publish books based on their mothering experiences.[58] But most mothers were not that venturesome. They had something to tell other mothers, based on their own experiences, but more usually as a brief response to or article on a particular concern rather than as a sustained volume. Mothers' advice letters and articles fall into three general categories: answers to technical problems, solutions to common quandaries, and responses to specific queries and experiences.

Initially letter writers presented readers with practical advice. One very popular topic in these magazines was "how to bathe the baby." Palmetta Goldsmith wrote the *American Agriculturist* with various hints to ease this chore for the nervous mother in the late 1880s. She went through the various steps she followed, from laying out the clean clothes and bath equipment to dusting the baby with a cheesecloth bag filled with fine starch, and ended with the reminder, "Always give the bath at the same hour, which should be as soon as possible after breakfast."[59] A few years later Julia L. Munger of Chicago, Illinois, provided a similar, but more detailed outline for the readers of *Babyhood*.[60] Other pragmatic suggestions included, for example, how to devise a home sterilizer, an improvised night lamp, and even a diaper box. The latter, properly constructed, would not only save drawer space but "it also makes a nice seat for an older child," according to its inventor, F.P.C. of Denver, Colorado.[61]

The most common problem discussed in mothers' letters and articles in this period was the question of infant feeding. Mothers who had successfully bottle-fed their children, such as Mulligan, used their experiences to instruct other mothers who might face a similar situation. For example, in 1898, "A mother" commented in *Farm, Stock, and Home* about the "great misfortune when for any reason a baby cannot be reared on the nourishment intended for it by nature." However, she assured mothers, an infant can grow healthfully on properly prepared cow's milk.[62] Another mother, in the *Herald of Health*, recommended condensed milk in cities where fresh milk cannot be trusted.[63] Others were more explicit about their purpose in writing. "Bell" had spent five months trying to find the right cow's milk formula for her baby. Finally, she used Baby Cream, which was 1 pint cream to 3 pints water. Her child thrived on this mixture and thus she recommended that readers of the *Ladies' Home Journal* try the formula, which should save them going "through the whole catalogue of 'Baby Foods,'" as she had.[64] Betty Allen was proud that "many experienced mothers say to me: 'What! A bottle baby and no colic?'" She was pleased to tell mothers that "the explanation lies in the absolute cleanliness surrounding his food."[65]

Some responses to the queries of concerned mothers spanned several issues with a variety of solutions proposed. C.L.C. of Topeka, Kansas, wrote to *Babyhood* in 1885, worried about her baby's constipation. Her problem and the solution proposed by the magazine, the use of a soap stick suppository, generated a flurry of letters from other mothers, who offered various alternatives. C.M.C. of Washington, DC, uneasily took issue with the use of suppositories. She normally appreciated the magazine's assistance, but in this instance disagreed because "in my own experiences with two very constipated children I found that the use of soap and roll of paper induced piles—quite as great an evil as constipation." Her method involved kneading the children's bowels with oil every night and morning and sitting "them on the stool at a regular time each day," as well as giving them "as laxative food as possible." E.C.C. of New York preferred following the directions given her by a physician: "Take loaf-sugar and dissolve in as little cold water as possible, thereby making a thick syrup. Give the baby one teaspoonful of this (or more as she grows older) *immediately before* nursing, or feeding if bottle-fed."[66]

In mothers' submissions to journals we see most clearly the transformation of scientific motherhood with its increasing emphasis on medically supervised infant and child care. Throughout the nineteenth and into the early years of the twentieth century, mothers continued to use their experiences to respond to the published concerns of others. They also continued to use their successes as instructional tales for less experienced mothers. What did change over the period was the source of this expertise, the source of authority for their mothering practices. With greater frequency and in greater detail, mothers such as E.C.C. acknowledged that they took their direction from physicians. Even when they gave advice based on personal experience, the advice often originated with a medical practitioner. Moreover, mothers used the imprimatur of a doctor to give added credibility to their advice.

Mothers utilized physicians for a wide variety of problems. In the late nineteenth century, the household of "Busy Mother" faced "a siege of measles." When the rash first appeared, she was alarmed and immediately sent for the physician, from whom she learned to keep the child warm and in a darkened room. The ill child, she was told, should stay indoors for two weeks until the rash entirely disappeared. "Busy Mother" related all the details of treatment to the readers of *Farm, Stock, and Home* "in order to save others that [doctor's] expense by giving them the benefit of my experience." As she explained, "If I had known what I do now I might have saved the doctor's bill."[67] Not that she could have done without the doctor's expertise, but she wanted to help others save on the expense.

An exchange in *Babyhood* exemplifies the critical transformation in relationships between mothers and physicians over the century. These late-nineteenth-century letters stand in sharp contrast to the *Maternal Physician*'s cavalier dismissal of doctors' advice and signify both medical advances in the nineteenth century and mothers' understanding of doctors' roles. A. L. Toland was pleased to present readers of the journal with Dr. John Forsyth Meigs' "most valuable receipt" for ginger cake, which she used when her daughter had a prolonged case of cholera infantum and could eat only a little at a time. Not only did she praise the recipe but even more significantly, she lauded Meigs' attitude. She strongly objected to physicians who mystified their craft and who refused to tell a mother the nature of the medicine given. Meigs, though, "read over every prescription to the mother . . . and also . . . explain[ed] to her thoroughly her child's trouble, so that she might not labor in the dark." This, Toland felt, was proper because "every true mother ought to know just what her child is taking."[68] Many women evidently agreed with this sentiment: physicians were to be consulted but they owed mothers an explanation. In the ensuing issues of *Babyhood,* several other correspondents responded specifically to Toland's letter, calling for "mutual confidence" between physician and mother. No longer were medical practitioners rejected as less knowledgeable than mothers. But mothers resisted being placed in the role of "medicine giving machines."[69] They celebrated physicians who recognized them as "an intelligent assistant."[70]

By the early years of the twentieth century, mothers generally had internalized the basic tenets of scientific motherhood. They accepted the idea that the best advice on child care came from medical and scientific experts, most usually physicians. Some women continued to depend on their neighbors, friends, and relatives for information on the best ways to raise their children. Some remained supremely self-confident in their own abilities, it is true. But more and more women looked to medical and scientific experts to inform them about the latest, most modern thoughts about child-care issues. Clearly they were convinced that physicians in particular held special knowledge that would improve their children's lives.

The concept of scientific motherhood—deference to medical and scientific experts and expertise—permeated American culture and influenced the infant- and child-care practices of mothers across the country by the turn of the century. Mothers' experience, physicians' counsel, neighbors' recommendations, nurses' instructions, these sources were not unique to the nineteenth century. Yet, in this period, it is the concerted efforts on the part of many mothers to seek out medical and scientific information on infant and child care that marks the century's break with past practices. The more women learned of the critical role of the "trained mother," the less competent they felt to care for their children without medical and scientific expertise.[71] The mothers whose voices we hear clearly in this chapter—the modern mothers who came to appreciate and embrace the medical direction of child care— were only a portion of women in the country. They were the literate segment of the population; they were undoubtedly primarily middle- and upper-class women. Yet their significance is greater than their numbers. In the coming decades, American mothers would follow in the path of these "scientific mothers," who were the harbingers of twentieth-century motherhood.

CHAPTER 2

"Mamma's scientific—she knows all the laws"

MOTHERHOOD IN THE EARLY TWENTIETH CENTURY

"A Modern Lullaby" (sung to the tune of "Rock-a-bye, baby")

Rock-a-bye, baby, up on the bough
You get your milk from a certified cow.
Before your eugenic young parents were wed
They had decided how you should be fed.
Hush-a-bye, baby, on the tree-top,
If grandmother trots you, you tell her to stop;
Shun the trot-horses that your grandmother rides—
It will work harm to your little insides.
Mamma's scientific—she knows all the laws—
She kisses her darling through carbolized gauze.
Rock-a-bye, baby, don't wriggle and squirm:
Nothing is near you that looks like a germ.[1]

$\mathcal{T}$his song, published anonymously in 1915 in a women's magazine that consciously sought to educate modern mothers, illustrates how completely and deeply the idea of scientific motherhood had permeated into U.S. culture. This was not a professional journal, yet it clearly expected its readers, laywomen, to know enough to make sense of the humorous lyrics. "Certified cow" referred to fears for the health of infants fed cow's milk that had spurred the creation of late-nineteenth-century medical organizations to carefully scrutinize special dairies. The milk from these farms was then certified as safe for infants and children. Parents who decided to give their children certified milk were making a definite statement about their knowledge of contemporary medicine. "Shun the trot-horses your grandmother rides" is an obvious reference to the practices of the previous generation that are now seen as injurious to the young child. Most importantly, "Mamma's scientific": this mother knows about the dangers of the old customs and new knowledge has taught her to fear not only the old ways but also newly discovered threats, such as germs. No longer were women assumed to look to their mothers, sisters, and neighbors. The modern, the scientific mother of the early twentieth century looked to medical and scientific experts for the information on how to raise her children.

Throughout the nineteenth century, self-confident women and women who lacked other options had depended on their own resources when deciding how to raise their families. Yet, many mothers, even self-assured mothers, found themselves referring to physicians. By the turn of the century, confidence and skill in childrearing did not blind mothers to the benefits of alternative modes of child care, nor did it lead them to brush aside new sources of information. Take, for example, the account of Marjorie A. Brown, who moved from San Francisco to the Nevada frontier in the early years of the twentieth century. In her small town, Tonopah, one enterprising man had brought in cows and established a dairy that supplied the town with fresh milk. Brown was pleased to have a local dairy; she used the milk for cooking and drank it herself, but she did not feed it to her children. She knew that cow's milk for infants should be pasteurized, which this milk was not. Writing about her infant-care experiences years later, she remembered: "Young mothers of Tonopah had no pediatrician to advise them. We relied mostly on instinct and the trial-and-error method." Her first child "did pretty well" on malted milk. However, "when my second boy came along, I was more fortunate. I had an English doctor who, knowing nothing about American baby foods, induced me to send to England for a food called Allenbury's. The little fellow flourished."[2] Brown's knowledge about the need to pasteurize milk and her use of malted milk indicates that she relied on more than "instinct and the trial-and-error method" with her children, though she leaves us no indication of her sources for this information. But even more striking is her relationship with the medical profession. She had raised her first child healthfully, and yet she consulted with a physician when one was available for her second and followed his advice, despite the fact that it involved a different food from a foreign land.[3] We do not know what impelled Brown to consult with a physician, but her story demonstrates that by the turn of the century even experienced mothers no longer expected to depend on their own knowledge and skill in child care.

From the perspective of medical authors, the ideal of an information-seeking mother was rapidly disappearing, to be replaced with the model of the mother dependent on the physician. The most eloquent example of this change is L. Emmett Holt's highly popular *Care and Feeding of Children: A Catechism for the Use of Mothers and Children's Nurses.*[4] It is truly a catechism. Gone are the paragraph-long expositions explaining the reasons behind the directions, which earlier physician-authors had included in their advice manuals. For Holt, child care was reduced to a series of questions with brief, but specific answers. For instance, his instructions for bathing an infant: "At what temperature should the bath be given?" Answer: "For the first few weeks at 100°F; later, during early infancy, at 98°F; after six months, at 95°F; during the second year, from 85° to 90°F."[5]

Holt expected mothers to follow his directions to the letter and, one might say, blindly, regardless of circumstances. The prose of other contemporary physicians was more verbose than Holt's, but to the same effect. Richard M. Smith's *The Baby's First Two Years*, published in 1915, seems almost lyrical when compared to Holt's. It was clearly directed to a middle-class mother with the modern technological facilities to carefully calibrate the temperature of the room and of the water. Wood-burning stoves and fireplaces were difficult to adjust and maintain at a constant temperature. With the new modern coal-, and later gas-burning equipment that brought hot water into the room, women could feasibly follow such instructions as: "A normal, healthy baby should be bathed daily. . . . The room in which the bath is given should never be below 70° Fahrenheit, but should not be much over this. . . . The temperature of the water should be between 95° and 98° until the baby is six months old; after that it can be as low as 90°."[6] Despite the affable style, the philosophy remained the same. Mothers should bathe their infants in this physician-directed manner; but, it was physician-directed, period, no further explanations and no further information needed.

This transformation to an authoritative style occurs simultaneously with the medical profession's efforts to create and enhance professional organizations and standing. In the nineteenth century, the profession was weak and fragmented and the typical physician, while respected, was not necessarily well-off. Efforts to strengthen physicians' professional stature resulted in the creation of a powerful professional identity through an invigorated American Medical Association (AMA). In addition, concerted disciplinary and legislative actions by physicians cultivated a strong, hierarchical system of medical specialization that was just emerging at the end of the previous century. The establishment of obstetrics and pediatrics, as defined medical specialties with their own organizations, journals, and board certification, signaled the importance of physicians socially and in the lives of women and children. Indicative of the increasing attention to children's health and well-being among physicians was the founding of organizations like the AMA's Section on Diseases of Children (1881), the American Pediatric Society (1888), the Association of American Teachers of the Diseases of Children (1907–30), and the American Academy of Pediatrics (1930), and the establishment of journals like the *Archives of Pediatrics* (1884), the *Transactions of the American Pediatric Society* (1889), and *Pediatrics* (1896).[7]

As the medical profession consolidated through the early decades of the twentieth century and its prestige and power grew, a steady stream of media informed the public of the latest medical and scientific discoveries. Such announcements glorified physicians. Newspapers, magazines, and later radio were filled with the news about amazing scientific and medical breakthroughs; they implicitly and explicitly promised that the power of science and medicine would improve everyone's lives and protect child health and well-being.[8]

At the same time, the growing maternal and child health movement brought unprecedented public and medical attention to the health problems of mothers and children. This movement engaged politicians, health practitioners, and health reformers in attempts on the local, the state, and even the national level to ameliorate appalling rates of maternal and child mortality and morbidity. Furthermore, as a result of the World War I mobilization of U.S. troops, the general public learned about the poor health status of many soldiers that was specifically linked to their health and nutrition problems during childhood. Such problems were often blamed on the failure of mothers. These movements and these observations resulted in three highly publicized White House Conferences in 1909, 1919, and later 1930, conferences in which physicians were given rising stature.[9] The combination of growing medical authority coupled with scientific discoveries and a changing social and political environment together served to influence not only the specifics of child-care advice but also its tenor.

A keynote of physician-authored texts in the early twentieth century was mothers' ignorance. Physicians were not alone in blaming high rates of child mortality and morbidity on women's lack of knowledge. This claim was the basis for many public-health campaigns and advertisements in the first half of the twentieth century. Physicians, however, were among the first to promote the idea and did so most vehemently. To them, mothers were people in desperate need of education, and the best education came from physicians, who taught mothers to look to them for advice in all aspects of child care.

Not limiting themselves to narrowly defined medical advice, physician-authors set out to convince mothers "just how to do best the ordinary everyday things that every mother has to do for her child" and "describ[ed] in the minutest detail the daily care of the baby."[10]

Some doctors preferred a more gentle approach than Holt's. Dr. Richard M. Smith wrote that he appreciated that "every mother with her first baby will be confronted with difficulties about which she needs help." He assured mothers that he understood their confusion and fears. You can almost see him patting her on the head reassuringly as he explained that help was at hand: "The doctor is the person to give her this assistance." Yes, infant care is difficult, especially alone. During this period, the American population was highly mobile and many young mothers found themselves far away from familiar social networks and family. But, Smith remarked, the mother need not be alone. "It is often possible," he maintained, "to prevent serious illness by frequent consultation [with a physician] about the apparently trivial affairs of the baby's life."[11] Whether friendly or autocratic in style, the substance was the same in these manuals: mothers needed not just medical and scientific knowledge, they needed to heed medical and scientific *experts* in order to raise their children healthfully.

It is not surprising that physicians endorsed the basic tenets of scientific motherhood. Doctors were at the heart of it. Scientific, modern mothers were encouraged to view doctors as their source of scientific and medical knowledge, the knowledge that would keep their families healthy. Whether doctors did this for humanitarian, professional, or financial reasons, it was in their interest to direct mothers to physicians. Others, though not in private practice, similarly promoted scientific motherhood. They sought to convince women first that they needed assistance if they wanted to be good and successful mothers. Second, that science and medicine had the solutions to the physical and the emotional problems of their children. Third, that the medical profession was the source of the latest scientific and medical knowledge. Among the most active advocates of scientific motherhood were health reformers and educators, who established formal and informal educational opportunities through which girls and women learned the social and cultural ideals of motherhood. Through their educational institutions, the ideal of scientific motherhood reached beyond the literate, primarily middle-class audience for medical manuals into the homes of working-class and immigrant mothers as well.

Horrified by high rates of child mortality and morbidity, health reformers and social commentators in the late nineteenth century blamed mothers.

In denouncing mothers, these critics echoed the sentiments of physicians and defined a societal problem—poor child health, as the problem of the individual—maternal ignorance. Their accusations were unambiguous and explicit. One of the most graphic was John Spargo, whose widely read *The Bitter Cry of Children*, first published in 1907, provided textual and photographic evidence of the problem. While delineating the linkage between the social conditions of health and poverty, still Spargo placed the responsibility for child mortality and morbidity squarely on the shoulders of the mothers, who, he believed, were incapable of healthfully caring for their children. He regarded "the tragedy of [the] infant's position . . . as its helplessness," and believed that such children suffer not only on "account of the misfortunate of its parents, but it must suffer from their vices and from their ignorance as well."[12] Dr. C.-E.A. Winslow, a leader of the public-health movement, went even farther and claimed that the 100,000 babies who died each year did not simply die, rather they were "killed by feeding them with dirty, uncooked cow's milk or some other improper food, killed by weakening them with heavy clothing and then exposing them to a sudden draft, killed by letting some one who was coming down with 'a cold' fondle them and pass on to them the deadly germs of some disease." This murder was not the result of malice. This slaughter was not done by strangers who hated children. No, he asserted, "most of them, these 100,000 [were] killed by their mothers or their grandmothers or their sisters, who loved them very much but did not know how babies ought to be cared for."[13] Seeing such devastation around them, health reformers and others believed that mothers needed education in the latest that science and medicine could offer to protect their families.

The promised benefits of scientific motherhood would be seen in several aspects. First and most obviously, children would be healthier. This would benefit the family and also society—healthier children would grow into healthier workers needed for the expanding factories and offices of the growing United States. Healthier children would also improve the condition of soldiers who defend the country. With the widespread practice of scientific motherhood, proponents also expected the creation of a population better able to cope with and even embrace the development of modern life. This is most evident in the educational efforts among immigrant and African American populations in the early twentieth century. Educators anticipated that mothers who aspired to the ideals of scientific motherhood would both raise a healthier family and help integrate the family into the wider U.S. culture.[14] Scientific motherhood magnified the significance of mothers for the future of the nation.

From the beginning, proponents considered scientific motherhood a solution to a social problem, namely, high rates of child mortality and morbidity that were a result of cultural, environmental, and communal conditions. Before World War I, both the medical constraints that separated public health and private medicine and the political realities shaped the sporadic and generally local efforts developed to address the problems of maternal and child health. The settlement house movement most clearly exemplifies that contemporary reform philosophy. In institutions such as Hull House in Chicago and the Henry Street Settlement House in New York City, middle-class, educated women established communities in the poorer areas of their cities through which they could learn about and evaluate the problems and needs of local residents, often immigrants. Settlement houses were not public institutions under the auspices of local or state government. They were developed by concerned citizens to encourage the socialization and education of those less fortunate than themselves. For example, they organized recreational and instructional programs, such as sewing clubs, at which mothers could prepare clothes for their children and exchange information. They brought nurses to the community to visit homes and provide health education.

Gradually, the focal point of the solution for infant and child health changed from communal to individual, a transformation that followed from new and increasingly sophisticated studies that clarified the sources of childhood illness, as well as a shifting focus in public health. In the early decades of the twentieth century, a "new" public health developed, one that emphasized each individual's responsibility for health and welfare. This significant shift is seen most clearly in the transformation of nineteenth-century milk stations, which morphed into twentieth-century well-child clinics.

Throughout the country, as physicians, public-health officers, and other concerned citizens recognized the connection between contaminated or adulterated milk and infant and child ill health, there were calls to insure that mothers had access to clean milk for their children. This led to the creation of "milk stations," to provide safe certified or pasteurized milk in urban areas. One example was San Francisco's Certified Milk Fund Committee, established in 1909 by a branch of the Association of Collegiate Alumnae (now the American Association of University Women [AAUW]). Local dairies worked with concerned women in the community to provide pure milk that was then distributed to mothers for infants and for toddlers.[15] By 1917, many reformers considered this an inadequate remedy to the problem of infant and child ill health. Consequently, the Committee expanded its program to include a Children's Health Center, which served as an educational institute for mothers with classes and conferences for prenatal and postnatal instruction. Indicative of this programmatic shift, the Committee was renamed the Baby Hygiene Committee in 1918, a label that encompassed its new multiple functions.[16] In this one city we can see how the initial concern with a specific problem—bad milk, led to a community solution—the production and distribution of pure milk. Continuing concerns, however, served to both broaden the practices and narrow the goals of the Committee. It expanded its mandate with the introduction of new services that increasingly focused on the education of the individual. With its concentration on teaching mothers how to best care for themselves and their children, the Committee privatized the solution to a social problem.

Not all applauded the establishment of milk stations, especially in their early years. With their distribution of milk and prepared milk bottles, they were often accused of undermining breast feeding, which critics reminded the public was the most healthful form of infant feeding. From the perspective of the twenty-first century, it is difficult to judge the truth of this accusation. What is clear, however, is the vehement reaction of milk station proponents to such claims, which demonstrates once again the growing emphasis on the need for contemporary medical knowledge to raise a child successfully. For example, Dr. Philip Van Ingen, one of the most vigorous defenders of milk stations, was pleased to report in 1912 that over 60 percent of children attending the milk stations of the New York Milk Committee were either entirely breast-fed or received some breast milk. This high rate of breast feeding, he explained, was because milk stations did much more than distribute milk. Rather, they insisted that infants enroll in the stations and report regularly for medical examinations. A nurse was sent to the family's home in order to instruct the mother on proper child care within that home environment. Van Ingen argued that milk stations such as these were required because mothers needed pure milk for the health of their children. At the same time, though, the physician-reformer did not see the solution to high rates of mortality and morbidity solely in terms of pure milk. "The purest milk in the world, alone," he noted, "will not solve the problem." The root of the problem lay elsewhere. "Ignorance kills more babies than bad milk," explained Van Ingen.[17] Again, rather than consider a communal solution to a communal problem, the doctor explicitly held the individual mother accountable.

This progression from communal to individual solution was repeated more and more as local branches of groups such as the AAUW, the American Home Economics Association, the National Congress of Mothers, and the Child Study Association of America as well as church groups and

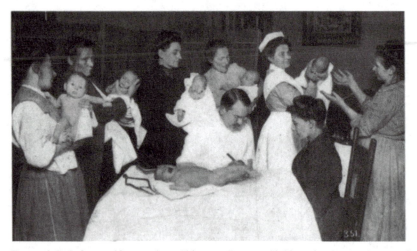

FIGURE 2.1. Infant welfare station, Chicago. *Source: Child in the City: A Series of Papers Presented at the Conference Held during the Chicago Child Welfare Exhibit* (Chicago: Hollister Press, 1912).

Children's Aid Societies established well-child health centers in settlement houses and neighborhood clinics across the country.[18] In many areas of the country, middle-class club women were convinced that the best way to protect the health of their families, and by extension their communities, was to sponsor clinics and lectures that elevated the role of physicians in child care. For example, in the 1920s, the Women's Club of Omar, West Virginia, working in cooperation with the West Virginia Coal and Coke Company, the community's primary employer, established two nurseries, a clinic staffed by company physicians and nurses, and a library.[19] In the racially segregated society of the United States at the time, most of these agencies were involved with Euro-American women. But African American mothers joined similar groups established by the National Association of Colored Women (NACW). In these too they were instructed in hygiene, health care, and other household issues.[20]

Those who believed that some mothers could not be educated sought to give the child the benefits of scientific motherhood in another setting. One alternative that developed was day nurseries. Yet, day care, particularly infant day care, was highly controversial in the early-twentieth-century United States. In this period, most reformers strongly believed that children should be cared for in their homes by their mothers and that the solution to health and social problems lay with the educated mother. Only the most dire circumstances could justify a mother's leaving her children in the care of others. Yet, during World War I, the need for workers to support the war effort led some groups to establish day nurseries in factories to enable mothers of young children to enter the work force. Again, in this venue, the benefits of scientific mothering practices were touted and could be implemented, at least within this controlled environment. Showing the class bias of the government agents, as well as the firm hold of the ideology of scientific motherhood on the public consciousness, a 1919–20 report of the Connecticut Department of Labor noted that "infants of as tender an age as four and six months were left in the factory nurseries where they undoubtedly obtained better and more scientific care and greater attention to their cleanliness than if their mothers remained at home and cared for them."[21] "Scientific" meant better, and working-class mothers could not provide "scientific" care, essential in the twentieth century. This example vividly demonstrates the paramount importance of science and suggests that not all mothers were educatable.

More typically, reformers of the period coupled the glorification of science with the absolute necessity of educating the mother. Efforts in Boston demonstrate how various groups within the city worked to improve the health of children through the education of women in scientific motherhood. There, as in San Francisco, well-child clinics grew directly out of the milk stations established throughout the city to furnish pure milk to bottle-fed babies. The activities of the stations grew beyond the distribution of milk and soon mothers of both bottle-fed and breast-fed infants were encouraged to bring their children to the clinic to be examined by physicians there and to receive instructions on mothering. Boston's Committee on Milk and Baby Hygiene, composed of public-health-oriented physicians and reformers, many of them civic-minded women, employed three different methods of education. Firstly, the committee held lectures for groups of mothers with demonstrations on bathing the baby, exhibits of suitable clothing for children, and the like. Secondly, there were the individual examinations, during which a physician gave advice to the mother. Thirdly, there were conferences during which one baby was examined in the presence of several mothers, who then heard the advice given the child's parent. Committee members believed that "in this way mistakes made by one mother are pointed out to her in a kindly way and made to do duty as texts for the education of other mothers, while those who have done well receive approbation and are encouraged to persevere, and the other mothers are persuaded to do likewise."[22] This teaching by example was considered the most effective and efficient course.

Another large, influential group was also taught by example. Health reformers such as Spargo noted that particularly high rates of child mortality

FIGURE 2.2. Young girl with her sibling. *Source:* John Spargo, *The Bitter Cry of the Children* (New York: Macmillan, 1907).

and morbidity were evident in areas of poverty where mothers went out to work, leaving their children in the care of siblings only slightly older. These so-called "little mothers," according to Dr. S. Josephine Baker, of the New York City Department of Health, were "an inevitable makeshift." In response to the problem, Baker designed an educational program for these girls with three interrelated goals. First and foremost, a little mother "intelligently trained" would be less dangerous to her charge. In other words, with instruction, these girls would be able to give their sisters and brothers more healthful care. This would have a beneficial effect with the next generation as well: educated little mothers would appreciate the advantages of medical supervision and scientific care and would more quickly seek medical attention when they became pregnant themselves. Moreover, Baker expected little mothers to be her "most efficient missionaries." With their knowledge of modern, scientific care, they would teach the mothers of the neighborhood, encourage them to attend well-child clinics, and to follow the instructions of clinic staff. This was especially important in immigrant families where the mothers spoke little or no English and their daughters acted as essential go-betweens, introducing their mothers and other women of the neighborhood to modern child care under the supervision of medical practitioners. In 1910, Baker established the first "Little Mothers' Clubs" and they rapidly spread throughout the city.[23]

Cities and states across the country quickly copied Baker's innovation. Wisconsin developed a course for "Wisconsin's Little Mothers." Schoolgirls learned about bathing, nutrition, cleanliness, and the utmost importance of scheduling infants and young children. They also learned the need for medical supervision. At the end of the course, each girl who successfully demonstrated her child-care skills was named one of "Wisconsin's Little Mothers." The Chicago Department of Health began to offer a similar course in the summer of 1919. By 1921 it enrolled 3,222 seventh- and eighth-grade girls in thirty-four schools. At the end of their classes, the students prepared a public demonstration of their child-care skills, including the appropriate ways to make up a baby's bed and to give a baby's bath, and the proper way to hold the baby. They also prepared skits and papers, which they presented to an audience of fellow students and parents.[24]

A different tack with similar results was evident in Madison, Wisconsin, through the work of a group of young philanthropic women called the Attic Angels. Founded in 1889 to address the plight of poor children, the Angels quickly expanded its mandate to the funding of a visiting nurse. In the early twentieth century, under the direction of Dr. Dorothy Reed Mendenhall,

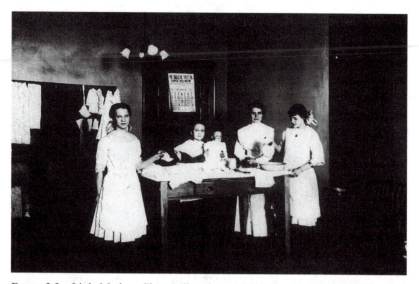

FIGURE 2.3.   Little Mothers Class, Milwaukee, c. 1915. *Source:* Wisconsin Historical Society, WHi–33794.

one of the first women to graduate from Johns Hopkins Medical School, the nurse attended the immigrant population of the community, while judiciously maintaining the separation of public health and private medicine. She visited them in their homes and directed them to physicians when they needed medical care. The nurse was soon overwhelmed with the magnitude of the problems among her clients, and Mendenhall convinced the Angels to establish a Well-Child Clinic that could more efficiently and effectively examine children and direct mothers to physicians to address particular medical conditions. Beginning in the summer of 1915, Mendenhall regularly supervised the clinic with the assistance of two nurses and volunteers from the Attic Angels. By February 1916, the Angels had established a number of permanent centers throughout the city. When mothers brought their children to be examined, they were also instructed in appropriate child-care practices.

Whether they grew out of a milk station, or the practice of an overworked visiting nurse, or some other agency, the end product was similar. The objectives of scientific motherhood were intimately woven into the structure and the practices of these clinics. Mothers viewed posters and films that depicted modern, healthful child care, usually presented as the scientifically, medically appropriate procedures to use in raising a child. They were given copies of pamphlets and brochures, such as the U.S. Children's Bureau's *Pre-*

natal Care and *Infant Care*. They were also instructed personally by the physicians in charge.

These agencies were distinctly class based. They were designed to address the situations of working-class, immigrant, and minority mothers, educating them specifically in the proper modern methods of child care. These practices, based on the ideals of middle-class, white urban families, would both improve the health and welfare of families and also, reformers hoped, inculcate the women with the principles of twentieth-century standards of hygiene and respect for experts and rigorous scheduling. Other groups reached out into the rural areas and small cities of the country. Philanthropic organizations like the Commonwealth Fund and the Milbank Memorial Fund supported demonstration health projects. In cities such as Syracuse, New York, and Salem, Oregon, these health projects brought together health department officials, private physicians, visiting nurses, and civic-minded women whose primary goals were to better community health through improved child health premised on the necessity of physician-supervised child care.[25] Whether located in crowded tenements or more rural environments, mothers were expected to learn practices that defined the dominant, urban, more affluent culture of the country. The NACW was most explicit about the promise of such education, insisting that through scientific motherhood, women would "uplift" their families and the "race." So too were reformers, who entered immigrant and working-class communities throughout the United States, spreading the word that scientific motherhood would bring them the benefits of modern medical and scientific knowledge.[26]

Not that all mothers reveled in these advantages or accepted the principle of scientifically informed maternal practices. Yet, their very rejection reflects the general popularity of scientific motherhood in the early twentieth century. A story in the 18 May 1916 issue of the *Milwaukee [WI] Sentinel* justifies this conclusion.[27] Baby contests were a common form of entertainment and an educational venue in the period. Health reformers and physicians assumed that the winners would be prime examples of modern child care and their mothers, exemplars of scientific motherhood. However, the results of one such contest confounded the experts. All three gold medals went to children of "working men," whose wives emphatically spurned such "new fangled ideas." The mother of George Carlin, winner in the eighteen months to two years category, told reporters: "I raised this baby to suit myself. I didn't listen to any faddish rules or read any books on how to raise a baby. I raised him myself and I guess I haven't made a failure of it." The mothers of the other winners similarly eschewed modern motherhood. The newspaper report, headlined "Best babies are blow to science," both pokes fun at the promoters of scientific motherhood and indicates the general public's knowledge of the ideology. Unless it was commonly known that modern mothers were expected to use contemporary science and medicine in rearing their children, this headline and the story it trumpeted would have made no sense.

Though middle-class mothers did not receive the same intense attention as their less fortunate sisters, they were not forgotten by proponents of scientific motherhood. They were encouraged to turn to scientific and medical experts through adult education in areas such as home economics, an emerging academic and vocational discipline in the first third of the twentieth century. Home economics grew out of the domestic science and cooking school movement of the nineteenth century. The Lake Placid Conferences, 1899–1908, brought together educators and reformers worried about conditions of modern life. They pointed specifically to massive immigration from Southern and Eastern Europe that was bringing into the United States peoples with strange languages and strange customs. They also noted widespread industrialization with its establishment of a factory labor force that introduced new consumer products powered by the innovative technology of electricity. Simultaneously, growing urbanization drew more people from the countryside into the already dirty and crowded cities of the country. Both immigration and urbanization brought rural people into the expanding metropolitan areas and required them to face new and unfamiliar modes of living. These conditions, early home economists feared, threatened the bedrock of U.S. society, the family. To Ellen Richards, Caroline Hunt, Marion Talbot, and other founders of the movement, the goal of home economics was a better world. Richards argued that home economics was "nothing less than an effort to save our social fabric from what seems inevitable disintegration"; "the Home Economics movement is," she believed, "an endeavor to hold the home and the welfare of children from slipping away over the cliff, by knowledge which will bring courage to combat the destructive tendencies."[28]

These efforts were centered in land grant universities, which were enlarging in this period and often used a comparable rationale when establishing their home economics programs. For example, the University of Wisconsin home economics program in the 1910s attracted students with a similar claim for social benefits, but one couched in economic and eugenic terms. In explaining the importance of a home economics education, the 1913–14 course catalog asked what the results would be "if the home environment were on a scientific basis" and concluded that "there is sufficient evidence to show that the savings to the state would be enormous, provided the women were trained in their chief business."[29] This oft-stated goal of political and social leaders of the Progressive era also echoed Richards' advocacy of "euthenics." As an alternative to eugenics, euthenics was based on the belief that "improved environment [through education] would improve the physical conditions of future parents and bring quicker results in race development" than selective breeding.[30]

Just as the development of scientific agriculture at land grant universities was teaching the sons of the nation's farmers to appreciate the application of science in their livelihoods, the development of home economics taught their daughters to appreciate the application of scientific and medical knowledge in their livelihoods, wifehood and motherhood.[31] College programs that offered degrees in home economics embraced modern science and medicine as its foundation. Most of these courses included a "practice house" experience. That is, a group of students would live together for several weeks or a semester in a specially built house, demonstrating to their instructors how well they had learned to apply in the domestic setting the knowledge they were taught in the classroom. A number of these experiences included baby and child care. For example, at Cornell University, orphaned infants lived in the practice house with the students, who learned how to care for them. Thus, college women were taught in home economics the basic tenets of scientific motherhood, namely the need for women to look to science and medicine for the experts and expertise to raise their families.

However, only a relatively few women could afford the time or the money to attend university. For those who could not, university extension in the form of short-term courses and traveling lecturers offered the opportunity to learn about the latest medical and scientific discoveries that could improve one's mothering practices. Mendenhall, for example, was hired by the director of home economics at the University of Wisconsin to travel around the state. Starting in 1911, she spent several months each year for the next two and a half decades speaking with women in the small towns and villages of rural Wisconsin about the importance of medical supervision of pregnancy and infant and child care.

For those who could not take advantage of these educational opportunities, and many who did, another source for "scientific motherhood" in the twentieth century was government pamphlets, especially the federal government's pamphlet *Infant Care*, prepared by the U.S. Children's Bureau. The Bureau was the brainchild of activists such as Lillian Wald, the nurse who founded New York City's Henry Street Settlement House, and consumer advocate Florence Kelley, Henry Street resident and president of the consumer and labor advocacy organization, the National Consumers' League. They were distressed by the problem of child mortality and morbidity and they reduced their concern to a simple question: "If the Government can have a department to take such an interest in the cotton crop [the U.S. Department of Agriculture], why can't it have a bureau to look after the nation's child crop?"[32] Wald was particularly galled by the contrast between attention paid by the U.S. Department of Agriculture to the damage done by the boll weevil in southern cotton fields and the lack of federal interest in increasing child mortality. These formidable women presented their idea to President Theodore Roosevelt in 1903 and lobbied other national leaders. Finally, in 1912, the U.S. Children's Bureau was established with a mandate to "investigate and report . . . upon all matters pertaining to the welfare of children and child life among all classes of our people."

Note, the agency was to investigate and report, not treat; the Bureau could not deliver medical care. Yet, within its limited charge the Bureau accomplished much in its first years, under the direction of Julia Lathrop, a former resident of Chicago's Hull House. It conducted well-publicized studies that highlighted the connections between infant and maternal mortality and morbidity and poverty in rural and urban areas. It produced popular childrearing brochures for general distribution to mothers across the country, among them *Prenatal Care* (1913) and *Infant Care* (1914). The latter proved to be the most popular of all the federal publications. By 1940 over 12 million copies had been distributed and by the 1970s distribution reached over 59 million in the revised and expanded version. People could and did write in for the pamphlet, but it was also frequently sent unsolicited by Congressional representatives.

Based on contemporary medical science, these brochures are indicative of the Bureau's faith in education and the reach of scientific motherhood in the early twentieth century, as the publication history of *Infant Care* confirms. Initially Lathrop appointed Mary Mills West (Mrs. Max West) to write the booklet. West was a mother of five and a graduate of the University of Minnesota. Significantly, she utilized her own experiences in preparing *Infant Care*. She also acknowledged the works of leading experts, drawing on, for instance, the behaviorism of J. B. Watson, which will be discussed further in the next chapter. Moreover, she warned readers that the booklet was not meant to replace the physician. In many ways, the *Infant Care* of 1914 represented an extension of the sisterly networks of the nineteenth century that combined maternal experience and professional expertise. However, this

Infant Care

Bureau Publication No. 8 (Revised)

U. S. Department of Labor

Children's Bureau

1924

FIGURE 2.4. Cover of *Infant Care*, 1924.

was soon to change. By October 1919, with the growing strength of medical organizations, such as the American Pediatric Society and the Pediatrics Section of the AMA, physicians wrote Lathrop and insisted that at minimum medical practitioners should review the work of laypersons in the area of child care. Moreover, they considered *Infant Care* a compilation of advice and therefore it should not list a single author. West, they admitted, could "write simply and pleasingly," but she did not have any particular qualifications for advising mothers. West, of course, differed: "I think there is a slight injustice in this attitude, for, after all, I had born five children and as I am not a hopelessly feeble-minded woman I must have learned a few things for myself by the process. Also, everyone learns from others. Even doctors."[33] Despite her disappointment, West understood the awkward position Lathrop was in. She agreed to the deletion of her name. By the 1921 edition of *Infant Care*, West no longer appeared as author; by the end of the decade all the compilers of *Infant Care* were physicians. No longer were women expected to learn for themselves about child care. Now, according to physicians, mothers were to listen to health-care practitioners: the twentieth-century rendering of scientific motherhood.[34]

Even greater numbers of women would have learned about scientific motherhood from child-care journals, such as *Babyhood* and *American Motherhood*, and general women's magazines, which prove to be among the leading proponents of the ideology from the late nineteenth century onwards. *Babyhood* was most explicit: "There is a science in bringing up children and this magazine is the voice of that science."[35] This was but one of many journals established in the late nineteenth and early twentieth centuries to instruct women in child care and family health and to celebrate the scientific mother. Other journals articulated the ideology of scientific motherhood through articles and advice columns, such as "Mother's Corner," edited by a trained nurse for the *Ladies' Home Journal*, and the "Health and Happiness Club," edited by a physician for *Good Housekeeping*.[36]

Mothers were pleased with the articles they read in journals and the magazines' responses to their queries. As an appreciative Mrs. R.M. wrote *American Motherhood* in 1914 regarding dietary instructions the journal published to treat her daughter's constipation: "I just don't know how to thank you enough. I only wish every mother might have such a wise and competent adviser. Thank you *ever, ever* so much for taking time to help me and my little one."[37] Mrs. O.K. also appreciated the role of physicians in child care, though she learned that they did not always have the answers. Her toddler daughter was interested only in milk and would not eat other foods. The mother consulted with "six of the most eminent physicians on the Coast, besides using Dr. Holt's *Handbook* as a daily guide." All to no avail. Then she consulted with a "very skillful physician who had, we felt, saved her life in a very severe illness." He suggested allowing the girl to drink all the milk she wanted "on the condition that she had at least one egg a day besides, and a small amount of solids." Following his suggestion, the mother established the rule that her daughter could have all the milk she wished if she would first eat "one good solid dish at each meal." This procedure worked well; the child's "health is one hundred per cent improved, and we do not have three night-mares a day trying to force an unwilling child to eat the food we think she ought to eat." Mrs. O.K. provided readers of *American Motherhood* with all these details not because she knew more than physicians but because she wanted others to benefit from this physician's knowledge.[38]

Some readers wrote to the magazines because they were frightened that untrained mothers were dangerous to their children's health. Acknowledging the importance of "maternal instinct," which she described as "love, patience, and unselfishness," one mother, signing herself "A trained mother," wrote to *Good Housekeeping* in 1911 and claimed that "maternal instinct left alone succeeds in killing a large proportion of the babies born into this world."[39] Soon, ill health, excessive crying, any negative characteristic of an infant could be, and was, blamed on maternal ignorance.[40]

Of course, this claim was not new in the twentieth century. Decades before "A trained mother" warned of the dangers of maternal instinct and promised the benefits of educated motherhood, other mothers had started looking to science and to physicians. In 1872 in *Hearth and Home,* a maga-zine directed to rural women, Ruth Freeman reminded her readers of the "utter helplessness [of] each human being when it starts upon its earthly career." She bemoaned the limited knowledge available on the care of infants, com-plaining about "what fools we have all been, ever since the foundation of the world" and urging women of "true womanliness" to pursue "the highest knowledge and the deepest science."[41] Two decades later, in *New England Kitchen Magazine*, Ellen Battelle Dietrick praised the new "race of mothers who equip themselves for motherhood as thoughtfully, conscientiously and zealously as any other scientist prepares himself for an exacting career."[42] Dietrick's use of "himself" is significant. A profession, whether law, medi-cine, the ministry, or science, was a masculine pursuit. In equating mother-hood with scientific activity, Dietrick was simultaneously enjoining women to seek advanced knowledge and affirming that women be considered worthy of such action and responsibility. Echoing Dietrick's call, Hannah Whitall Smith demanded that women "change instinct into insight. We need, in short, to study the science of motherhood as carefully and as intelligently as we would study any other science."[43] New in this period was the vehemence of the hyper-bole and the even more forceful emphasis on the need to listen to doctors.

The reasons that mothers turned to contemporary science and medi-cine in the twentieth century are varied. Throughout the century, mortality and morbidity rates continued to fall. Popular knowledge of these declines further enhanced the prestige and status of medical science and physicians, which had been rising since such earlier discoveries as germs and vaccines.

At the same time, the average family size was shrinking. In the nineteenth century, children were economically beneficial, especially in rural areas, where they could assist with the labor necessary to sustain the family. In the city, and urbanization was increasing in the twentieth century, children were less likely to be in the labor force, jobs for children were less common, and laws that required children to attend school also drew them from the labor market. Over time, families had fewer and fewer children. It is likely that in smaller families, each child was much more precious. This is not to suggest that parents felt any less sorrow on losing one child within a large family, but that in smaller families emotional commitment was focused more tightly on one or two children. In the words of historian Viviana A. Zelizer, children by the early decades of the twentieth century were "defined as emotionally priceless assets."[44] At the same time, science and medicine promised the health and well-being of the child.

Each ill child made well under the direction of a private physician further enhanced the reputation of modern medicine as women told their friends about the events. The successful treatment of ill children at clinics also added to the aura of the profession. Some clinics affected whole communities. In 1915, the well-child clinic in Madison, Wisconsin, faced a severe challenge. Because vegetables were difficult to obtain at the time, the immigrant families of the area faced an epidemic of scurvy. In some unspecified manner, the clinic alleviated the condition and in so doing established itself "on a firmer basis and inspire[d] trust in the people that ran it."[45]

An article by Mrs. W. R. Hollowell of Goldsboro, South Carolina, in the *Progressive Farmer* in 1916 embodies the faith of mothers at the turn of the century in medical and scientific expertise and reveals just how the ideology of scientific motherhood had permeated U.S. society. Hollowell appreciated the knowledge and education of medical practitioners but not so much that she blindly accepted all they said. Her piece "Why the young doctor is to be trusted" relates with disgust the story of one young woman faced with an old-fashioned doctor who laughed at her when she objected to his use of "not even sterilized, just old, common, dirty cotton" to dress her infant's navel. Faced with such an authoritarian physician, the young woman felt "helpless; they make out like they know more than I, and they do, of course, and say that I had better quit reading all that mess in *The Progressive Farmer* and *Ladies' Home Journal, The Woman's Home Companion*, etc." The mother knew about modern scientific and medical practices, she was well read in the literature of the day, but she could not overcome the authority of the physician.

Hollowell commiserates with the unfortunate mother and her child, noting that "the most ignorant member of the laity that ever read a newspaper would know about germs and the serious danger of infection." She does not fault all physicians, but she stresses the necessity of carefully selecting the right physician and following his advice. (Hollowell consistently employs the male pronoun in referring to doctors. Given the relative scarcity of women in the medical profession at this time in the United States, this was an understandable grammatical practice as well as an indication of the gendered nature of the professions and of the study of science and medicine.) Hollowell recommended finding a doctor who combines experience with new knowledge. Identifying a well-educated physician was only one important maternal task. In addition, every mother should send a postcard to the Children's Bureau requesting copies of its publications because, Hollowell insisted, "in this day and time, it is little less than criminal to thrust into being a life without this knowledge by the mother who gives that soul being." Trustworthy doctors trained in modern medical studies were necessary, but that did not relieve the mother of the responsibility of evaluating the advice they gave her. The epitome of early-twentieth-century scientific motherhood, Hollowell confirms maternal responsibility for family health and well-being, while simultaneously enjoining women to learn from the latest scientific and medical authorities. As she concluded:

> May every little mother in the country know that she is right in reading all she can for the baby's welfare and practicing what she learned! God has given the care of the tiny baby only to the mother's arms; He has given that mother the intelligence of the man [*sic*], and with it an added quality—intuition. And what can be God's purpose in this but that she has been entrusted with the care of the world's welfare—the future of the human race? Therefore, all hail to the intelligent doctor, . . . and the mother who is both young and intelligent![46]

By the early years of the twentieth century, mothers had internalized the basic tenets of scientific motherhood. They accepted the idea that the best advice on child care came from medical and scientific experts, most usually physicians. Some women continued to depend on their neighbors, friends, and relatives for information on the best ways to raise their children. Some remained supremely self-confident in their own abilities. But more and more women looked to medical and scientific experts to inform them about the latest, most modern thoughts about child-care issues. Certainly they were convinced that physicians in particular held special knowledge that would improve their children's lives.

CHAPTER 3

"Follow my instructions exactly"

EXPERTS TO MOTHERS IN THE INTERWAR PERIOD
AND DURING WORLD WAR II

*In December 1932, a seventeen-month-old infant was brought to the San Francisco Child Health Center. The examining doctor reported with disapproval that the baby was still being bottle-fed and the mother was "told to stop." Two months later, the examining physician wrote that the mother "took ¹/₂ hr of Drs' time which was a repeat of the last Drs'. [She was] Told not to return unless she does as she was told." The mother and her infant did return in April and there was no more mention in the file of bottle feeding.[1] This and numerous other examples make it clear that by the interwar period, physicians expected and demanded that both poorer clinic patients and middle-class mothers attended by private doctors follow their doctors' orders without deviation. The ideal of scientific motherhood now consisted of a dominant physician and an obsequious mother.

This transformation is evident in published sources as well. Dr. Frank Richardson's 1925 child-care manual carried the reassuring title *Simplifying Motherhood.* Mother "simplified" her tasks by turning all control over to the physician. There was no doubt about whom Richardson considered the authority. He regarded his advice as the product of "a 'keep-well' system, in which all responsibility rests, not on the mother but on the shoulders of the doctor who is directing the baby's whole regimen."[2] An article in the 1938 volume of *Hygeia,* the popular health magazine published by the American Medical Association, reinforced this physician-mother relationship, telling mothers that regular doctor visits are "the best insurance you can buy" for protecting a child's health.[3] During this period, the rhetoric of doctors and other proponents of scientific motherhood became increasingly strident as they insisted on the crucial role of scientific and medical expertise and experts in the healthful rearing of children. In their hands, the hierarchical relationship of scientific motherhood with the authoritarian physician, usually male, who gave directions to the passive, submissive mother was solidified. Mothers, wanting the best for their children, were often convinced of the necessity of medical supervision but they are not always as acquiescent as the contemporary version of scientific motherhood demanded.[4]

Physicians were openly disdainful of mothers. One of the nation's leading pediatricians, Joseph Brennemann, was extremely hostile to mothers who would do anything more than follow his directions. He granted that women needed some instruction to insure that they successfully acted on the physician's advice. But too much instruction would create a mother who might question her doctor and such a woman, he believed, was an obstacle to the health of her child. He warned other physicians in 1930, "That lay education is desirable may be granted as an axiom. . . . [But] in actual practice the young mother with a nutritionally untutored mind who frankly states that she knows nothing about babies and leaves the instruction to me is a treasure; the mother who has perhaps specialized in dietetics while in college, or who approaches the subject with a McCollum in one hand and a Gesell in the other is sometimes more of a problem than is her baby."[5] By the mid-twentieth century, an educated woman could be a threat to her child's physical and psychological health.

Mothers needed education—but not too much education—and also they needed the right education. That meant education from a physician, not out of newspapers or magazine columns written by nonphysicians, and not according to neighbors or friends or relatives. From the vantage point of 1944, Isaac Abt, a Chicago colleague of Brennemann, looked back fondly to a mythic past when mothers depended on instinct and were not misguided by confusing advice from nonmedical sources. Take the question of fresh air for the baby, he explained:

> In the matter of regular airings, it is possible that children fared better before mothers had read in the papers that every baby should be taken out of doors every day. When we had horses, we hesitated to drive them in a high wind or a snow-storm; and if this was unavoidable, we saw to it that they were blanketed and sheltered as much as possible. Today, many people seem to think a baby is stronger than a horse. When I was a child, the question of keeping the baby in the open air was determined by common sense; and that was well

developed in the mother of sixty or seventy years ago. She used her own judgment—happily unfortified by long-range advice delivered daily by the newsboy—and did not imagine that her child would lose vitality by being kept in the house for a day.[6]

In Abt's eyes, the proliferation of bad advice had perverted the common sense of mothers. Both he and Brennemann were concerned that maternal education of the wrong sort threatened the health of the child and made their jobs much more difficult. Abt concluded, "From a doctor's point of view, the mother of long ago was, in general, easier to work with than the mother of today. Although she was often garrulous, she was quick to observe deviation from the normal and report them exactly, permitting the doctor to interpret the facts. She said, 'Baby sniffles every night and has a rattle in his throat.' The modern mother, on the contrary, is inclined to make her own diagnosis. 'Baby is allergic,' she says."[7] Maternal education was the solution to the problems of child care, education that directed the mother to the physician, but not too much education so that she might question or second-guess the physician.

By the 1920s and 1930s, then, with the further consolidation of the medical profession, with the coalescence of medical specialties such as pediatrics, and the cultural authority of medicine at its height, physicians presented an image of supreme self-confidence.[8] Mothers, physicians insisted, must look to them, not to instinct, not to neighbors, friends, or relatives, not to advertisements. Furthermore, mothers were to follow the physicians' instructions to the letter, to passively acquiesce to medical instructions. Earlier, physicians had accepted the idea that mothers would learn from medical practitioners, and also that mothers and medical practitioners would work together to some extent. Physicians were dominant but not the be-all and end-all for advice on child care. Now, however, mothers' role consisted solely in selecting the medical practitioner. "If you have picked your doctor intelligently and have faith in his skills," the popular magazine *Modern Priscilla* reminded women, then "do exactly what he says, no matter what contrary advice you may have. . . . Obey his orders absolutely, because his experience and his knowledge is superior."[9] Physicians expected blind obedience to their instructions, promising good health and happiness if the mother accepted medical direction.

In their 1932 pamphlet *Instructions for Expectant Mothers and the Care of Infants*, Whiteis and Anthony, doctors in Iowa City, Iowa, addressed the details of daily care, ranging from the appropriate layette and the perennial how-to-bathe the baby, to the importance of regular feeding. They instructed mothers to read the publication carefully and save it for reference. However, "whenever a point comes up concerning the care of the mother or child, which is not fully covered or understood, your doctor should be consulted at once."[10] And they reminded their readers that "your baby needs and deserves a good start in life. Fortunately, it is easy and inexpensive to assume this by seeing that he has frequent medical attention during his formative years."[11] Whether this patronizing attitude of Whiteis and Anthony resulted from medical self-assurance or possible frustration with the continued existence of alternative sources for child-care advice, the effect was the same: mothers were enjoined in no uncertain terms to follow the directions of their physician.

Like Whiteis and Anthony, many physicians promoted the importance of medical supervision in booklets written for their patients in private practice. These ephemera enable us to see medical practice from the perspective of the practicing physician. The earliest of these booklets appear in the 1920s, when they were directed at middle- and upper-class patients who could afford to act on the emerging consensus that the health of women and their children required regular office visits during pregnancy and for child care. Though limited to this target group, the booklets reflect physicians' views of their role and they make quite clear the behavior expected of mothers; they illustrate the idealized mother-physician relationship.

Take, for example, *Instructions for Expectant Mothers*, written by Frank O. Wood, of Hartford, Connecticut, an obstetrician who expected his patients would return to him after delivery. Wood urged his patients to faithfully observe the advice in his booklet. He was emphatic that he and he alone held the answers to their questions. "Unless I recommend them, do not buy books on pregnancy or infant care, as they tend to confuse," he wrote. Moreover, "please do not accept advice from friends or relatives, however well-intended. I cannot be responsible for your well-being unless you follow my instructions exactly."[12] The tone and the specific instructions clearly established the dominant position of the physician and the subordinate, if not submissive, role of the patient. Wood depicted himself as the "fount of all knowledge," not an unusual stance for a physician of the period. Not that he denied women access to knowledge about health matters, but that knowledge must come from him. Echoing other counselors, Wood warned that nonprofessionals based their advice on individual situations, which can and do vary greatly. Only physicians have observed the wide range of cases necessary for informed judgment. In this private publication, Wood insisted that his instructions were to be obeyed, or the patient risked her health and the health of her future child.

"Many times women wish to know whether or not they may travel to various out-of-town places," Wood noted. "The answer is no, and if you go you must be entirely responsible." Here Wood gave the patient the appearance of choice: she could choose to follow his counsel or not. But if she went her own way, she faced a fearful future. In this pamphlet, the physician is presented as the guardian of health and safety; the patient, representing danger, must acquiesce to all his instructions.

Some physicians explicitly omitted any discussion of specific areas of child care in their booklets for patients in order to bring the mother back to the doctor. In the 1920s, when William M. Hanrahan provided his patients with the pamphlet *General Instructions to Prospective Mothers*, he was most insistent that infant feeding was not a topic that mothers could decide for themselves. Each infant was unique; there were no general rules that could be laid down for a mother to follow. To him it was clear: infant feeding "must have the careful judgment of the pediatrician."[13]

Not all physicians were as dogmatic as Wood and Hanrahan. H. Kent Tenney, for decades the preeminent pediatrician in Madison, Wisconsin, took a slightly different approach, yet one characterized by a similar relationship between physician and patient. In the 1930s, Tenney privately printed and distributed to his patients a chatty book entitled *Let's Talk about Your Baby*. It proved so popular with patients and other physicians who saw it that a second edition was published in 1940 by the University of Minnesota Press. Tenney's style was less authoritarian than Wood's and Hanrahan's, but no less authoritative. In his first chapter, he has the mother querying "Doc" about the baby's room and furniture. The physician opened his remarks with the statement: "There are some things that are really important and some that can be left to your judgment." He then went on to explain about beds, bedclothes, bath table, scales, shirts, diapers, care of diapers, nightgowns, dresses, sweaters, bootees, rubber pants, and woolen trunks. It is not clear what could be left to the mother's judgment. Once again, the physician is the person responsible; the mother follows his instructions, even in the minutiae of daily life.

Many forms of maternal education steered mothers towards doctors. In addition to physician-authored books, a wide array of other sources such as government pamphlets, well-baby clinics, and visiting nurses instructed mothers on the importance of physician supervision. However, the mother's exposure to these sources was not systematized. Some upper- and middle-class mothers took their children to see a physician regularly, which undoubtedly reinforced the message. Manuals and magazines with the latest medical information and celebration of physicians were available to the literate. Visiting nurses entered the homes of the working class and of immigrants, but frequently only when the children were ill. In other situations, mothers attended well-baby clinics when they were available. By the 1930s, though, a new, more focused venue for educating mothers came to dominate the scene: widespread utilization of hospitalized childbirth.

Few women birthed in U.S. hospitals in the nineteenth century. The trend to institutionalized childbirth grew in the early years of the twentieth century as doctor-attended hospital births promised safer and less painful labors and deliveries with the increased use of anaesthesia and antiseptic routines. By the advent of World War II, approximately one-half of all births in the U.S. took place in hospitals; by 1955, the number had reached 95 percent.[14] This institutional setting placed women in an unfamiliar environment without their families and friends. It provided an unparalleled opportunity to educate impressionable new mothers in the most modern of child-care practices and in an appreciation of medical supervision. Health-care practitioners recognized this as a "teaching moment." One, speaking at the annual meeting of the American Academy of Pediatrics in 1928, maintained that the maternity unit was a prime location for such education because the mother

> is an unusual patient in that she is intimately under the care of her physician for approximately a year, if we include her prenatal and post-partum care. It is possible by collaborative effort with our existing knowledge, hospital, and clinic facilities, to do a much more complete and better job in this regard, giving the mother a lasting impression of the advantages of modern obstetrics and pediatrics for herself and her baby. The advantage[s] of such a program in time-saving and services rendered are obvious.[15]

Women who learned to depend on medical practitioners in the hospital would continue to look to physicians in later years, fostering a lucrative career for the physicians and fixing in mothers' minds the basic tenets of scientific motherhood.

Hospitalized childbirth at midcentury was very different than it is now. Today, mothers are released from the hospital within twenty-four to forty-eight hours after the birth, sometimes earlier. In the first half of the century, the stay was seven to ten days. Today, the newborn is next to the mother during their entire hospital stay; previously, newborns were swept from the delivery room into the nursery, from which they were brought to their mothers for feedings only and on a strict schedule. As one doctor described the ideal

FIGURE 3.1. Mothers and infants at doctor's office. Caption: "A return visit to the doctor is almost a form of insurance, for here a careful check-up is made to determine the baby's weight, growth, and general health and the condition of the mother. Advice is given about artificial feeding, if necessary, and about questions which may have arisen in the mother's mind about the baby's bath and other features of baby's care." *Source: Hygeia* 16 (1938): 423.

hospital setting, "The new-born baby in the modern hospital nursery is clothed and covered lightly. Proper ventilation is maintained, the temperature of the nursery is 70°F or less. The infant is not picked up except for his bath, when diapers need to be changed and at feeding time."[16] Under such a regimen, women saw little of their infants before going home with their "little stranger." Doctors and hospital administrators offered both institutional and medical rationales for these routines. Hanging as a cloud over every maternity ward was the fear of epidemics. Before the discovery of sulfa drugs in the 1930s and later the widespread utilization of antibiotics after World War II, infections could, and often did, sweep through hospital nurseries. Isolating babies from their mothers and any other possible source of contamination was considered critical in the control of potential epidemics. Also, especially in large urban hospitals, stringent routines were needed to keep the hospital running smoothly, routines that reinforced the commonly accepted practice of scheduling all aspects of child care, such as feeding on a fixed schedule of every three or four hours and bathing at a set time every day.

Such scheduling was an institutionalized form of Watsonian behaviorism, the form of child management named for psychologist John B. Watson.[17] After an academic career, Watson applied his theories in the emerging arena of Madison Avenue motivational advertising. Even from his position in commerce, he continued to promote behaviorism in child care as the way to protect the child. For instance, he discouraged mothers from kissing their children. Previously, mothers had been warned that kissing was dangerous because it might spread germs. For Watson, kissing was a sign of emotion, which had to be dampened before it engulfed the child and the mother. Children should at most be kissed once a day, but should quickly be taught to

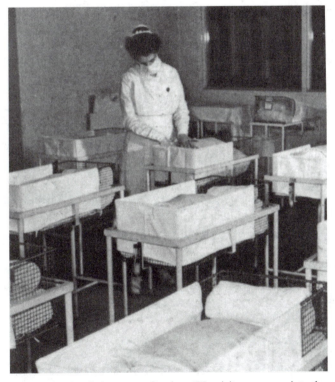

Figure 3.2. Hospital nursery. Caption: "No visitors may go into the nursery, for babies are peculiarly susceptible to infection. Specially trained nurses, individual equipment, and no contact between the babies are factors in promoting a program of protection." *Source: Hygiea* 16 (1938): 422.

greet their parents in the morning with a respectful handshake. In this way, as with rigid scheduling, children would be protected from their mothers, both physically and emotionally.[18]

Despite this nomenclature—Watsonian behaviorism, its practice significantly predates the work of Watson. In 1907, Dr. Emma Walker explained that in order to prevent the development of bad habits, the baby must learn to sleep through the night. Therefore, she advised, if babies cry at bedtime, let them cry. Even if they cry for seventeen nights or more, let them cry. Eventually they will learn to sleep through the night.[19] A few years later, Dr. Francis Tweddell told mothers that they should begin bowel training when their children were two months of age, with some children successfully trained by age three months. He explained that "the comfort of forming this habit at the earliest possible age will be readily appreciated, as it means a great saving of labor; and it is also beneficial to the child's health, as it will be conducive to regular movements of the bowels throughout childhood."[20] Bladder training, he admitted, was more difficult but with perseverance could sometimes be accomplished in the first year. He also discouraged play. Playing with young infants could, he warned, be "injurious, and may be the means of making [the infant] nervous and irritable." Even past the age of six months, he expected children to amuse themselves.[21]

Roger Dennett, in his confidently titled book *The Healthy Baby*, indicates the lengths to which physicians went in outlining schedules in the early twentieth century. In the chapter on "Daily routine," he explains that with a newborn, first of all, the doctor will decide the length of time between feedings; he (Dennett) usually begins the child on a three-hour schedule. This then determines the flow of the day, which he explained as follows:

> We start the first feeding at a given time, say six o'clock in the morning, thus beginning the day right. This will give the nurse or mother time to dress, have her breakfast, give the baby a bath, and even make up the bottle-fed baby's feedings before nine o'clock, when the next feeding is due.
>
> After the nine o'clock feeding, the baby is taken out for his airing and morning nap. If there is a yard or fire escape available for this part of the day's program, the mother has this interval free for other duties. At twelve comes another bottle, followed by the mother's luncheon and baby's afternoon nap and airing. At three there is another feeding, followed by an interval, during which baby has his recreation hour, lying on the bed or sitting on the floor to play by

himself. During the hour before six he may be held in the lap or entertained, if one has the inclination, or if he gets restless and fussy by himself. After the six o'clock bottle, he goes to bed for the night and is not taken out of bed again until morning, except for his feedings.[22]

Clearly then, even in the nineteenth and early twentieth centuries, physicians did not limit their pronouncements to the physical care of children; they considered other aspects of the child within their purview, including everything from how long a baby should cry to the psychological dangers of thumb-sucking. Well in advance of the profession of child psychology, physicians

FIGURE 3.3. Time cards, c. 1935. *Source:* Division of Child Hygiene, Minnesota Department of Health, with the permission of the Children's Bureau, U.S. Department of Labor.

explained the importance of rigorous regularity in terms of child development and habit formation, consciously linking the physical and emotional in their insistence that regularity in infancy would produce a well-adjusted adult.

The insistent and extensive demands of physicians would have been mere footnotes in history if they had not been promoted through U.S. society by others as well. Popular culture and popular education attest to the pervasiveness of the ideology of scientific motherhood throughout U.S. society, especially in the twentieth century. The importance of scientific and medical expertise to appropriate mothering was noted in passing in literature ranging from ephemeral advertisements through human interest stories to government reports. The tenets of the ideology were casually included in media such as Hollywood films and later television programs. The significance of scientific motherhood to the image of the good mother underpinned contests at agricultural fairs and was evident in school and after-school programs. In some sources, such as child-care books and formal education, scientific motherhood was in the foreground, explicitly articulated as the underlying rationale for modern motherhood.[23] In other sources, scientific motherhood appears as a passing mention or part of the general background in the discussion of another topic, documenting that it was common knowledge, if not common practice.

One example of the former was the Emergency Maternity and Infant Care (EMIC) program developed through the Children's Bureau during World War II. Initially it received limited funding through the Social Security Act, but by 1943 all states had set up programs with special congressional appropriations designed to "raise the morale of enlisted men by relieving them of concern over the uncertainty of the availability of maternity care for their wives and medical and hospital care for their infants, and of anxiety as to how the cost of this care would be met." Prenatal, maternity, and post-partum care was available to wives of enlisted men, who were encouraged to apply early in pregnancy. Similarly, and most significantly, well-child and other medical care was available to their infants for up to one year of age. As a result, in state after state, more and more women were directed to hospitals for their children's birth and mothers were persuaded to continue this medical supervision in the following months. By 1947, almost 1,200,000 mothers had been attended along with their children and more than 200,000 children received additional care from authorized hospitals, physicians, nurses, and social workers, as well as state and local health agencies that often handled the massive paperwork associated with these efforts. To facilitate this work, new mothers' classes were sponsored by the USO and local health departments. This instruction also emphasized the need for maternal education and the assumption of medically supervised child care. In regions of the country where segregation was practiced, separate classes were established for white and black women. Though it was difficult to conduct detailed follow-up studies of this highly mobile war-time population, instructors were proud to announce that as far as they could determine all their students returned to physicians for post-partum examinations and that they adopted the practice of early childhood immunization, indications of the widespread acceptance of scientific motherhood in the 1940s.[24]

Other forums too acknowledge this ideology in U.S. society. I have already discussed home economics at the turn of the century. The discipline became even more influential in the interwar period and the middle decades of the twentieth century. As in the earlier period, home economics was championed as the educational solution to critical social problems plaguing the United States. After World War I and the Immigration Restriction Acts of the 1920s, massive immigration ended and home economics moved from "Americanization" to "modernization." New equipment, such as vacuum cleaners, electric refrigerators, and automatic washing machines; the growing popularity of automobiles, which fostered the spread of suburbs; the explosion of national brands of convenience foods, such as canned fruits and packaged rice; and the recent developments in nutritional science, such as the discovery of miraculous micronutrients like vitamins; all changed domestic labor. Mothers lacked the experiential knowledge to teach their daughters how to cope with this complicated modern life. Home economists eagerly took on that role. By the end of the 1910s, federal funding under the Smith-Hughes Act of 1917 had firmly established home economics in the primary and secondary schools across the nation.[25] In 1919, home economist Alma Binzel noted: "Much of what is unwise in the rearing of children is due to the indifference, the inertia, and the lack of insight that rise from unpreparedness for the responsibility. Each generation of graduates from the eighth grade and high school courses in home economics should increase the number of homes in which babies and children will have better chances of survival and health."[26] Such rationales helped generate support for home economics among politicians and school administrators, but at the same time changed the tone and content of this education for girls. They moved home economics from the general-education, science-based program of the early twentieth century to one more focused on the development of domestic skills.[27]

Like home economics education, Girl Scouting adapted to the new expectations of twentieth-century America. Between 1920 and 1970, millions

FIGURE 3.4. Seventh-grade girls participating in demonstrations preparing children's food, clothing, and toys, and in bathing infants. *Source:* National League for Nursing Archives.

of girls joined Girl Scout troops—some stayed only a year or two, but many others maintained their membership into adulthood.[28] Most critically, both Girl Scouting and home economics consciously sought to prepare girls for their future as women of America. Singly and together, Girl Scouting and home economics sanctioned, sanctified, and reinforced a specific domestic image of the American woman. In both, experts—typically medical experts— played an expanded role in defining and limiting the extent of girls' and women's domestic role. Moreover, a loss of autonomy occurred as girls' activities in both Girl Scouting and the home economics curriculum called for less and less self-reliance. In its place, impressionable adolescents were taught to follow the directions of experts.

Girl Scout manuals explained the various aspects of Girl Scouting and, most importantly, outlined the specific requirements for acquiring merit badges, the focus of most Girl Scout activities. Girl Scouts would have read them very closely.[29] Hence, Girl Scout manuals, like home economics text-books, reached millions of suggestible girls. During Girl Scouting's early

years, in which the organization grew slowly, girls consulted a manual entitled *How Girls Can Help Their Country* (1913), adapted from the British
Girl Guides' handbook, *How Girls Can Help the Empire*.[30] This handbook,
which like home economics texts assumed that girls would grow up to become mothers, included a short section on the "Care of children" and listed
"child nurse" as one of the badges girls could earn. This skills-oriented domestic badge required the Scout to take care of a child or infant, to make
poultices, to do patching and darning, and to know how to test bath heat, use
a thermometer, and test the pulse.[31] The 1914 badge requirements natural-
ized motherhood, encouraged girls to *do*, but not to *think* through the problems and questions of child care.

Following World War I, the manual changed significantly as Girl Scouting became more popular (the number of Girl Scouts increased by a factor
of ten, from little more than 8,000 in 1917 to over 83,000 in 1921). In the
post–World War I period, the manuals insinuated that a woman's success in
the domestic sphere and beyond often derived from her ability to learn from
scientific and medical experts, a conclusion supported by the tremendous explosion of advice literature emanating from commercial publishers, physician-
authors, and governmental agencies as well as the growth of parenting
education, hospitalized childbirth, and child study clubs. The 1920 edition
of the Girl Scout manual, *Scouting for Girls*, epitomized the new model of
womanhood with themes of domesticity and female self-sacrifice that are traditional enough to harken back to the nineteenth century.[32] Yet, at the same
time, the methods recommended are modern. Household chores will take less
time when the girl learns the "scientific, business-like way" to accomplish
them "with the quickest, most efficient methods, just as any clever business
man manages his business."[33] Thus, by marrying traditional roles with modern methods, the 1920 Scout manual simultaneously and subtly denigrated
women's ways and elevated those associated with men.

The manual continued to reinforce the idea of female as traditional and
male as modern in its discussion of badge requirements, which often involve
scientifically informed domestic tasks. Household Economics, for example,
will be "the great general business and profession of women, if it is raised
to the level or [*sic*] the other great businesses and professions, and managed
quickly, efficiently and economically, will cease to be regarded as drudgery
and take its real place among the arts and sciences."[34] Similarly, the discussion on child care valued contemporary medically sanctioned practices, such
as behaviorism, over women's traditional experience. In order to earn the child
nurse badge in 1920, a Scout had to care for a child under two for at least

two hours a day for four weeks (a minimum of fifty-six hours). During this time, she had to handle all the necessary work of routine care, including feeding, bathing, and dressing. Other required activities for the badge were more "academic": the scout was expected to answer questions such as "How can a baby be encouraged to move itself and take exercise?" Several reference books were listed, but answers to all these questions were included in the manual's discussion of child care. The clear expectation was that by 1920 the Scout should *think* about why she does certain things with a child. Thus, these badge requirements were in stark contrast to the earliest requirements for a child-care badge. A Girl Scout earning a child-care badge after World War I is expected to have hands-on experience with a child *and* to demonstrate her ability in problem solving.

The emphasis on learning by doing, especially in relation to child care, persisted in the 1929 edition of the manual, which also connected good mothering with nationalism, a reminder of the patriotic furor that swept the country during World War I and that remained a common theme through the 1920s. Girl Scouts were reminded that "there always are and always will be children to be taken care of. There is no way in which a girl can help her country better than by fitting herself to understand the care of children."[35] To earn the child nurse badge, a Girl Scout still needed to demonstrate that she could independently and responsibly care for a child, but by 1929 the child could be older (any age up to five) and the period of care was reduced from fifty-six hours during one month to twenty-four hours spread over three months. Still, the Scout was expected to "perform all the necessary work covering daily care of a child, including feeding, bathing, dressing, preparing for bed, arranging bed and windows, amusing, giving fresh air and exercise, and so forth." She again had to exhibit her knowledge of the rationale for these tasks, leaning on contemporary scientific and medical expertise. One of the activities, for example, required her to "bring a chart or a poster, which you have drawn or made of pictures you have cut out, showing the foods suitable for a child up to five years of age." While this version of the child-care badge demanded less in the way of "academic" knowledge than earlier badges, the Girl Scout continued to learn by doing and by being responsible. Other badge requirements were more creative and active, requiring the Scout to plan and give a party with games and refreshments for a group of children.

While these early manuals show the impact of scientific and medical knowledge on the activities required for child-care badges, the growing influence of medical practitioners in baby and child care became more evident in later manuals. The 1940 requirements again specify a minimum of twenty-four hours of care over a three-month period. Now, however, Scouts would only "be responsible for the care that the baby's doctor feels you can safely assume."[36] Now, information about child care should come from physicians—undercutting female experiential learning; so too should permission to care for children come from a medical practitioner—not the mother. By the end of the decade, the requirement that a Scout be responsible for the daily care of a child had been dropped. In order to earn the child-care badge, she needed a *doll* to demonstrate how to bathe, dress, and feed a baby.

A similar trend is evident in advertisements of the period. The very casual and frequent inclusion of medical and scientific expertise and experts to sell an incredibly wide range of products indicates that the ideology of scientific motherhood was commonplace in U.S. culture. We would expect an encyclopedia on child care to promote the use of scientific and medical knowledge; a 1938 advertisement for it (fig. 3.5) does that. The modern, up-to-date mother replaces traditional advice networks with scientific advice. As the advertisement proclaims, "Instead of blindly following instinct alone or laboriously duplicating the tedious methods of previous generations, you turn to specialists and authority," which implies that without them mothering would be a dismal failure. "Specialists and authority" replace "instinct" and the knowledge of "previous generations." The appeal to science is strengthened with the grandmother extolling the virtues and benefits of modern motherhood. The copy underscores her advice: "Add science to love and be a 'perfect mother.'" At the same time that this advertisement elevates modern science and medicine, it subverts traditional and family methods as the grandmother sadly relates that she did not have such modern information.

Physicians and scientific discoveries are used to convince consumers to purchase an exceedingly diverse array of goods and services, some with tangible connection to health, such as food products, soap, and household cleaners, and some more tangential, such as toilet paper. A 1928 Scot Tissue advertisement (fig. 3.6) is unambiguous about who should judge the best product. Basically, the advertisement implies that mothers who care about their children will listen to medical practitioners on many, many issues, even on the topic of toilet paper. By this period, doctors had not only intervened in the home routines of mothers, they had also entered the bathroom. Sometimes advertisements even coupled physicians' solutions with mothers' ignorance. The two are graphically illustrated in a Lysol advertisement from 1936 (fig. 3.7), in which the mother is clearly blamed for her child's illness. She did not listen to scientific and medical experts and her child suffers.

Other manufacturers presented less threatening scenarios, but were

FIGURE 3.5. Advertisement for child-care class, 1938. *Source: Parents Magazine* 13 (Nov. 1938): 77.

FIGURE 3.6. Scot Tissue advertisement, 1928. *Source: Good Housekeeping* 86 (Feb. 1928): 233.

FIGURE 3.7. Lysol advertisement, 1936. *Source: Good Housekeeping* 102 (May 1936): 107.

similarly based on "medically informed" child-care advice. The seventy-eight-page booklet *Baby's Outfit* provided mothers with counsel from "eminent scientists of motherhood" and exhorted mothers to depend on physicians' advice in areas such as baby's sleep, mother's diet, baby's weight and growth.[37] It was published for Vanta, manufacturer of diapers, vests, training pants, and the like, and so not surprisingly ten pages were devoted to a discussion of these products. Moreover, in its promotion of modern, scientific motherhood, *Baby's Outfit* consistently lauded the knowledge of physicians and denigrated the knowledge of others, particularly grandmothers. For example, the reader learns of new clothing products that have won the approval of "doctors, nurses and infant workers." However, such items might not meet the approval the grandmother and the booklet warns that "it may be hard for you to disregard the advice of your own mothers or dear friends but the health and happiness of your Baby are much more important than the opinions of friends and relatives."[38] Once again, women are told that ignoring medical advice and depending instead on female experience can be dangerous for their families. How convincing were these arguments we cannot judge. What is significant is that we see these claims are widespread in advertisements and brochures of the period, claims that are echoed in other areas of U.S. culture.

Hollywood writers, too, assumed the public's familiarity with the ideas of scientific motherhood. The concept was so well established that they could use it for comic effect. Take, for example, the 1939 film *Bachelor Mother*, which starred Ginger Rogers and David Niven. Rogers is a sales clerk in an urban department store; Niven is the son of the store owner. Through a series of complicated events, Rogers becomes the caretaker of an infant. Rogers is unmarried and therefore, in Hollywood's world, an uneducated mother. Niven, who is interested in Rogers romantically, offers to help her. The telling scene opens with Rogers feeding the child. Niven enters and asks how she knows what she is doing is correct. Rogers replies that there is nothing to it; she puts food on the spoon, puts the spoon in the baby's mouth, and the baby swallows it. Niven is not so sure. He pulls out a child-care manual, written by a doctor with "twenty years' experience," that he has picked up in the book department of the store. Moreover, he insists that Rogers stop feeding the child until he has read the pertinent section on feeding. What he finds is that the mother is told to rub some warm food into the child's navel. From Rogers's face the audience can tell she is torn: the baby was happy as she was feeding it, but an "expert" is advising something quite different. She puts the spoon down and starts to undress the child as if to follow the doctor's instructions. Then, rethinking the situation, she takes the book from Niven and begins to read the same section. Though still bewildered, she announces that she will not put the food on the child's navel. Then, looking more closely at the book, she realizes that several pages are stuck together. When read in the correct sequence, they provide the mother with a treatment for colic, involving the rubbing of warm oil into the baby's navel. Ultimately, Rogers returns to feeding the child as she had been doing. This scene shows that the idea of buying a book written by a physician in order to learn how to take care of a child was widely accepted by the 1930s. It was so recognizable a part of U.S. culture that it could easily be dropped into a Hollywood film. The misreading or misinterpreting of the advice was fodder for the comedy writers, as was the mother's skepticism about expert claims. But the writers had this fodder because the concept of scientific motherhood was so common by this time.

The reasons that mothers turned to contemporary science and medicine in the twentieth century are varied. In the interwar period, social scientists turned their attention to the lives of "ordinary people." Health reformers too were studying the details of everyday life in order to highlight the correlates of morbidity and mortality. Drawing on their work we can develop a typography of factors that influenced the acceptance and rejection of scientific motherhood and that shaped its dimensions. Throughout the century, mortality and morbidity rates continued to fall. The trends of rising literacy rates, the widening spread of public education and mandatory schooling, the growing numbers of books, magazines, and newspapers continued to alert the reading public to the latest medical and scientific advances. This news, in turn, enhanced the prestige and the status of medical science and physicians, which had been rising since such earlier discoveries as germs and vaccines. To note just one example: by 1925 the City's Bureau of Child Hygiene claimed that through the use of mass inoculation against diphtheria and smallpox, major communicable diseases had been virtually eradicated in New York City. In a similar continuity, the average family size kept shrinking through the Depression and the years of World War II. Science and medicine in this period signified the promise of the health and well-being of that "priceless" child.[39]

The critical question is the extent to which mothers actually turned to medical and scientific experts and expertise in the period. In order to evaluate maternal practices, we need to look at a range of different sources. Literate mothers have left us written records in the form of published and unpublished letters, diaries, articles, and books. These personal accounts will be discussed in the following chapter. To assess the experiences of others—

mothers who lacked the skills, the time, or the inclination to record their lives—social scientists and government agents undertook a series of surveys and studies that examined the health and health practices of these often silent groups. Granted these investigators were not unbiased observers. They were often maternal and child health advocates and typically proponents of scientific motherhood. Yet, even reading their reports through that lens provides us with some indication of the popularity and spread of scientific motherhood in that era. For instance, in order to assess the health and welfare of America's mothers and children, the Children's Bureau sent researchers to many different sections of the country, urban and rural, where they conducted comprehensive neighborhood surveys, talking with mothers and health-care practitioners. The data suggest the range of sources women used in developing their child-care practices and document the uneven, nevertheless persistent spread of the ideology of scientific motherhood across the country. Despite the perspective of the interviewer, the voices of working-class women and women in poverty in the United States come through clearly.

The Children's Bureau study of rural Mississippi undertaken in the 1910s is instructive. In conducting the survey, Helen M. Dart learned that only about one in six mothers had any prenatal care, despite the insistence of the Children's Bureau and other proponents that scientific motherhood, including a medically supervised pregnancy, was critical to the health and well-being of children. Most of her informants lacked a knowledge of "modern" child care and the resources to follow medical advice. For example, these rural mothers breast-fed their infants into the second year and often longer, at a time when contemporary medical advice recommended much earlier weaning. Also, the diets of even very young infants were augmented with food from the table, primarily bread or crackers soaked in milk or gravy, a definite negative in contemporary guidance. Dart noted some differences in feeding patterns by racial groups but more often merged "whites" and "Negroes" in her analysis. Few mothers looked for child-care advice beyond their immediate circle of friends and relatives: twenty had received some instruction from a physician and two from a "trained nurse." Despite the high rate of illiteracy among these rural informants, however, Dart found that fifty-eight mothers had gained some knowledge from literature: two mothers had read Holt's book; one, a pamphlet from the Department of Agriculture; twenty-five, some current magazines and papers; the remaining depended on advertising pamphlets and almanacs. Consequently, "the methods of caring for children were in accordance with the customs handed down by other generations," Dart reported and, she added, "many mothers were very glad to receive the Children's Bureau pamphlet on Infant Care."[40] Mothers who recognized the benefits of medical practitioners were constrained by their poverty, even in cases of illness. The report relates numerous instances in which mothers had neither the money nor the time nor the household assistance to take their children to physicians or to carry out medical directions, if they had seen a doctor. As one mother told Dart: "A farmer only gets money twice a year, and if the children get sick between seasons they have to get along."[41] In another case, a newborn became ill but the family lived in the woods, four miles from the doctor and almost inaccessible from the main road. Consequently, all the family could do was consult the physician by phone. Despite the delivery of medicine, the baby died the next day.

Viola Paradise surveyed families in Montana in the same period.[42] There she found physicians were generally inaccessible and public-health nurses, rare. Yet, mothers in rural areas of Montana in the late 1910s were reaching out for medically sanctioned information on child care. Of the 463 mothers interviewed in this desolate area, 162 reported that their information on child care came from printed sources. Some used physician-authored books, such as Holt; others depended on brochures and booklets distributed by federal and state agencies; still others turned to advertising material. One mother told Paradise that "she had followed exactly" a government booklet. Another reported that she raised her child according to physician advice printed in a women's magazine, "though she had to fight the prejudices of grandparents and neighbors," who preferred traditional methods of childrearing. Paradise concluded that the majority of mothers realized that they needed child-care instruction.[43]

Health conferences held irregularly in this very poor, rural region attested to the mothers' appreciation for medical direction. Given the distinction between public-health efforts and private medical practice in the United States, these conferences offered no treatments. If treatment was needed, parents were directed to take their children to a local physician. Though they knew no medical care was available, still many mothers attended the conferences, eager to have a physician examine their children. The women wanted a medical practitioner to reassure them of the health of their families. Many families traveled more than fifteen miles to attend a conference; others drove twenty-five miles in each direction in open wagons. Mothers were not only eager for information, they also promised to follow the medical instructions they were given. And evidently they attempted to do so. Paradise saw one mother six weeks after she attended a conference with her baby where the physician had advised her to feed her child with cow's milk rather than condensed milk. The mother had changed the child's formula and was extremely pleased to see her infant begin to gain weight. Moreover, this advice on medically approved infant feeding reached beyond the conference attendees because "this mother said that she had written to all her relations whose babies were given condensed milk, telling them what the change to cows' milk had done for her child."[44] This woman's practice reflected the long tradition of woman-to-woman counsel but was based on medical direction, not personal experimentation.

Reports such as Dart's and Paradise's disclose women struggling with their responsibilities for family health.[45] Even in the rural areas of Mississippi, Montana, Wisconsin, and Kansas, slowly mothers were learning of the ideology of scientific motherhood. This awareness spread through the distribution of books, such as Holt's *Care and Feeding of Children*, and magazine articles, as well as the publications of the Children's Bureau and state and local health authorities, and face-to-face encounters with conference physicians, visiting nurses, and the representatives of the Children's Bureau. Over the decades as book, magazine, and pamphlet publishing grew and as funds became available to send visiting nurses into more homes across the country, women learned to use these sources in shaping their child-care practices.

Later surveys confirm that increasing numbers of women embraced these sources. Arguably the most comprehensive survey of the period was an outgrowth of the White Conference on Child Health and Protection of 1930.[46] This cross-sectional analysis conducted during the depths of the Depression suggests distinctions between socioeconomic classes and between racial groups, while highlighting the uneven, yet extensive spread of scientific motherhood across the country. The survey involved nearly 3,000 families, 2,758 white and 202 black. From this data, we can develop a picture of how American women were responding to the demands of scientific motherhood. It is evident across groups that women acted on the tenets of scientific motherhood within their abilities.

The first striking finding of Anderson's study is the extent to which white mothers, who were identified within seven standard socioeconomic classes, from class I: professional, to class VII: day laborers, read child-care literature. Over half of the sample had read a child-care book in the past year, ranging from a high of 80 percent of the professional class compared with barely 25 percent of the "laboring class." The contrast between classes is less, though still visible, when we turn to other print material. Over 70 percent of the families surveyed had used pamphlets, for example, with nearly 50 percent of the professional class reading five or more pamphlets in the past twelve months. Though mothers in the laboring class did not read as much, nevertheless almost one-half had read at least one pamphlet. Significantly, over one-half of the mothers in the survey cited pamphlets as an important source for information on child care.[47]

Anderson's statistics on the sources of information reported by white mothers is most critical for our appreciation of the pervasiveness of scientific motherhood in the late interwar period. For example, in addition to utilizing pamphlets, mothers took their children to doctors, invited nurses into their homes, and talked with neighbors and relatives. By far the most frequently cited source was pamphlets, with books a popular second. However, interestingly, by the mid-1930s, many mothers reported pediatricians as their source.[48] Within the more affluent groups, more than half looked to "pediatricians"; among the "farming group," where medical specialists were less common, less than 20 percent referred to these doctors; among the laboring class, only 7 percent saw pediatricians. Studying the survey's figures for nurses shows a reverse relationship. Barely 12 percent of mothers in the professional class used nurses for information on child care; over 60 percent of the laboring-class mothers did. While documenting the widespread employment of health-care professionals for help with childrearing, Anderson's figures even more significantly illustrate the fact that "grandmothers" and "other mothers" ranked fairly low as sources for information. The overwhelming majority of women surveyed reported sources outside traditional female networks. Pamphlets and books were the most popular sources across classes, followed by medical professionals. Though a relatively large proportion of women reported relying on their own experience, it is very likely that these were experienced mothers, not mothers of newborns. We have no indication from what sources their initial child-care information came.

The figures for African American families were separated in Anderson's study from those of white families. Because the black families spanned fewer socioeconomic classes, the information was analyzed and presented in one or two categories rather than the seven categories used for white families. Frequently, the results are compared with whose derived from the analysis of white families, particularly the findings for the white laboring class, because Anderson found that the characteristics of the African American families surveyed most closely resembled this class. There were differences, of course. For example, "a smaller proportion of Negroes than of whites have read no books and pamphlets on child care during the past year." Moreover, since library facilities were less accessible to blacks due to segregation in many parts of the United States, African Americans were more likely than whites to own the books they read. Clearly, literature was an important source for black mothers surveyed. As with the white sample, health-care practitioners were significant sources for information, though African American mothers were more likely to attend clinics and consult with nurses and less likely to confer with physicians, particularly specialists. Moreover, black mothers overall were less likely to consult with no one.

Though the 1936 survey has its limitations, and though the surveyors did not always pose the questions we in the twenty-first century might want asked, still it does provide critical evidence of the extent to which scientific motherhood had become a part of many women's lives. Across class and racial lines, the families Anderson studied clearly expected that mothering practices should be informed by contemporary medical and scientific expertise and health-care practitioners. There were differences among groups, with those in higher socioeconomic categories more able and likely to follow the tenets of scientific motherhood. Nonetheless, the overwhelming majority of mothers read books and pamphlets, attended clinics, consulted with physicians and nurses. Only a minority turned to traditional sources of knowledge such as relatives, friends, and even their own experience.

Early-twentieth-century surveys, such as those developed by the Children's Bureau, and reports of public-health agencies made clear the significance of location also. They described rural families, miles and miles from the nearest medical facility or health-care practitioner, with virtually nonexistent or impassable roads. Montana mothers in the 1910s had to ride fifteen, twenty-five, even fifty miles in a day to attend health clinics. A few decades later, a Wisconsin County Demonstration nurse colorfully recounted making a call on a family living deep in the woods of north central Wisconsin:

> It was necessary to leave the car at a neighbor's, and walk through several fields, in one of which a bull was tethered. He seemed only mildly interested in the nurse, who luckily was wearing blue, not red! After walking through woods, up and down hills, and crawling under two fences, in twenty minutes or so the house was reached. Then the whole process was repeated on the return journey. It was a very hot, tired, and perspiring nurse that finally reached the car and relaxed somewhat behind the wheel.[49]

Though written from the perspective of nurses who understood that traveling conditions impeded their ability to delivery optimal health care, such reports are indicative of the problems faced by rural families as well.[50] If public-health nurses had difficulties getting to mothers and children, how likely was it that a private physician would make frequent calls? That families could maintain easy contact with the larger world? Accessibility was a major limiting factor in a woman's ability to act on the tenets of scientific motherhood, especially the direction to have a physician regularly examine her child and to supervise her infant care.

The crucial intersection of class, race, and geography positions mothers within the larger social and cultural environment. It provides one perspective for analyzing the growing popularity of scientific motherhood in the United States in the twentieth century. However, in order to understand the dramatic transformation of mothering practices we need to investigate the agency of women. Why did women in the interwar period embrace the principles of scientific motherhood? Why did they come to believe that the best, the most healthful child care required the intervention of health-care practitioners? Though the surveys give us some indication of mothers' motivations, it is the voices of individuals that most explicitly articulate women's beliefs and reasons for their child-care practices. Their reports enable us to see mothers struggling to provide their children with the best, most healthful care, which increasingly involved the application of modern science and medicine in their everyday lives.

CHAPTER 4

"The modern way"

MOTHERS CIRCA 1920–1945

*R*uth Williams Thompson was extreme-
ly self-assured about her mothering practices—so self-confident that in 1929
she justified writing *Training My Babies* with the explanation that "as my
friends see my girls [aged four and three] and learn of their early accom-
plishments I am continually asked, 'How did you do it?' I decided that if my
ideas and suggestions were worth anything to a few intimate friends and relatives, many other young mothers might care to read my interesting experi-
ments and experiences."[1] The epitome of scientific motherhood in this period,
Thompson used contemporary science to inform her childrearing practices
and insisted that "too much emphasis cannot be placed on the necessity of
establishing regular habits for the child." These "regular habits," she noted,
were the very basis of "the physical and mental happiness which my little
girls now enjoy," beginning in their infancy when "after the six o'clock feeding
I always put my babies to bed regardless of our plans for the evening. After
they were tucked in, the window was opened wide and the light turned out.
They were left then to go to sleep alone." Even at two months, her infants
did not cry at bedtime because "already the sleeping habit had taken its
hold."[2] Thompson was not your conventional mother of the 1920s.[3] Urban,
college educated, professional, she represented a minority of women raising
children in the U.S. in the period. Despite her distinctiveness and because of
her self-reflective nature, her experiences bring into sharp focus the effect of
scientific motherhood on the maternal customs. Most importantly, her decisions about child-care practices demonstrate how women accepted and
adapted the dominant ideology.

Contemporary medical thought demanded the regularity of Watsonian behaviorism, which Thompson applauded. However, household requirements and experience influenced the schedule she set for her children. When she came home from the hospital, she continued the regime she had observed there, feeding the babies at 6 a.m., 9 a.m., noon, 3 p.m., 6 p.m., 10 p.m., and in the first month also at 2 a.m.. Shortly thereafter she found several reasons for altering the schedule. Firstly, she discovered that the infant was nearly always asleep at 10 p.m. and she "hated to disturb her." Secondly, Thompson was ready to retire before 10 p.m. She considered her rest important as well as the child's. Consequently, she decided not to awaken the baby, but to let her wake up if she needed to feed. The first night, baby did not awaken until midnight and following her feeding, she slept until 5 a.m., nearly the time for her first morning feed. Thompson found that gradually the night feeding came later and later. By five months of age, the baby went from 6 p.m. to 6 a.m. without feeding. Though flexible at night, the mother would not deviate from the schedule during the day and "never hesitated to awaken [the infants] either for their bath or bottle."[4] In this process, we can see how at least one interwar mother managed to maintain self-confidence—she determined that "it was more important that our baby learn the art of sleeping all night than that she should get an extra feeding"—while at the same time upholding her belief in the medical directions of the day—she was very rigid about the day-time feeding schedule.

Though we cannot generalize from Thompson's experiences to all mothers, her book provides critical insights into how a 1920s mother constructed her child-care routines and what sources she felt were most significant in doing so. Her balancing of expert advice and familial and personal needs is clear as she adjusted the feeding schedules for her growing girls. She conformed to every other aspect of dietary advice advocated by contemporary medicine. For example, at three months she added orange juice with "ten drops of cod liver oil as prescribed by my doctor. . . . My doctor impressed upon me very strongly the importance of cod liver oil in a child's diet, and seemed pleased to hear me report that I gave it faithfully with the orange juice *every day* [stress in the original], and not just once in a while." But, when it came to feeding schedules, she tempered medical directions with experience. On the one hand, contemporary advice books advocated establishing a four-hour schedule for infants five to six months old. On the other hand, Thompson believed that to "have changed to a four hour schedule then would have meant a complete disruption of my earlier schedule, and I felt that it would be very unwise to do that." Instead of totally rearranging her day, then, she added some thin cereal before the 6 p.m. bottle at six months; at eight months, some vegetable soup or baked potato at the noon meal. She gradually increased solid foods and replaced the 3 p.m. bottle with a graham cracker and cup of milk. Then, she replaced each bottle with a cup, and found that "at thirteen months both babies sat up at the table with Daddy and mother and fed themselves like grown-ups." Once again, she did not reject modern medical and scientific advice. She studied the topic and decided that the regularity of a fixed three-hour schedule slowly modified to a three-meal-a-day plan was more significant than following the recommended schedule. In other words, she accepted the general philosophy of regularity and found the best way to fit that into her daily life.[5]

A similar combination of science and pragmatism dictated Thompson's toilet-training methods. In this case she specified her source: the Children's Bureau pamphlet *The Care of the Child*, which at this time was a resolute advocate of regularity and Watsonian behaviorism. When her first daughter was three months old, she began by holding the child on her lap on a "very small toilet, more like a large cup, but easy to handle," for ten to fifteen minutes. "Of course at first it was just a game of Luck or no Luck, and there were times when I felt perhaps it was a waste of time. But I was determined to give the thing a fair trial, so kept at it day after day." By the time her daughter was six months of age, she was putting her on the toilet "about every forty-five minutes during the day, when she was awake, and once during the night." Moreover, Thompson was proud to report, "I was having fewer and fewer diapers to wash." She found this method so successful that with her second daughter she embarked on toilet training at the age of six weeks. Previous experience helped her streamline the routine: "It does not pay to hold the baby on the toilet for several minutes at a time and does not make the training any easier. As soon as the baby becomes accustomed to the sitting posture the organs will act immediately if there is a desire to urinate. . . . My babies learned to urinate as soon as they touched the toilet." She treated her daughters' bowel movements similarly. When they were inclined to constipation, that is, they did not move their bowels daily, she would resort to a soap stick, prune juice, milk of magnesia, or even an enema.[6]

Thompson's experiences reveal how profoundly medical supervision reached into the domestic sphere and dictated a mother's everyday practices. After all, Thompson pleased the doctor by feeding her children cod liver oil and orange juice every day, and she was proud of her physician's approval. She understood the critical role of contemporary science and medicine in shaping routines necessary for the creation of habit formation. Nonetheless, she also felt comfortable interpreting scientific and medical directions for herself, in modifying schedules to fit better in her household routines.

For Thompson, the practice of scientific motherhood actually enhanced her self-confidence. Other women experienced the spread of scientific motherhood much differently. For them, the pursuit of the ideals of scientific motherhood led them to doubt their own observations and abilities. One such woman, Mrs. L.J.R. of Anaconda, Montana, wrote the Children's Bureau in 1923. Mrs. L.J.R. had been dutifully following the child-care practices outlined in the agency's pamphlet *Infant Care*. Though she appreciated the popular pamphlet, she did not rely on its advice alone. During the summer she had visited a well-child clinic in St. Paul, where the head nurse gave her a diet schedule suitable for a child of her son's age. "The diet seem[ed] to agree with him splendidly," Mrs. L.J.R. was pleased to report. Despite her confidence in the advice she had received and her observation that her year-old son was "in excellent health," she sought confirmation from a recognized medical expert. She explained in her letter that she had recently had her child "examined by a baby specialist here simply to assure myself that there was nothing wrong with him." She does not say what the physician concluded from this examination but he did tell her that her child's diet was inappropriate. This advice directly contradicted the diet schedule she was following and the information supplied in *Infant Care*. Given her admiration for *Infant Care*, she looked to the Children's Bureau to tell her what she should believe because "when authorities and specialists disagree to such an extent, how can a mother have confidence in them?" she asked plaintively.[7]

Mrs. L.J.R's letter exemplifies another strand in the evolution of scientific motherhood: she learned appropriate child-care practices from a variety of personal and published medical sources. She visited a baby clinic in St. Paul on more than one occasion and received literature from it. We do not know how she obtained a copy of *Infant Care*, perhaps through the St. Paul clinic, perhaps she asked to have it mailed to her, as many mothers did in this period. She also recognized the growing importance of "baby specialists," as the medical specialty of pediatrics was spreading at this time. And she knew or suspected that the staff of the Children's Bureau had exceptional knowledge about children. She was actively involved in the search for useful knowledge. She visited the clinic and made the appointment with the specialist. Whether she paid for these medical visits is not known, but clearly she accepted the importance of physician-directed well-baby care. However, she was given contradictory advice and sought assistance in evaluating the specifics of the problem. Recognizing the importance of scientific and medical expertise in defining a healthful diet regime for her infant, she needed help in identifying the right answer. As she plainly stated: "I want to know whether he [the physician] was right or not."

Thompson and Mrs. L.J.R. represent two poles of twentieth-century scientific motherhood. Along with growing numbers of mothers, each accepted the critical importance of contemporary science and medicine to her child-care practices. They welcomed the involvement of medical and scientific experts, usually but not always physicians, in their families. For Thompson this intervention was empowering: she found her own voice in the development of her child-care practices and was impelled, as were her nineteenth-century sisters, to educate others from her experiences. For Mrs. L.J.R., it was disempowering: she looked at her son and saw a healthy child, but she distrusted her own judgment and needed an expert, a medical practitioner, to confirm her opinion. Their stories make clear that scientific motherhood was not a single ideology or practice. It could and did vary depending on the circumstances of the mother and her personality; it could be an affirmation of a woman's mothering skills or a source of doubt.

In order to understand women's mothering practices and their relationship to scientific motherhood, we need to listen to how individuals defined their problems and where they sought their solutions. As we have seen, nineteenth-century mothers left their words and their ideas for us in a variety of published and unpublished sources. Twentieth-century mothers also described their experiences and their concerns in books and magazines. In addition, hundreds of thousands of parents wrote to the Children's Bureau in the years before World War II. Letters came from poor and working-class mothers as well as middle-class ones, from rural and farm women as well as those living in small towns and urban areas.[8] More recently sociologists and historians have interviewed women who had their children in the interwar period. Their memories too broaden our knowledge of women's mothering experiences and why they cared for their children as they did.

Most useful in this regard is a study of Philadelphia mothers in the interwar period by sociologist Jacquelyn Litt that highlights the significance of class and race for an individual's mothering practices.[9] Her interviews with Jewish American and African American mothers who birthed in the 1930s and 1940s demonstrate a differential acceptance of scientific motherhood. For the middle-class Jewish American women, "the faith in modern medicine and the desire to become modern mothers were taken for granted, commonly accepted and understood," Litt concluded.[10] They used scientific motherhood to distance themselves from their parents' immigrant culture and to move visibly into the American middle class. Among Litt's informants were highly motivated women who actively sought out the best child care they could find for their children. Having identified that "best care," they diligently followed its prescriptions. For them, best care was modern and that meant medically supervised. As one of her informants expressed it: "Just because your mother and your grandmother did it I didn't think that was the best thing. I was a modern mother and the modern way was to go to a specialist."[11] Another recalled vividly the contrast between her mother's way and the modern, scientific way. If her daughter awoke before her next scheduled feeding time, she would let the baby cry. This behavior horrified her mother, but she would not feed her daughter before the scheduled time. "This was the way it had to be," she told Litt. "If [the doctor] said every four hours, every four hours. It was the right thing to do." In her eyes, this practice constituted "perfect" motherhood.[12] For some, "perfect" motherhood meant accepting the direction of their physician and only their physician.

And many doctors, not only Wood, insisted on such obedience. Reminiscing about her early infant-care experiences, one middle-class Jewish American mother remembered a home visit by their highly respected physician. As she related: "You know you read baby magazines. How to take care of your baby and all. And I had them on my chair in my bedroom. [The doctor] walked in, he said, I'll never forget, 'If you want me to be your doctor, you'll get rid of all those magazines.' . . . So I said, 'Okay.' Because I heard that he was good pediatrician and I was glad that I was able to get him because he was in a great deal of demand." These women acquiesced to medical surveillance because so doing was reassuring and "help[ed] them secure their positions as good, American mothers."[13]

Science had the answers to successful, healthful childrearing, agreed Litt's Jewish American informants. Moreover, the practice of scientific motherhood separated them from previous, immigrant generations. It made them modern, it made them American. The African American informants raising their children in the same time period present a less homogeneous picture. On the one hand, the middle-class African American mothers utilized scientific motherhood in much the same way as the Jewish American mothers. They too were likely to follow medical prescriptions and find pride in their abilities to know and to do so. On the other hand, the working-class African Americans were alienated from the institutionalized medical system of the North, in which hospitalization with white doctors and nurses replaced the home births and African American midwives of the South. These women had moved up to the North during the Great Migration; they were fleeing the Jim Crow South in search of better economic situations and sought to avoid the discrimination evident in medical and hospital practices in the North as well as the South. At the same time, they endeavored to re-create the extended relationships of caretaking familiar in the South. In this network, the most important source of child-care information was experience—their own, their mother's, or that of relatives and neighbors.

One African American informant was a working-class single mother struggling to raise her child during the 1930s. She drew her mothering knowledge from previous domestic employment during which she cared for the family's children. A combination of confidence in her own experience and limited financial resources deterred her from routine doctor visits. She relied instead on a close social circle, including neighbors and relatives. "You had to know things yourself. My mother did. . . . [My grandmother] pulled us through when the flu was raging," she remarked, remembering the fearful influenza pandemic that followed World War I. Yet, she was not immune to the push to be modern and scientific. She did not use traditional remedies with her son: "You get modern, I guess. I mean you go and buy, you don't make, you don't bother with all these remedies. You go and buy."[14] Within the limits of her financial situation, this working-class woman, and others, reached out. If physicians were too expensive, then they reached for the products of modern science and medicine, in place of traditional, homemade ones.

Women's relationship with scientific motherhood is contingent on a multiplicity of factors and can be viewed from a range of perspectives. Litt's fine-grained analysis points to the significance of class, race, and ethnicity in this regard. Historian Carolyn Carson's study of similarly positioned African American mothers in Pittsburgh highlights other critical defining factors.[15] These women also typically moved North during the Great Migration, but their experiences were quite different from those of their sisters in Philadelphia, largely due to the critical role of the Urban League and black professionals who fostered the women's use of medical services and medical personnel. In effect, organizational and professional groups replaced the more traditional and informal social networks of the mothers Litt interviewed. In Pittsburgh, women were encouraged, even pushed, to turn to medical and scientific authorities, even when those authorities were white physicians in segregated hospitals. Because of a lack of finances or desire or the discrimination of northern urban institutions, many undoubtedly resisted this drive and continued traditional practices. Yet, Carson found, increasing numbers of African American mothers "did indeed utilize available medical facilities from the 1920s onward." Litt concluded from her study of Philadelphia working-class African American mothers that social networks were the critical element in shaping women's child-care practices and in their search for, or rejection of, medical and scientific authority. The same can be said for the Pittsburgh mothers, but in this case the social network—the Urban League and black health professionals—mobilized the community to seek answers in the modern medical world rather than one of traditional practices. In other words, the community expectations in Philadelphia and Pittsburgh were different and as a result so too were mothers' views and child-care practices.

Though scientific motherhood was becoming increasingly popular throughout the interwar period, not all women felt the need to become "scientific" or had the resources to follow its prescriptions. Before studying why women did turn to scientific and medical experts for assistance in child care, it is instructive to note why some women did not. Since these mothers did not actively seek out advice, they have left us little in the written sources. However, the records of visiting nurses and other public-health officials who entered women's homes in an attempt to persuade mothers of the efficacy of modern scientific methods give us some idea about those who rejected scientific motherhood, some for personal reasons, others for material reasons, some proudly, some sadly.

Self-confident women, especially women who had raised previous children successfully and healthfully, saw little reason to change their ways. A County Demonstration Nurse in northern Wisconsin was baffled by Mrs. M.F., who would not accept the importance of medically directed well-baby care. Mrs. M.F.'s rationale was quite simple and straight forward: "It is not necessary—all my children are well."[16] Though the nurse could see the need to supervise even healthy children, this mother could not. In other instances, the opposition of a grandmother, or even a father, thwarted the introduction of scientific motherhood principles into the home. In June 1940, nurse Constance Carmody visited a nineteen-year-old mother in Marathon County, Wisconsin. Mrs. W. had used a midwife for the birth "since that was her mother's custom. Her mother-in-law looked askance at any suggestions for regular feedings or outdoor naps," the nurse reported, which limited the nurse's ability to influence the mother in the ways of modern child care.[17] Mothers who resisted the imposition of scientific motherhood frequently had identified alternatives to medical supervision, alternatives that resonated with their lives. Mrs. M.F. was confident in her own abilities; Mrs. W. looked to a different authority, the authority of family traditions. Other mothers based their decisions on folklore and community norms. Though such practices were not in accord with contemporary scientific motherhood, the mothers themselves were clear that they were making a rational choice.

Some mothers failed to follow the tenets of scientific motherhood not because they were unwilling, but rather because they were unable; they lacked vital resources. For instance, the routines of scientific motherhood demanded water—copious amounts of water for bathing, for drinking, for cleaning. This simple requirement was well beyond the means of many, especially rural families in the interwar period. A 1919 study of northern Wisconsin found that few had water in the home and fewer still had running water. For many, their water supply was twenty-five or even one hundred feet from the house. In describing the typical situation, the investigator noted, "In this county it is the usual thing for the mother to have to carry the household water herself. The hardest feature of the situation is that in most instances every bit of water must be carried up several steps, often of the roughest construction. Moreover, all household waste must be carried down these same steps."[18] Lack of sanitation facilities plagued urban and suburban mothers as well, as the development of public water works spread slowly and unevenly through the country in the late nineteenth and early twentieth centuries. The sanitation standards of scientific motherhood were extremely difficult to achieve in such an environment.

In other cases, women lacked the time and money necessary to support the routines of scientific motherhood. The studies of the Children's Bureau documented how isolated many families were, far removed from medical institutions and practitioners. And though the presence of health-care providers could ease the situation, it was not sufficient. For example, in November 1937, in rural Wisconsin, Mrs. E.S. gave birth to a daughter. When the nurse visited her in mid-November, the parents and two children were living in "two very small, dirty rooms above a vacant store building." The mother was not interested in post-partum care and well-baby instruction. "Mother says she has to work very hard. It is necessary for her to carry water from a store across the street as her husband refused to do this," reported the nurse. Fortunately, the baby appeared well. During another visit in early December, the nurse reported that the home conditions remained poor and the mother's "diet inadequate. Bread, meat, and milk are all she gets to eat. She says if she purchases other foods, her husband scolds her. Patient appears very tired and undernourished." Since the baby was having trouble breathing, Mrs. S. had gone to the doctor, who prescribed treatment. The nurse assisted by demonstrating the proper method of applying nose drops, but she could have little effect on the depressing home situation.[19]

Poverty-stricken cases like these were probably fairly typical, especially during the Depression. Whether rural or urban, many families lacked the money, the resources, the time to follow the detailed instructions that comprised modern medically directed child care. Visiting nurses and well-child clinics came and went, depending on the financial condition of state and local governments and the generosity of private philanthropies. But in the home, it was the mother who took care of the children, the mother who followed, or not, the dictates of medical supervisors.

Even mothers committed to the tenets of scientific motherhood could not always follow through on its prescriptions. A striking example of this quandary was Peggy Gesell, daughter-in-law of Professor Arnold Gesell, the developmental psychologist. He was widely published and quoted in contemporary women's magazines and his books, including *Infant and Child in the Culture of Today* and *The Child from Five to Ten*, brought his theories to a broad audience. Though he did not advise the strict regularity of Watsonian behaviorism, Gesell did insist on the significance of maternal guidance and structure, especially in the early years of a child's life. In his laboratory at Yale, his staff used scheduling and coding charts to map the development of his subjects. He offered these to his daughter-in-law and she tried dutifully to follow them. However, as she found, the pressures of daily life forced some deviance. When she returned the charts to her father-in-law, she warned that there was "wide variation here and there in [the child's] feeding schedule" that she explained was due to the demands of "housework or sleep." The professor also advocated regular weighing, which his daughter-in-law sometimes neglected, especially in the early morning "because the scales make quite a distinctive noise and Pete [her older child] at that hour is easily wakened by it. And frankly, Science is nothing to me when compared to a few minutes more sleep."[20] The realities of everyday life could disorganize even the most avid followers of scientific motherhood.

For those who adopted the ideology, motherhood continued to be described in the flowery language of the previous century but with a twentieth-century twist that acknowledged the general acceptance of the tenets of scientific motherhood in American culture. The up-to-date mother was scientific. Mothers were both extolled for their position and told that "motherly affection has its seamy side," especially "blind and unintelligent mother love." As one mother, Estelle Reilly, advised her pregnant readers in 1935: "Your first important and most intelligent step is to put yourself in the hands of a good doctor. . . . Be very sure you understand [his instructions] and do exactly as he tells you." Not that physicians should be a mother's only source. Reilly presented mothers with a conundrum; on the one hand, she insisted that a woman should "rely on [the doctor's advice] completely; he must lay down the laws you are to follow out and you are to ask no one else about them." On the other hand, she noted that in "every-day details of pure experience Grandma is clearly indicated as your source of information."[21]

Other mother-authors were less confusing in their advice. "The mere physical fact of motherhood gives us no claim to honor," noted May Whitaker, who published an advice manual based on her mothering experiences. "In bringing forth the young of our kind we do not more than the brute mothers." To be successful, mothers must lift themselves "above the plane of brute creation."[22] It is the application of scientific advice that separates the modern mother from the lower animals; she will consult with physicians and nurses "and follow their directions intelligently and accurately." She will also read a few books written specifically for the inexperienced mother. But with these she needs some assistance lest she misinterpret the advice. Whitaker suggested that the new mother have her husband read the books as well because "a man's clear insight will help you in applying [their instructions]. Being less hampered by 'old women's notions,' the science and commonsense of the approved methods will appeal to him."[23] Science, gendered male, was the supreme authority for child care.

Evidently many women considered the embrace of scientific motherhood symbolic of modernity; scientific advice was the most modern, most up-to-date, most healthful advice. Scientific motherhood became part of their self-definition; it separated them from a traditional, premodern past and it enhanced their status as well as their child's health. Litt's informants talked of visiting physicians, particularly specialists, as the "modern way." Similar sentiments were heard from all over the country. Though women with fewer financial resources found it more difficult to consult specialists, they still wanted—and believed they needed—contemporary scientific advice if they were to be good mothers. Writing from Dallas, Texas, to request that the Children's Bureau send information on child care, A.E.F. was unambiguous about the reasons:

> We have a baby boy one month of age to whom we wish to do justice in regards to feeding and care to get the best possible results.
>
> As it is our first child, every friend and neighbor feels it their sacred duty to advise us in all matters pertaining to its care, and though

perhaps given with the best intention, it would be sometimes amusing were it not for the thought that perhaps in the past thousands of infants have lost their lives for just such advice.[24]

Lois Waggoner received a hundred-page booklet at a lecture on infant care in rural Indiana. She called it "my baby 'Bible.'" Before having children of her own, she had lived with a family and cared for their children. Despite this experience, she remembered, "I wanted to learn some new ways of caring for my baby."[25] Upwardly mobile women "whose maturing years were spent in college dormitories and New York offices," Lenore Pelham Friedrich reported in *Atlantic Monthly* in 1939, "were scientific, even if it was expensive."[26]

Underlying all these calls for scientific motherhood was the expectation that modern science would result directly in more healthful child care. A.E.F. wanted the information because traditional social networks were not trustworthy about such an important issue. Reilly insisted that a good doctor can set a baby on the road to good health. Author and essayist Kathleen Norris personally enthused over the joy and "fun" of being a mother, yet was concerned that many women looked upon childrearing as drudgery and dreaded the prospect of raising a baby. From her experience, modern motherhood eliminated such fears. The prescriptions for scientific motherhood "with regular hours, baths and meals on schedule, . . . with top-milk and spinach and bran toast in place of the old sugar-sucks, doughnuts, and pickles that used to be given to wailing child, with plenty of black 'physic' from large bottles to follow," she assured mothers, are healthy; we "don't know what chronic ailments are nowadays."[27]

Many mothers felt that they lacked even the basic information and experience in childrearing. Feeling overwhelmed by the demands of motherhood, they believed they needed the best advice for successful child care. Mothers who wrote letters to the Children's Bureau frequently lamented how little they knew about contemporary child care methods. In July 1915, Mrs. H.A.C. of Augusta, Georgia, requested of the Bureau, "Please send me your bulitin [*sic*] on summer complaint or infant care or babies & any other littiture [*sic*] you all may have that would give me any information on how to raise children & care for them as I live out in the country & cant get Dr's advise [sic] without a good prise [*sic*]. . . . Any information would be greatly appreciated."[28] From the other end of the country, Mrs. J.S., mother of a two-month-old son living in Inglewood, California, echoed similar sentiments in 1929. She explained that "I do not know much about taking care of babies but am trying my best to get along with some information, but know that you have the correct information and would be glad to give the best advice as to the care of children." Rather than depending on their own advice, her friends had recommended that she write the Bureau with her questions because she "would like real authoritative information."[29] The Bureau's position as "authoritative" and responsive to the concerns of mothers continued through the interwar, and the letters kept pouring in to Washington. Mrs. H.L.'s request for copies of the agency's literature is typical: "I have never had a baby before and I know nothing whatever about caring for them."[30]

Mothers' search for trustworthy scientific and medical advice is evident in many other sources as well. In 1930, the magazine *Nebraska Farmer* asked women to respond to the topic "My biggest job." From the flood of letters, the editors concluded that "children are the greatest problem homemakers have." One woman, keenly aware of the breadth of knowledge she needed for successful mothering, wrote, "Child raising does not end with food and clothes. I wish we mothers could study more child psychology. Many mothers think it is foolishness. One woman said to me, 'I was able to raise my children without reading books.' But she didn't raise them they just 'grew up.'"[31] A succinct rationalization for contemporary scientific motherhood.

Publications were one source, but increasingly through the mid-twentieth century, physicians played the pivotal role in the development of scientific motherhood. Mothers were consistently reminded by the Children's Bureau, by women's magazines and child-care magazines, by books and pamphlets how important it was to trust their physicians and to take their infants and young children to the doctor or clinic on a regular schedule. It was not just the articulate and self-confident manual writers, such as Whitaker and Reilly, who spoke highly of their physicians. Scattered through the literature and reports of the period, mothers' paeans to doctors are evident. Mothers committed to the tenets of scientific motherhood could and would follow the directions of their physicians, even when the medical recommendations contradicted the mother's own sense of what was appropriate. Doris McCray was eminently qualified to tell other mothers about the importance of medical supervision, particularly of infant feeding. Her faith in physicians' directions grew directly out of her own experiences. Her son would eat virtually anything offered to him, but her doctor limited the boy's diet. McCray feared that the "doctor was slowly starving him, but my confidence in the judgment of the doctor was so great that I followed his directions exactly." McCray observed that her son did very well on this regime, thriving and consistently gaining. Her trust in the medical profession was so great that she had no problem insisting that women follow "the instructions of the physician meticulously."[32]

At other times, the results were less satisfying. Advances in vitamin research in the early decades of the twentieth century proved the efficacy of vitamin D in the prevention and treatment of rickets, a widespread childhood disorder of the time. Cod liver oil was the most frequently recommended source of vitamin D for children in this period. During a series of well-baby clinics held in south-central Wisconsin, the state's visiting physician was horrified to discover several cases of rickets. She soon learned that the mothers were "staunch advocates of a near-by practicing physician." He, however, provided little prenatal or pediatric care and, moreover, advised that cod liver oil was unnecessary.[33]

Other mothers consulted with physicians but needed assurance that what they were told was correct. Mrs. L.J.R. questioned the "specialist's" advice about her child's diet, for example. Cases in which medical authorities disagreed sent mothers to request clarification from a trusted source, often the Children's Bureau. In 1927, Mrs. M.G.P. of New York City wrote concerning her six-week-old infant. She had questions about night feedings and worried that if she let the infant cry, it could "cry itself into a rupture." Unfortunately, the physicians she had seen were indecisive on the issue. She wanted "a definite stand" and would "act according to the advice I receive from your office," she told the Bureau.[34]

Mothers turned to scientific motherhood because they believed that following its tenets assured the healthiest childhood for their children. Sometimes they knew this because of their own experiences. In 1930, Mrs. E.L.H. wrote to the Children's Bureau from Harrison, Arkansas, for a new copy of *Infant Care*. She had reason to feel confident in its directions because "I used the book for my child now nearly four & had almost perfect results in infancy with her due to the clear & Thorough information." With her second child, now five weeks old, she anticipated a repetition of her success by once again following the latest scientific and medical information.[35] Litt's informants in Philadelphia were convinced that physician-supervised child care was the best that they could provide their children. In other cases, it was the faith of others in the benefits of medically directed child care that drew mothers into scientific motherhood. For example, friends would tell friends about their successful childrearing and specify their sources. In 1925, Mrs. E.O.T., from Richmond, Virginia, wrote to the Children's Bureau with her questions about the diet for her infant because a "friend of mine in this city having advised me that she had obtained such benifical [*sic*] results, from your suggestions in the care of her baby, I thought I would write you in behalf of mine."[36] In 1928, Mrs. B.R.N. of Kansas City requested another copy of *Infant Care* because "mine is so used by everyone I feel it will help [to have a new one]."[37] Sometimes, a concerned woman observed a worrisome situation, but she was not in a position to intervene personally. Under such circumstances, she might write a trusted source and ask for assistance from that organization or person. Mrs. H.M. of Ocean Park, California, was very anxious about the seven-week-old daughter of a neighbor. Her detailed letter to the Children's Bureau graphically described the family's living conditions: "They are living in one room and the baby sleeps there, even during the evening when the lights are on, and perhaps friends come in. They close all their windows at night for fear of a 'draft' . . . [sic] and the baby gets very little of this glorious outdoors and sunshine." Their apartment is in a crowded building and so when the baby cries, she "is given catnip tea! [sic]." Mrs. H.M. explained that the mother is only nineteen years old and "does need advise [sic]," but "resents this word coming from me [Mrs. H.M.]." Accordingly, she asked the Bureau staff to help by sending a complete set of booklets on how to care for a new baby directly to the mother.[38]

Public-health nurses and community organizations, as we have seen in the Pittsburgh story, also encouraged mothers to utilize medical and scientific expertise in their childrearing. And mothers then used health-care professionals to learn the principles of scientific motherhood and to validate their childrearing practices. In Amery, a small town in far western Wisconsin, nurse Sadie Engesether found the mother of baby E. "very anxious about her baby, worried that baby is getting along o.k." Since the nurse found a baby who was on a four-hour breast-feeding schedule and received the appropriate doses of cod liver oil and orange juice (all in accord with contemporary medical advice) and who seemed in good health, she "advised mother to continue same routine and stop worrying."[39] This is not to say that mothers were passive in the presence of health-care professionals; they did, though, use them as a check on their own sense of appropriate child care.

Convinced of the need for modern, medical supervision, mothers then looked to physicians and nurses to tell them how to carry out correct practices. Mrs. H. was adhering to a three-hour feeding schedule for her one-month-old infant. When she noticed that the baby often slept longer than three hours, she queried the nurse about using a four-hour schedule. This mother obviously had been convinced of the importance of regularity in feeding and also the importance of regular bowel movements because she had been giving her very young child enemas. Endorsing the four-hour schedule and reassuring the mother that "a stool every other day is all right with the breast fed baby," a public-health nurse suggested prune juice, orange juice, and cod liver oil, rather than an enema.[40]

Many mothers then were attracted to scientific motherhood because of their general conviction that science and medicine could help them improve the lives of their children. Others were drawn to medical supervision of child care because of specific problems that demanded specific solutions. Sometimes they were nervous because of prior experience. When nurse Lelia Johnson visited a home in western Wisconsin in the fall of 1939, she reported, "Demonstration baby bath was given to [Mrs. H.], as this mother lost a baby two years ago with naval [sic] infection and now is afraid to handle and bath [sic] the baby."[41] In another case, County Demonstration Nurse Cook found that with two previous babies dead, Mrs. S.B. was fearful about the outcome of her current pregnancy and she appreciated the nurse's help.[42] Such mothers knew the dangers and potential problems of child care. They did not want a repeat of their horrific previous experiences. They looked to scientific and medical experts to tell them how to avoid these dangers.

In other instances, mothers were looking for solutions to current problems. In early January 1940 in north-central Wisconsin, Kathryn Lynch, another County Demonstration Nurse, visited the tar paper shack of five-week-old Virjean, "a crying, tiny, starved unkempt baby with buttocks so excariated [sic] they were bleeding." Virjean had five older siblings, "all sick with colds, and with no clean clothes, and very little to work with." By the end of the month, following numerous home visits, the nurse reveled in the family's transformation: "Virjean, while a long way from a perfect baby physically, is clean, buttocks almost health [sic], is sleeping in her own pasteboard box bed. The pile of dirty clothes in the corner has been washed and put away. The pillows have clean covers. The floors are shining, and the dishes are washed."[43]

We can track how groups such as the Urban League of Pittsburgh, the Wisconsin State Bureau of Maternal and Child Health, and many other governmental and private agencies reached out to women to promote scientific motherhood. From extant records, it is clear that when they did, mothers often responded positively to the call. The "Better Babies Club" of Garfield, Wisconsin, was organized in the mid-1930s, suggested by a county nurse but developed and run by community women who "were eager for knowledge and better living."[44] In many other situations we do not know how women first learned of the importance of scientific and medical expertise in raising their children, but we do know that they actively sought out the information in the belief that contemporary science and medicine could help them. Mothers attended health conferences and took their children to well-baby clinics. They also wrote to agencies such as the Children's Bureau with their specific problems and expected authoritative answers. Moreover, they gratefully acknowledged the assistance they received.

The Children's Bureau files are filled with letters from desperate mothers seeking advice from an authoritative source. The case of Mrs. M.B. is illustrative.

> I am kindly writting you for incristian of health am the mother of 4 childrens and this one mak me 5 and the 4 I all ways gave enought milk for them from my brest and this one are now in 4 weeks old and I haff to nurse him from a bottle I have not been able to give any milk from my brest and i nurse him off of bordens baby brand condensed milk and does you think this is a good milk for him or not[45]

In a similar case, we know not only the circumstances that worried the mother, but also the resolution to the problem. "Your recently issued pamphlet, tital [*sic*] 'Infant Care' which I requested you send me arrived safely and i [*sic*] am very much pleased with it, a doctors book could not prove more valuable and would cost considerably. I have studied the book carefully," Mrs. M.B.W. of Skowhogan, Maine, informed the Bureau staff in 1915. She had had a serious problem. Under the direction of a physician she had attempted a variety of different foods for her infant daughter: the milk from three different cows; Mellin's Food, a popular manufactured infant food; and Borden's condensed milk. Nothing seemed to satisfy the infant. Then, "when your book came which must be nearly two months ago I started giving baby cows milk prepared as described in your book, and she slept better & has been a different child ever since, the cows milk satisfies her whereas the Condensed didn't."[46]

Some mothers have left us reports that display their great appreciation for the principles of scientific motherhood. In the period, applause for Children's Bureau pamphlets was not limited to letters of congratulations to the Bureau staff. Mothers told others through the pages of women's magazines, for example. J.B., writing in *Cosmopolitan* in 1940, pronounced *Infant Care* "that Bible of the 1940 young mother."[47] Other women from all across the nation used different sources with equal praise. Interviewed years later, women talk with pride and gratitude of their physicians. Others remembered books and magazines. Mary Breckinridge bore a son, Breckie, during World War I. Born into a wealthy Tennessee family, she trained as a nurse in the early years of the twentieth century. Recalling her years as a mother of an infant, she wrote, "Dr. Holt's book on the feeding and care of infant was the classic for babies when he was born. I followed its direction in raising him."[48] Mrs. R.E.D. of Virginia was a regular reader of the journal *Farmer's Wife*. She used the information in its articles to good effect and she called on other women to do likewise, explaining that this advice will "help you and you in turn give baby the best chance possible for a good start in life."[49]

Contemporary surveys and reports of public-health workers, oral histories, mother-authored books and magazine articles, as well as letters written to child welfare agencies, such as the Children's Bureau, all bear witness to women's growing awareness of and allegiance to scientific motherhood. Throughout the interwar and beyond, mothers turned increasingly to health-care practitioners for advice on child care; they came to believe that medical direction would insure the best chance for their children's health. This is not intended to suggest that scientific motherhood made the modern mother's tasks any easier. For a variety of reasons, a conscientious mother committed to scientific motherhood faced tremendous obstacles, some medical and some practical, in selecting her methods of child care.

Some mothers used chronology to make the decision: how old or new the advice was. An article in *Atlantic Monthly* in 1933 describes the predicament "modern parents" faced in light of information overload and their solution: "We had a baby specialist inspect the baby almost as soon as it had begun to breathe, and we engaged him to preserve its health indefinitely. This, however, did not prevent us from investing in the latest books on the care of babies. Our generation was full of respect for the printed word. We bought all the standard books in the very newest editions. Earlier editions might say bananas at eight months. The latest said three. We were careful to get the latest."[50] Scientific motherhood meant the most up-to-date advice possible: out with the old, in with the new.

The underlying principle of the ideology of scientific motherhood was clear and unambiguous. By the interwar period, mothers were told they should take their direction from health-care practitioners. Nonetheless, the practice of scientific motherhood was fraught with inconsistencies and contradictions. Mrs. L.J.R. was in a quandary; she needed to navigate between two different sets of dietary advice, each from expert sources. Visiting public-health physicians in rural areas found local doctors, often older practitioners, instructing mothers in ways that directly contradicted their counsel. "The situation here is rather difficult," related Dr. Bessie Mae Beach after a health conference in DeForest, Wisconsin. "There is one physician in the village. He tells the mothers that if God intended for the baby to have cod liver oil the baby would be born with a bottle of it in his hand and if He intended for the child to have orange juice God would send a crate for him from Heaven." She was pleased to report, however, that "despite his advice we found quite a few of the mothers following the *Infant Care* book and giving the babies cod liver oil and orange juice."[51] Clearly mothers were making significant choices between diametrically opposite views of child care. Why these rural mothers decided that cod liver oil and orange juice were necessary, Beach does not report.

In terms of practice, scrupulous adherents to scientific motherhood faced a maze of time-consuming tasks. Being a scientific mother in the interwar period could be exhausting. Just as mothers in the nineteenth century worried that they were not effectively following the requirements of modern medical motherhood, so too did mothers in the twentieth century worry that they might not be conscientious enough in their mothering practices. And yet, where to draw the line? In letters to the editor of health and women's magazines, in correspondence with the Children's Bureau, we see mothers questioning not the scientific basis of their practices, but rather the extent of them. R.W.B. had breast-fed her child until her seventh month. Now in her ninth month the baby had bottle feedings as well as cereal, vegetables, orange juice, cod liver oil, apple sauce, and bacon in her diet. R.W.B. explained that she prepared a two-day's supply of vegetables at a time, keeping one jar in the refrigerator for the next day. She also went through an elaborate process of sterilizing all the cooking and feeding equipment. And she believed that the second jar of vegetables "should be sterilized before using just as I sterilize the bottles for milk." Writing in to the editors of *Hygeia*, the popular health journal of the American Medical Association, she plaintively inquired: "My task is becoming endless and I should like to know whether I am doing unnecessary work. At what age may I safely stop boiling bottles for the feeding of milk?"[52] Clementine Wheeler found herself overwhelmed on her first day home from the hospital with a newborn. The first task was to prepare the baby's formula, which she began "armed with four standard handbooks on baby care and the twenty-three articles they agreed were essential in preparing a bottle for a baby. Two embattled hours later," she wrote in *Parents Magazine*, "I was ready to offer my son his first home-cooked meal." Frustrated by the time and aggravation, she asked for a visiting nurse and was grateful to learn from her a ten-minute method of formula preparation.[53]

Faced with the day-to-day tasks of child care, even scientific mothers found it necessary at times to modify the counsel they were offered. Thompson rearranged the feeding schedule to fit better into her life; Wheeler found simpler, though still medically sanctioned, methods to make formula. Pragmatism dictated mothers' choices in instances such as these. But what was a mother to do when the advice given from different, but respected sources clashed in every aspect? One mother in rural Wisconsin in the early 1940s had decided before the birth of her child that she would bottle-feed. This decision upset the public-health nurse, who was adamant that maternal nursing was the best form of infant feeding. However, the mother had also learned of the importance of cleanliness, even sterility, in all objects surrounding the baby. Considering these two precepts of healthful infant care, the mother described a scene she had recently observed: "At sugar rationing Mrs. X was sitting there nursing her baby in the warm crowded room. Every time the baby would cry, the mother very obligingly would nurse the baby. Needless to say, no breast hygiene was observed. Now, I thought and read in all the books that the breast should be clean and that babies weren't supposed to be taken in crowds, let alone be fed there. I'd rather wash bottles and nipples and be sure my baby is being fed properly."[54] Though the nurse could not agree with the mother's decision, she could not deny that the mother had selected her mode of infant feeding in light of contemporary tenets.

Throughout the period, increasing numbers of women were entering the hospital for childbirth. In 1929, already nearly 29 percent of births took place

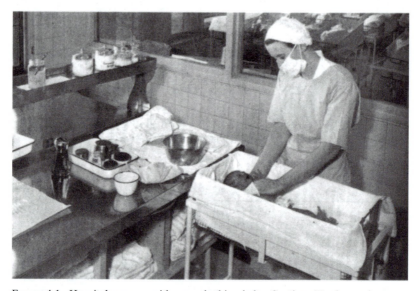

FIGURE 4.1. Hospital nursery with nurse bathing baby. Caption: "In the modern maternity hospital expert care is furnished for the newborn baby, who also benefits from the finest scientific equipment." *Source: Hygeia* 23 (1945): 510.

in hospitals. By 1940, though there were differences by income, race, and geographical area, the overall hospitalized childbirth rate in the United States had risen to 56 percent, a number that increased rapidly during the years of World War II.[55] This structured and controlled sanctuary gave new mothers a measure of security, but at the same time contributed to the lack of self-confidence many women were articulating by the 1940s in the face of scientific motherhood.

The situation at Lenox Hill Hospital, New York City, was typical. After birth, infants were taken away from their mothers to the hospital nursery. Mothers, even breast-feeding mothers, saw their children only to feed them at regular intervals. Nurses would wheel the babies into the maternity ward on a large cart and mothers were instructed to "listen carefully when the nurse calls out your baby's name" at nursing time. Then the nurses would "give out" the babies and mothers were told to "keep your hands clean. . . . The alcohol sponge given to you each time your baby comes to breast is to be used to clean your fingers thoroughly." The sense that the baby needed protection from its mother was further reinforced with the warning, "If you develop a head cold, tell the Nursery nurse so that the proper steps may be taken to protect your baby." Note that the nurse needs to safeguard the baby from the mother. As the hospital patronizingly tells the mother: "We know that you do not want your baby to be sick and we are asking for all these things in order that you may help us in keeping your baby well and in so doing protect all the other babies who are under our care."[56] Note that the hospital expected the mother to follow these instructions so that the institution could keep the baby well. The mother served as merely a necessary accessory to the hospital, which was responsible for the health and well-being of the child, not the mother.

The arrangement of this security could intimidate all but the most confident of mothers. Typically newborns were immediately whisked away to a closed nursery, where they were bathed, changed, and displayed by white-uniformed nurses in face masks. Mothers received their infants on a fixed feeding schedule, usually every four hours, but sometimes every three hours. Today new mothers are released from the hospital forty-eight or even twenty-four hours after delivery. In the interwar period and into the 1940s, however, women stayed one, two, or more weeks in the maternity ward before returning home. As very new nervous mothers, they were highly impressionable; cut off from alternative child-care advice and convinced of the efficacy and appropriateness of hospital-offered medical direction, they gratefully absorbed the routines and schedules they observed in these early weeks.

FIGURE 4.2. Hospital class; notice the face masks on the mothers as well as the nurse. Caption: "During their hospital stay, mothers attend demonstration class in care of newborn infants. Similar classes are also given during the prenatal visits of clinic patients." *Source: Hygeia* 23 (1945): 509.

Confident women religiously followed the advice they received from nurses. Leaving a Los Angeles hospital in 1945, G.L. remembered clearly being told that "the baby should be burped after each bottle feeding." At home, G.L. continued to practice what she had learned in the hospital: she gave the baby a bottle and she burped her. However, after the second bottle at home, G.R. found that her daughter would not burp. She kept, in her words, "pounding," but to no avail. Finally, in frustration, she called her doctor's office, expecting to speak with the nurse. As it turned out, the physician answered the phone. G.L. asked him, "How long should I burp the baby?" Rather than replying directly, the doctor asked, "How long have you been trying?" G.L. answered, "Thirty minutes." Blinded by the medical directions she had been given, G.L. could not stop until the doctor told her, "Stop and put that baby down. Use some common sense."

A 1942 *Parents Magazine* article typifies the hospital experience for mothers and its after-effects.[57] Lois Huntington's infant spent most of her days and all of her nights in the nursery; consequently, during her last week in the hospital, the mother "spent a good deal of time peering through the nursery windows." In her peering she "gained useful knowledge of changing, bathing, and so forth." She learned more about these techniques through demonstration classes given by the nurses. When the infant was brought to her for feeding "I practiced picking her up and putting her down, bubbling, and so forth." Armed with this information and detailed instructions from the doctor telling her "exactly how to make the baby's formula," which she wrote down carefully, "it all seemed too simple and we [she and her husband] patted our selves on the backs for being such good planners." It did not take long for reality to rear its ugly head. She found her first day home "pretty hectic and my husband returned after a hard day to find me in a state of physical and mental exhaustion." Having been insulated in the hospital from the mundane tasks of bottle making and baby bathing, she had had no idea about how intense modern mothering was. Moreover, she had not "realized how very much on my own I was and how little I really knew about babies." Her solution was to work out a meticulous schedule with her husband in which they shared child care. Gradually, caring for her daughter grew to be enjoyable. Yet, throughout the trauma of homecoming, the exhaustion, the worry, Huntington never doubted the medical directions under which she organized her life. The rules and routines she had learned in the hospital and from her physician defined her motherhood practices.

Nurses often stood as surrogates for physicians, the conduit through which women learned the basic practices of scientific motherhood. Public-health nurses entered the homes of the poor in rural and urban areas, intervening directly in the daily lives of new mothers and infants. Middle-class mothers used private nurses to ease their way into daily mothering and into scientific motherhood. In the spirit of sisterhood, Sarah Hepburn offered her experiences as an example for others to ease the transition to motherhood.[58] She advocated hospital stays of two or three weeks. And when at home with her infant, she needed a trained nurse. Hepburn considered a nurse "worth every penny she costs." Hepburn knew from her own experience how nervous a new mother was when alone with her baby. A nurse, she found, could give "practical hints about all kinds of everyday problems" when home from the hospital. New motherhood was stressful and exhausting, Hepburn found. Therefore she was grateful for the presence of the nurse. "The baby was fed from a bottle, so her mother could sleep all night serene in the knowledge that baby would get her feedings," Hepburn reported. However, "if the baby had been breast-fed her mother could have had the nurse bring her in to her at two and at six in the morning so that she could nurse her without having to get out of bed." After Hepburn's first week home from the hospital, the nurse did not stay all day, but instead came in the evening and remained throughout the night. This relieved Hepburn not only of night feedings and formula-making, but also of bathing the baby, until she felt more comfortable taking on these responsibilities. Moreover, after spending the day with her infant, Hepburn "was full of questions which the nurse could answer. When the need for an enema arose, for instance, the nurse was there to show me how to give it."

Though Hepburn paints a picture of a mother dependent upon others for directions in infant care, this process enabled her to gradually develop a self-confidence and willingness even to question medical authority. It was on the issue of crying that Hepburn breaks with contemporary medical authority. Both doctors and nurses tell her that babies get exercise crying; they insist that even an hour of crying will not hurt infants. Hepburn demurred: if a "baby cries over twenty minutes, I believe there is something wrong." Consequently when her daughter started to act "fussy" in the afternoon, Hepburn rearranged her schedule. She still maintained a schedule, as any virtuous scientific mother would do, but "I changed the play time so that she plays from three until four, dropping off for a little nap until five when she has her rub." Like many other mothers of the period, Hepburn was a scientific mother, but a pragmatic one.

Whether they could afford a private nurse or depended on public-health nurses or managed the struggle on their own, by the late 1940s, mothers found themselves intimately intertwined with the ideology of scientific motherhood. Generally, contemporary scientific and medical advice replaced traditional social networks, and good mothering, modern mothering, meant following the directions of your health-care provider. The increasing use of hospitals for childbirth facilitated a greater homogeneity of child-care practices across the United States. Whether or not the labor and delivery were highly medicalized, and many were, babies commonly were taken away immediately after birth and returned to their mothers at set times for feedings and little else. Women came to believe that the hospital personnel knew more about their babies than they, the mothers, did. Moreover, the scientific institution, the hospital, knew more about child care than they, the mothers. In other words, mothers were the pupils of scientific motherhood, learning at the feet of scientific and medical practitioners. Yet in the privacy of their own homes women had to, and did, negotiate the demands of scientific motherhood, rearranging schedules and adjusting procedures to fit their lives and the lives of their families. It is in the postwar era that these private, individual actions would become public as new voices demanded that women's experiences and knowledge be incorporated into the ideology of scientific motherhood.

CHAPTER 5

"Now I know that an authority has the same opinion as mine"

MOTHERHOOD IN THE POSTWAR PERIOD

The "Spock Generation": a familiar motto in postwar United States and into the Cold War. From some it was a tribute: the work of Dr. Benjamin Spock released mothers from the tyranny of Watsonian behaviorism and acknowledged women's everyday life experiences. For some it was a profanity: the children raised according to Spock's books were blamed for undermining the social structure of the nation through the civil rights movement, the environmental movement, the women's movement, and, most especially, the anti–Vietnam War movement. There is truth in both versions of Spock's influence and more. Spock was not the first to protest strict behaviorism and its emphasis of rigid schedules. His name, however, is iconic of so-called permissive childrearing of the post-war era which was associated with youth who criticized their elders, who challenged authority, and who caused dissension throughout the nation. Spock's name became shorthand in the popular media for modern child-care advice—the mid-twentieth-century version of scientific motherhood.

The ideology continued to insist on the primacy of scientific and medical experts and expertise in child care and the need to educate mothers. By the 1940s and 1950s psychology had become an even more important component of its advice. And, advocates of scientific motherhood increasingly broadened their mandates while seeking to foster confidence in mothers. Advisors expanded their sphere of influence to include new topics such as "Adopting a child,"[1] "How to have a comfortable home,"[2] and "Sibling rivalry."[3] In so doing, they further opened the door to the home, interjecting experts and expertise in areas previously unrelated to medical advice manuals.

We know that mothers read this literature, especially Spock, because in articles and correspondence in women's magazines, in letters to the Children's Bureau and survey results, and in mothers' recollections of the period, women frequently raved about Spock's book and his advice columns in magazines such as *Ladies' Home Journal*. Scientific motherhood did not remain static through the period. As hospital routines changed, as women became more directly involved in childbirth decisions, as the women's movement empowered individual mothers and groups, scientific motherhood moved from the idealized hierarchical relationship of dominant physician and submissive mother to one in which the medical profession slowly began to take into consideration the needs and demands of mothers and their experiences. Spock was a potent symbol of scientific motherhood in the second half of the twentieth century, when the baby boom raged and women were encouraged to find their happiness in domesticity, but he was not the only force shaping the ideology.

By the 1950s, scientific motherhood and Spock were so deeply entrenched in U.S. culture that the mother-dependent-on-scientific-and-medical-experts had become a stock character in the media. A *Newsweek* article in 1955 described a purportedly common scenario: "The bowl teetered, tentatively, on the edge of the milk-spattered table. In the next instance, propelled by the firm pushing motion of two plump hands, and accompanied by a loud yell, it tumbled to the floor, liberally sloshing the surroundings with its full cargo of hot cereal, curdled orange juice, and half-chewed bits of toast. Young Johnny Norm, aged 15 months, was mad." Moving the focus from child to mother, the article continued with Mrs. Henry A. Norm as "she whipped a paperbound copy of Dr. Benjamin Spock's 'Baby and Child Care' from the kitchen shelf and turned to the appropriate section on Feeding (page 206). . . . She went for a cross-check to a larger volume, 'Infant and Child in the Culture of Today,' by Drs. Arnold Gesell and Frances L. Ilg, for a look at the Behavior Day (page 137)." After glancing though these authorities, and recalling the words of more, Mrs. Norm still had a quick decision to make. Was Johnny's activity just one of the normal, healthy "gross motor impulses" that Gesell mentions, common in youths of his age? Was it a situation where she should follow Spock's advice to be "jolly and doting even to the point of gushiness"? Or was not the fault, somehow, her own? For solving her dilemma, the columnist pointed to the "5,067 top-flight American pediatricians, plus thousands of psychiatrists, psychologists, sociologists, anthropologists, educators, and child development experts" and over 7,500 books published in the past several decades vying to provide expert advice to such a beleaguered mother.[4]

This acceptance of maternal education was so common that Hollywood could and did play it for comic effect in films such as *Rock-a-Bye Baby* (1958), with comedian Jerry Lewis as Clayton Poole and Connie Stevens as Sandy Naples, his friend. For a series of ridiculous and complicated reasons, Lewis is left caring for triplets. The movie, of course, makes much of the incongruity of a man caring for infants and how he learns what it means to be a modern mother. For example, after Lewis "finds" the babies on his doorstep, he calls Sandy to help him. He asks her to pick up some bottles for the babies on her way over and in the meantime he, in Jerry Lewis style, fashions a temporary feeding device from a rubber glove with holes in the finger tips. Once Sandy arrives, she is the one who changes the diapers and hangs out the wash. Then, while she watches Clayton bottle-feed one of the infants, she picks up another one, explaining: "See, this is the first thing you learn in Home Economics, Clayton. After they eat, they have air bubbles and you hafta pat their backs and get them out." Sandy then proceeds to show him how to burp a baby and watches while he practices, the clear expectation of sex roles in the mid-twentieth-century United States. As the rubber-glove bottle and education on burping a baby illustrate, men can handle child care, but women do so more efficiently and appropriately, with education.

The story quickly gets more complicated. Clayton is an unmarried man, and there is a well-to-do couple in town interested in adopting the triplets, so Clayton has to appear in court to defend his caring for them. The judge is sympathetic but with traditional gender roles in mind, he informs Clayton, "The court recognizes that you have been a very good foster father, but these children need more than that. They need a mother as well." Clayton is not deterred. He stands and in addressing the court he announces, "Your Honor, sir, if you want me to be a mother, I'll be a mother, a real mother . . . I'll become a mother, a real mother, if you only give me a chance." Needless to say, the judge is unconvinced and the spectators in court giggle, but Clayton insists.

The question remains: How does a man, an earnest man, "become a mother"? How can Clayton prove that he can be both a father and a "mother"? We next see him enrolled in the University Child Care Clinic in Chicago. The scene opens with a classroom of well-dressed women and Clayton; they are addressed by a formidable nurse. Her introduction, "As we all know, a healthy, happy baby does not just happen. A healthy, happy baby happens when there is a healthy, happy mother to take care of that baby," reiterates the basic tenets of scientific motherhood. Of course, this school is the place to create those healthy, happy mothers, as she happily reports to the class, "That's what we at the University Child Care Clinic are dedicated to: healthy, happy, and efficient mothers. I'm so proud to see our classes filled with women who are interested in the future welfare of their children. All of you women, mothers, and expectant mothers are to be commended." Clayton, who cannot be ignored in this sea of female faces, receives special commendation from the teacher, who remarks that "I am also happy to see in our midst a member of the opposite sex who had the courage and fortitude to want to be both a father and a mother. Oh, if there were more fathers like you, Mr. Poole, a woman's work would get done." She closes with a particularly cheery note: "And now in just a moment we will be on our merry way to proper child care." Though we do not see any other scenes at this University Child Care Clinic, we can surmise what instruction is like from the fact that the students are directed by a nurse.

Clayton returns to the court and hands his diploma to the judge. For the benefit of those in the movie audience, he elaborates on his education: "I passed all the requirements of the child-care course. And, well, this diploma is only awarded to the very best of mothers. I was first in my class for overall child care and I placed second for formula mixing. But I set a new record for diaper folding. And I did everything any other woman can do." Sorry to report, despite his impressive achievements, the judge did not consider him a "mother," and awarded the triplets to the couple. This being Hollywood, mayhem ensues following the announcement of his decision and eventually the triplets are reunited instead with their biological mother. At the end of the film, Sandy and Clayton marry and have quintuplets.

The film plays maternal education and the contradiction of man-as-mother broadly, providing an ideal set-up for Lewis's comic flair. But more than that, the movie is critical in understanding the place of scientific motherhood in the United States in the postwar era. The comic scene at the University Child Care Clinic is possible because the idea of maternal education for women was familiar to audiences throughout the country: women, not men, were educated in scientific motherhood. The movie may seem like an exaggeration of maternal education and for many people it probably was. But there were tertiary educational institutions, such as the Merrill-Palmer School, that trained mothers along with nursery school teachers, psychologists, and others who worked with children; there was home economics education available on many campuses of land-grant universities and, for a time, even Vassar offered courses in euthenics for their students. There were increasing numbers of hospital classes; home economics was spreading throughout U.S. elementary and secondary schools; and, as we saw previously, even the Girls Scouts were teaching girls about motherhood practices. Exaggeration or not, in *Rock-a-Bye Baby* we see that scientific motherhood, the idea that women needed scientific and medical advice for raising their children "properly," was part of the mainstream of U.S. culture.

Rock-a-Bye Baby depicted the expectations of idealized motherhood in mid-century. Women were to be mothers, girls were trained to be mothers, children were to be raised in a two-parent home with a father who worked outside the home and a "stay-at-home" mother. This picture ignored the reality of many women's lives: the increasing number of women, even of mothers, who worked outside the home and the increasing number of single-parent families; not every family lived the lives of popular television programs such as *Father Knows Best* and *Ozzie and Harriet*. This disjuncture between popular image and lived experiences provided fuel for the mother-blaming of the postwar era, when social critics denounced women who stepped out of their traditional role for creating many of the problems of the day, such as juvenile delinquency, the decline of the American home, and even child mortality and morbidity. Such criticism could, in turn, intensify the lack of self-confidence some mothers felt about their childrearing and the belief that they needed maternal education. However, just as earlier in the century, hope could be found in the promises of science and medicine. Scientific breakthroughs, such as new antibiotics, which were released seemingly daily, loudly announced through newspapers, magazines, radio, and television, assured worried mothers and others that cures were near at hand.[5] Once again, mothers were directed to physicians and other experts for instructions on healthful, appropriate child care.

A critical venue for this instruction continued to be the hospitals. Throughout the postwar period and later, during the baby boom and its aftermath, increasing numbers of women entered hospitals for their births. There, as we have seen, hospitals prided themselves on the educational opportunities they afforded new mothers in prenatal classes and in postnatal hospital demonstrations and classes before returning home. In addition, hospital routines themselves, such as separating the mother and child immediately after birth and insisting that babies be cared for in separate nurseries by trained nurses, had deleterious effects. For experienced mothers, such an environment of peace and quiet away from the demands of their frenetic home life was to be enjoyed to the fullest. For new mothers, though, the situation sapped the self-confidence of many and reinforced the belief that medical practitioners knew better how to care for children than mothers.[6]

As mentioned before, hospitals in the pre-antibiotic period and later were especially worried about the possibility of epidemics sweeping through maternity wards and nurseries. To prevent such disasters, pediatric nurses wore face masks and encouraged mothers to do the same, implying that babies needed to be protected even from their mothers' germs. Though not all hospitals insisted that mothers wear masks, many did. And some women were encouraged to buy face masks to wear at home. One woman I spoke with remembered her mother returning from the hospital with twin newborns in

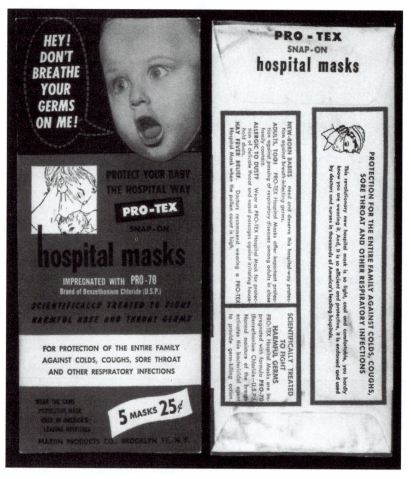

FIGURE 5.1. Package of face masks, c. 1940s.

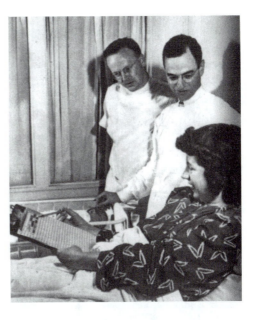

FIGURE 5.2. Mother and physicians in hospital rooming-in ward. Caption: "The perfect team for a baby's welfare: mother, father, obstetrician, pediatrician, nurse. Doctors make rounds together and here inspect 'behavior' chart kept by mother." *Source:* "Babies Welcome Here," *Woman's Home Companion* 76 (Jan. 1948): 116.

the early 1950s. To assist in the transition from hospital to home, the family had hired a nurse. "Nursie," as the family called her, had very definite ideas about appropriate infant care. No one was allowed to enter the babies' room without a face mask. In this family, as soon as the nurse left, the face masks were thrown away.[7]

But the medical profession was not monolithic and there were those who saw the dark side of the increasingly bureaucratic and impersonal hospital routines; they focused more on the psychological side of child care than previous advisors. For example, Dr. Edith B. Jackson accepted the advantages of hospitalized childbirth but looked for ways to "humanize" hospital medicine.[8] In the 1930s, Jackson had concluded that the emotional circumstances of the home environment of many of her patients caused their infants' feeding problems, problems she linked back to contemporary hospital practices. When mothers returned home from the hospital with their infants, they rigidly followed the four-hour feeding schedule they had been taught. Jackson saw anxious mothers caring for babies they scarcely knew because they had hardly seen their infants when in the hospital. As a clinical professor of pediatrics and psychiatry at Yale University School of Medicine, Jackson determined to improve the home situation by altering the initial newborn period in the hospital and fostering a more confident attitude among new mothers.

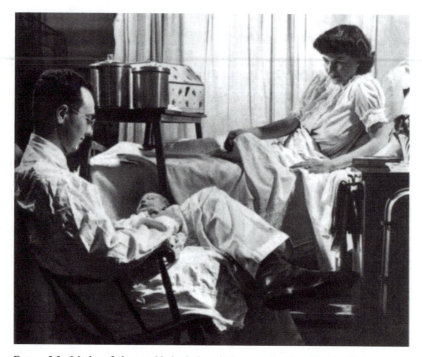

FIGURE 5.3. Mother, father, and baby in hospital room. Caption: "Looks like your own room but is actually the corner of a four-bed ward in a modern hospital. Homelike atmosphere and comforts help new families off to a good start." *Source:* "Babies Welcome Here," *Woman's Home Companion* 76 (Jan. 1948): 117.

Between 1946 and 1952, she established two unique four-bed units in Grace–New Haven Community Hospital, wards that housed both mothers and their newborns. In this situation, mothers could get to know their children before going home from the hospital; they could nurse their infants as needed, and they could learn their habits, all under the watchful eyes of specially trained nurses and pediatric fellows, who demonstrated infant care and were ready to answer every question the mother raised.

Undoubtedly, Jackson's practices did serve to humanize the childbirth and postnatal experiences for women fortunate enough to participate in the short-lived experiment. As historian Silberman points out, this practice of rooming-in was "enormously satisfying for its participants and enthusiastically endorsed by physicians, nurses and hospital administrators familiar with it."[9] Numerous articles appeared in women's magazines, child-care magazines, and health magazines extolling the virtues of rooming-in and quoting enthusiastic new mothers. One woman, Carol, was the focus of a photo essay in

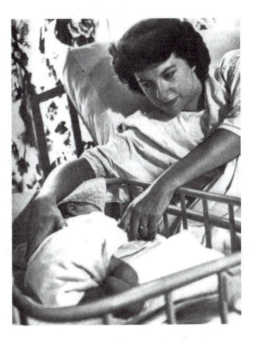

FIGURE 5.4. Mother and baby in hospital room. Caption: "Each baby has movable crib next to mother's bed. She soon learns his needs—when to move him, feed him, comfort him or play with him. Nurse is available if she tires." *Source:* "Babies Welcome Here," *Woman's Home Companion* 76 (Jan. 1948): 119.

Hygeia, the magazine that the American Medical Association published for lay readers. Poor Carol, before she entered the hospital for childbirth, was at a loss. She was an only child, and so had no experience with babies as siblings; she trained for a profession, and so had no courses in high school or college on how to care for children. Now she was faced with a newborn. Fortunately, Carol was admitted to George Washington University Hospital, which was experimenting with rooming-in. She was delighted. She found "the learning process painless and pleasant." She was particularly pleased with the instruction she received from the nurse, who "demonstrates such procedures as holding and feeding the baby, diapering, taking his temperature and bathing him." Then, the article explains, "As Carol's strength permits, she is learning to perform each step herself." Consequently, Carol happily asserted, "I believe I'm going home fairly well qualified as a baby tender."[10]

But while actively involving mothers in the care of their infants, and in the process enhancing their self-confidence, rooming-in also served to solidify the authority of health-care practitioners. Though Silberman considers that Jackson's rooming-in schema exemplified the "notion that obstetricians, pediatricians, and nurses should help parents to trust their own nurturing instincts," a contrary interpretation is more likely. As Jackson herself described the rooming-in environment: "During the first two or three days the nurse lifts the baby for the mother, changes his diapers while the mother watches, helps make the baby comfortable at the mother's breast and, in general, takes care of both the baby and the mother. The mothers all know the nurse is ready to help in any way, and they need not hesitate to call her at any time. But as soon as they feel ready to take care of the baby themselves, they are encouraged to do so."[11] Other doctors, too, found that mothers "appreciated that they were really learning these procedures under the best possible guidance."[12] Mothers in these rooming-in units did gain confidence in handling their children. But the routines there reinforced the authority of the health-care practitioner and the impression that experts know best how to care for children.[13]

At the same time that Jackson established rooming-in at Grace–New Haven, Benjamin Spock made similar pronouncements in his incredibly popular manuals, first issued in 1946 under the title *The Common Sense Book of Baby and Child Care*. His dominant position in the postwar era eclipses the works of others who preceded him. Many mothers in the 1930s and early 1940s were familiar with Arnold Gesell, psychologist, who with Frances Ilg wrote *Infant and Child in the Culture of Today*.[14] Gesell and Ilg called for children's "self-regulated growth" and stressed the mother's role as "guidance." Other mothers mentioned Aldrich and Aldrich, *Babies Are Human Beings*, which moved away from the mechanical images of children in Watsonian behaviorism.[15]

Just a few years before Spock, Dorothy V. Whipple, a doctor and mother, published *Our American Babies: The Art of Baby Care*. Whipple introduced her book with a description of the rigidity in child care that she had been taught in medical school in the 1920s, the heyday of behaviorism. She reminded readers that in that period early conditioning was mandatory and took place in a germ-free environment where "an infant's needs were attended to with stop-watch regularity by a well-trained attendant."[16] These practices she had advocated until she had her own children. Then, "I soon found that it made a lot of difference to me whose baby was crying. I had been able to go away with equanimity from some other mother's screaming child, with the knowledge that a skilled nurse would see that he lacked nothing; but to go away from my own crying baby, and stay within earshot for an hour or more before the clock said I could give him milk I knew he wanted, that, I confess, I found to be a different matter."[17] For example, in toilet training, she combined experiential knowledge with scientific and medical expertise. Whipple had accepted the ideal of a strictly trained child who would be toilet trained in the early months of life. Yet, her lived experience as a mother showed her that children do not necessarily follow the routines established in child-care manuals. She admitted that it would be nice to not have to bother with the laundry problems of an untrained child, a particularly onerous burden in this period before the widespread adoption of automatic washers and dryers. But she cautioned against "try[ing] to accomplish the impossible."[18] Whipple coupled her family observations with the experiences of her patients and with contemporary science, noting that a child cannot voluntarily control bowels and bladder until eight to ten months of age. Not that schedules were not useful. Babies have their own schedules, she explained, and the baby "is a better guide than the clock upon the wall." It is better for the child, she told readers, that mothers watch the baby carefully and follow the baby's clock. Whipple acknowledged that mothers can and do learn from their children, but that does not remove the need for the direction of experts. In disclosing that she based her advice on both experience and the latest scientific and medical knowledge, Whipple explicitly demonstrated that the mother should learn from experts what to look for in her child and how to follow her child's lead in training. We can hypothesize about why Whipple's book never gained the popularity of Spock's. Perhaps it was published at the wrong time, or by the wrong company, or written by a woman. For whatever reason, it is Spock's name that we associate with this intense form of mothering.

Spock often discussed his motivation for writing the book, beyond the fact that the publisher approached him to do it. The doctor explained that he felt psychology was an important element, but one that was typically lacking in contemporary child-care manuals. His claim was, of course, more self-serving than enlightened. He was well aware of other books that incorporated psychology, such as Aldrich and Aldrich; he even asked Aldrich to review the manuscript for *The Common Sense Book of Baby and Child Care*. Though Spock was not the first, he was certainly the most popular. The book's initial price—twenty-five cents, at its time of publication—at the beginning of the baby boom, its down-to-earth-style—he wrote in colloquialisms and short sentences, made the book an immediate best-seller. It first appeared in May 1946; within ten months it had sold 6,478 copies in hardcover and 541,460 copies in paperback. This was as many copies as Holt's *Care and Feeding of Children* had sold over thirty-nine years. Within three years, paperback sales reached a million copies a year. And, despite many competitors in later years, by 1998, Spock's book had sold over 50 million copies and had been translated into thirty-nine languages.[19]

His method of writing the book is most revealing. Whipple had joined the experiential and the professional in one person; Benjamin Spock (the professional) and Jane Spock (the experienced mother) jointly wrote *The Com-*

mon Sense Book of Baby and Child Care. During the war, Benjamin was in the Navy and traveling across the country. Each evening he would call back home and dictate the text to his wife, Jane, who had cared for the children in their family. As his biographer Lynn Z. Bloom tells his story:

> "If it's easier to sterilize formula right in the bottles than to boil the bottles, nipples, and formula separately, why would anyone do it the hard way?" Dr. Spock would wonder, wearily.
>
> "Because in the 'easy way' the milk scum clogs the nipples, and it's hard to clear the bottles inside," Jane answered. "They break, too."
>
> "O.K. Let's put in the reasons." He dictated: "The main difficulties are from scum which clogs the nipples ... breakage of bottles, and milk which sticks to the inside of the bottles and is hard to scrub off."[20]

It was many years later before he admitted that in this process they had integrated his medical knowledge with her practical experience. He had the training in Freudian psychology, but she had the practical knowledge of pinning diapers, sterilizing formula, and realizing "that a baby's sweater should have shoulders that unbutton so you don't skin his nose putting it off and on."[21] The topics they considered ranged from circumcision and breast and bottle feeding through the ever popular daily bath and on to "Separated parents" and "The working mother," some more directly medical than others and yet typical of the broader issues handled in contemporary child-care manuals.

Spock's advice was a reaction against strict behaviorism and he was, like Jackson, influenced by his involvement with the introduction of Freudian psychoanalysis into U.S. child development theory in the 1930s and 1940s. It is not clear how much Spock expected mothers to absorb his psychological perspectives. One could very easily read *Common Sense* and take only the practical suggestions, ignoring the psychological underpinnings. As a matter of fact, Spock suggested just that in his opening section as he informed the reader, "You don't have to read the whole book ahead of time. . . . Use the Index at the back when you are troubled. It's arranged to help you find the answers."[22] And the presentation of his advice also differed sharply from his predecessors'. In contrast to the authoritarianism of advice manuals such as Dennett, Tweddell, and Holt's catechism, Spock's style was more conversational as he urged mothers to watch their children and to follow their lead. Rhetorically, it was more inclusive than earlier popular manuals. Spock's posture suggested that he was a friendly advisor who considered mothers' opinions in his writing. Mothers were no longer strict disciplinarians; in the intense mothering of Spock's book, they were supportive nurturers. They must not rush their children prematurely into weaning, eating solid foods, tub bathing, or toilet training and the like. Rather, modern mothers carefully observed their children and followed their lead.

It is critical to note that not all child-care manuals of the period advocated this form of intense mothering. There were some, a minority, that insisted mothers needed to train their children, not indulge them. The Spock form of child care clearly annoyed Dr. Walter W. Sackett, Jr. His *Bringing Up Babies: A Family Doctor's Practical Approach to Child Care* (1962) was typical of this school, reflecting more of the outlook of earlier in the century than the psychologically informed child care of Spock and others. The mother who did not impose a schedule on her child, who watched and waited until the baby was ready, would create "the adult who expects others to bail him out of trouble." We were at the height of the Cold War, the First World against the communist world, and Sackett warned, "If we teach our offspring to expect everything to be provided on demand, we must admit the possibility of sowing the seeds of socialism."[23] Consequently, the doctor urged "mothers to walk away from a crying baby (unless it's really time for eating, and after checking for wet diaper, an offending pin, or other irritation) and to ignore the crying baby at night as well as in the daytime." He did not deny the psychological elements of child care but rather than focusing on the emotions of the child, he focused on the mother, explaining that "rocking or fondling the baby should be done primarily for the mother's pleasure."[24] In general, Sackett maintained that the children must learn to be good citizens, which they would do if their mothers followed the rules he, the good doctor, laid down. At the same time, the autocratic Sackett spoke of the need for "each mother [to] exercise her own good judgement in many situations lest her own common sense grow weak from disuse like a broken leg in a cast."[25] But, as with Tenney, the space within which the mother could "exercise" her common sense was very limited. For example, with feeding he detailed that cereal should begin on the second or third day; strained vegetables at ten days; strained meats at fourteen days; fruit juice at three weeks; cod liver oil at four weeks; eggs at five weeks; sweets such as fruits, custards, and puddings at six weeks; and bacon and eggs at nine weeks. Directions in such minutiae surely undermined a mother's ability to think the problem through for herself, despite his warning that he did not "want to set forth any strict rules that mothers will follow blindly."[26]

However, Sackett was a member of a minority of child-care advisors. More typical was the transformation that occurred in the popular literature of the Children's Bureau. Over the decade of the 1920s, Mary West had been eased out by the organized medical profession and laywomen were no longer directly involved in the production of pamphlets like *Prenatal Care* and *Infant Care*. Throughout the interwar period, the Children's Bureau had used Watsonian behaviorism to explain the need for rigidly scheduling children. By the mid-1940s, the medical practitioners who worked for the Bureau were clearly aware of the changing content of advice and particularly the increased reliance on psychology to address problems of child care. In one typical case, Mrs. S.M. of East Orange, New Jersey, wrote of her concerns about toilet training:

> My baby is 10 months old now and since he was 3 months old he always went on the chamber when I set him on it to move his bowels and now for a month he simply will not go on his chamber at all. When I see he struggles, I put him on and he just won't move his bowels. No sooner I take him off he'll move them in the diaper & I try to get him on again to complete it [but] he just won't move them. No matter how long I keep him on no sooner I take him down he completes it again in the diaper. I believe it makes me feel bad about it being he was so wonderful until about a month ago.[27]

Did Mrs. S.M. read a previous version of *Infant Care* that had urged this early training? Did she rely on the experiences of family and friends? Her letter does not tell us. But the mother was attempting to follow the instructions that had been popular for decades, and that the Children's Bureau itself had expounded. By the postwar period, though, the advice had changed and the rationale for toilet training routines as well.[28] As Spock and many other writers were suggesting, three months old was too early developmentally for toilet training the modern child. Dr. Katherine Bain, director of the Bureau's Division of Research in Child Development, answered Mrs. S.M.'s letter, suggesting that the frustrated mother look in the current edition of *Infant Care*, which advises not to start training the baby before eight to ten months old. Quite a switch from early admonitions. Moreover, Bain does not explain that the theory of toilet training has evolved; rather she blames the mother for the problem: "Your difficulty is that you have attempted to train him too young with the mistaken idea that the younger you train him the better." This disparaging tone was not unique to the physicians of the Children's Bureau, or Sackett. It was common among health-care practitioners at that time.[29]

The prime example of this is Benjamin Spock, who in his 1946 book and subsequent editions opened with a section entitled "Trust yourself," the first sentence of which is the often quoted "You know more than you think you do." Such a sentiment may or may not have been comforting to a nervous new mother but it does remind the reader of the mother's importance in child care. What follows in Spock's manual, though, is equally important for understanding the doctor's views of mothers and of the relationship between physician and mother that the doctor promoted. Spock urges, "Don't take too seriously all that the neighbors say. Don't be overawed by what the experts say. Don't be afraid to trust your own common sense. Bringing up your child won't be a complicated job if you take it easy, trust your own instincts, *and follow the directions that your doctor gives you.*"[30] Mothers may have some instincts, mothers may "know," but that does not mean that they are in control of their childrearing. Like Holt and Tenney and many others before him, Spock continues to insist on the primacy of the physician in child care, who gives advice on everything from how many sheets to buy and of what type through to adoption. For all his supportive statements about mothers' "common sense," he warns women away from neighbors and directs them to their doctors. He explains the importance of regular visits to the doctor, a growing phenomenon in the booming post–World War II era, while he belittles the mother at the same time. "On your first visit you will have hundreds of questions," he informs mothers, "and you'll probably forget most of them until you are home again. It's good to make a list—for days beforehand—and then try hard to remember not to forget to bring the list. You needn't be bashful about asking the doctor questions, no matter how silly you may feel they are. It is important that you be satisfied that things are going along all right and that you are doing the job properly."[31] For all his trust in maternal "instincts," he presents the mother as incompetent, an attitude that is even more apparent in the 1957 revision of *Common Sense*. The section on "The bath" is a good illustration. The 1957 edition provides step-by-step directions for a tub bath, details not found in the first edition. The 1957 edition elaborates:

> Before starting the bath, be sure you have everything you need close at hand. If you forget the towel, you'll have to go after it holding a dripping baby in your arms.
>
> Take off your wrist watch.
>
> An apron keeps your clothes drier.[32]

In his chatty style, Spock positions the mother as so nervous and inept that she needs to be reminded to take off her watch. He puts the mother in the same quandary as his predecessors did: you know how to care for your child, but the doctor knows best.

There is an implicit contradiction here. On the one hand, physicians published advice manuals and columns; on the other hand, they insisted that mothers place their children under the observation of a "competent and sensible doctor." If mothers listened to their physicians, why should they read books and magazine columns? For physicians in the late nineteenth century there had been no inconsistency. They did not expect to intervene in the everyday life of the well child. They expected to give instruction, but instruction that the mother could follow without the personal intervention of a physician. Educated motherhood was the key to lowering infant mortality and morbidity rates, and that education established parameters that defined the role of the mother and of the physician.

This insistence on physician supervision, especially personal supervision, grew more resolute throughout the twentieth century. In order to take their advice directly into the homes of their clients, some physicians went beyond books and pamphlets and office visits to printed pads that prescribed the feeding schedules by age. They specified when the child should be fed, what the child should be fed, and how the child should be fed. For example, Dr. Manuel S. Hirshberg of Bloomfield, Connecticut, instructed the mother to feed her two-month-old infant cereal at 10 a.m. and 6 p.m., and at 2 p.m., cracker mush, which was "crumbed up crackers to which formula is added. You may use zwieback, graham crackers, arrowroot & milk crackers."[33] In other instances, preprinted pads for the same purpose were distributed by manufacturers of products such as Vi-Penta vitamin drops and Carnation Evaporated Milk. The companies often supplied these pads with the name and address of the physician or hospital already printed on them.[34] At the same time there continued to be a booming market in prenatal and child-care manuals, both commercial and governmental, many with authors who were not physicians. In addition, more and more institutions such as schools, girls' clubs, and hospitals were offering prenatal, child-care, and parenting classes; this instruction could be seen to undermine the influence of physicians in the area and even provided an implicit, if not explicit, challenge to the physicians' status and prestige.

As doctors reminded their public, contradictory advice circulated by these sources could make the physicians' job more difficult and time-consuming as they needed to re-instruct their patients. Moreover, such information, these doctors feared, could be erroneous or even dangerous. The Chicago pediatrician Isaac Abt believed that the mother of the mid-twentieth century was "neurotic," and "the neurotic mother [of today] is probably the greatest victim of free advice. Afraid to rely on her own judgment, she becomes utterly confused when the advice in the morning paper is at variance with that in the evening paper, and neither article agrees with the point of view of the writer of her favorite women's magazine."[35] The readily available and growing number of alternative sources fueled these concerns.

In other instances, physician-authors explained that they were writing for those mothers who did not have access to a physician, either for financial or other reasons. They were not writing for women who had their own doctor, but for those unfortunate women who did not. Spock, for example, urged parents to visit and to phone their doctor not only when their child was ill but "for all specific directions about formulas, vitamins, etc." He insisted that mothering "with only the help of a book is not satisfactory," but, he admitted, "it is better than nothing."[36] By the second half of the twentieth century, the ideal was a middle-class mother who cared for her child under the direct supervision of her private physician. But, when a physician was not available, then physician-authored books could stand in for the authority of the doctor.

There were other reasons that mothers utilized published advice rather than or in addition to medical practitioners, reasons that mothers explained in their many letters to Spock. Though these letters are a limited sample, in their praises of Spock we see a diversity of experiences and mothers' opinions about the role of the expert in child care. Many women learned about Spock and his books through their own physicians or the hospital in which they birthed. One mother was pleased to inform Spock that his work was "of wide use with Army families. It's even recommended by the staff of the hospital here, Madigan Army Hospital, almost as part of the necessary equipment."[37] In previous decades, some physicians had written their own booklets for patients; by the 1950s and 1960s it was common for doctors to instead distribute Spock's. As another grateful mother wrote Spock: "Having had a nice healthy son, 5 months ago, my doctor, [R.S.C.], presented me with your book, 'Baby and Child Care,' for which I have been most thankful and would not be without for one second."[38]

Women recorded many reasons for embracing child-care manuals and the directions of experts such as Spock. Foremost among them was unfamiliarity with children. With the shrinking of family size through the century and across the country, many new mothers of the baby boom generation, like Carol in the *Hygeia* article cited earlier in the chapter, found themselves facing a small stranger with little or no previous experience with younger siblings. They had many questions, for which they wanted expert advice, but they did not want to bother their own physicians with what might be trivial concerns. Typical was Mrs. R.D.S. of Concord, California, who wrote Spock in 1954:

> I am a young mother of two children—ages 20 months—(boy) & 7 weeks (girl). Myself and several other of my friends refer to your book as our "Bible of Child care"—& also call our babies "Dr. Spock Babies." We refer to your book very often—& usually answers [*sic*] all our questions & eliminates an unecessary [*sic*] call to the doctor. . . .
>
> Many young mothers, particularly like myself who have never been around a small child before our own children our [*sic*] very thankful for a reliable source like your book to refer to when a problem arises.[39]

This letter also suggests that mothers were not reading child-care manuals through from cover to cover. When a "problem" arose, Mrs. R.D.S. looked through the book. Other mothers might look to friends and neighbors rather than a book, but these were often not available to them. The United States is a highly mobile society, and more so during the middle decades of the twentieth century, when families looking for employment moved during the Depression and when mobilization during World War II sent young parents away from their families and friends. In such cases, a new mother could find some level of comfort in the details of modern child-care books. One woman whose husband was stationed at Fort Leonard Wood was especially thankful, assuring Spock, "I think that your book is wonderful. Especially for a new mother away from home who doesn't have her mother to run to every time something new arises."[40] Other mothers complained that they were geographically isolated. They wanted expert advice, but did not have access to it. Typical of these forlorn letter writers was a mother from Montana who wrote to Spock about her three-and-a-half-year-old who stuttered: "I doubt if you realize how limited life is in Montana. There are no nursery schools here & unless a child is sick the doctors feel your [*sic*] wasting their time. It 1000 [*sic*] miles to any city."[41] The tone of modern child-care books represented a further extension of sisterly advice networks. For instance, Spock's conversational style and his inclusiveness mimicked earlier woman-to-woman discourse. Mothers felt comfortable including him and believed that he included them. They sent him letters describing their experiences with the expectation that he would pass them on to others. In other words, they included him in their circle.

One of the stated goals of Spock and other writers of his ilk was to inspire confidence in mothers. W.S.B. of Long Beach, California, for example, reported to Spock that "your book on the care of babies added a great deal to our courage and knowledge in the rearing of our two boys."[42] Mothers revealed self-confidence in several different situations. For some mothers, self-confidence enabled women to ignore advice they felt was inappropriate or simply wrong. For others, it meant greater reliance on their own resources and less use of experts and expertise. And for others, self-confidence enabled them to overtly challenge directions and practices that they believed were wrong. Emblematic of the many letters Spock received was one from Flemington, New Jersey:

> [Your book] was invaluable to me, especially is [*sic*] a new mother. I had a college education, a fine job as a bacteriologist[?] and quite a share of knowledge in almost any field but babies, when I first became a mother 3 1/2 years ago. Some well-meaning friend gave me a "Baby Book"—not yours, but I won't mention it's [*sic*] name. I have never read anything more frustrating! Their baby ate, slept, and so on, on a perfect schedule, it didn't have colic, it slept all night. My baby did none of these things! Then your books came my way. I discovered that there was nothing wrong with me or the baby. He was just different. The line I best remember is "Most babies go to sleep after their feeding, but some babies don't." Light dawned. My baby was one of the "don't"s. I relaxed, discovered his own pattern, things were much easier. I was a Spock convert. I love you! . . .
>
> Thank you so much, Dr. Spock, for all your help and the belief in good old common sense that you gave me.[43]

By the late 1950s then, aspects of scientific motherhood were shifting, most especially in the relationship between mothers and physicians. American medicine was slowly being transformed through the second half of the twentieth century with movements such as Grantly Dick-Read's "childbirth without fear" and Lamaze "prepared childbirth," which gave women a voice in the conduct of their labor and childbirth. Rather than imposing predetermined labor and childbirth procedures, physicians began listening to the needs and wants of their patients in these two increasingly popular practices. The advent of the women's health movement, with its call for de-centering the physician and empowering the patient, also prompted doctors to present the relationship between mothers and physicians in a new light.

The changes are most evident when we compare various revisions of Holt's long popular *Care and Feeding of Children*. When L. Emmett Holt, Jr., revised his father's book in the 1940s, he carefully incorporated new theories of child care, as well as added mentions of immunizations and other preventative health measures and some consideration of behavioral problems, such as temper tantrums and sleep disturbances. He retained sections on bowel training that advocated regularity by the third or fourth month and illustrations on how to pin a diaper. He also continued his father's authoritarian catechism format. In later editions, however, he eliminated the catechism format with the explanation that "the times have changed and with them mothers' attitudes." He understood that "the mother of today [1957] is a very different person from the mother of yesterday. She lives in a world with greatly increased facilities of communication, a world with a thirst for medical knowledge, where medical facts and advice are freely broadcast and where conflicting opinions are often encountered. She wants more than a dogmatic statement of *what* to do. She wants to know something of the *why*, the factual basis for the opinion given."[44] These transformations did not abruptly alter medical practice or the relationship between mothers and physicians throughout the United States. They did, however, introduce changes that gradually spread across the country.

By the mid-twentieth century, writers universally promoted the idea of physician-directed child care, with the physician close at hand. Some, like Herman Bundesen, longtime president of the Chicago Board of Health (1931–60), explained that the mother should keep his book on hand to answer day-to-day problems, but, he cautioned, it was to be used in conjunction with her doctor because "the mother can take care of her baby best under the guidance of a physician trained in the care of infants."[45] Drs. Litchfield and Dembo maintained that the purpose of their book, *A Pediatric Manual for Mothers*, was "definitely *not* to supplant the doctor." Instead, they sought to ease the work of "the busy physician and anxious mothers" by anticipating worrisome questions and answering them "quickly and clearly."[46] Physician-authored magazine columns reiterated this same message.

We can see that the authoritarian stance of these writers slowly receded. Physician-writers encouraged mothers to use literature to supplement their physicians and they understood the advantage of the educated patient. But they wanted education that corresponded to their practices. After all, an appropriate class or book that was supportive of the physician's practice could make physician-patient interactions briefer and more effective. Concluded one New York physician discussing childbirth classes in 1952, "I am certain that good teachers who consult with the obstetrician in the community in preparing their program, can sound the knell of doom to professional opposition. The aim of the teacher should be to preach the same sermon as the physician. Parents' classes then serve their true purpose in helping the public and in making the complicated practice of medicine easier for the obstetrician."[47] Physicians did not object to educating the mother; they simply did not want her confused. With appropriate education, she would be compliant with medical supervision.

Similarly, the booklets that physicians wrote for their patients presented the medical practitioner as somewhat less authoritarian and patients less subservient. The physician-mother relationship was more collaborative, though by no means equal. As the Chicago Lying-In Hospital and Dispensary informed its patients in the 1958 *Information for Expectant Mothers*, "Adequate prenatal care is possible only when there is close co-operation between patient and her physician and nurse." This being a publication of the Chicago Lying-In, the nurse is sometimes used as a stand-in for the physician, though the physician held final authority in this relationship as well. In this more collaborative environment, women were not forbidden to read unapproved books or listen to nonprofessionals; rather the hospital suggested that patients use their office visits to query their physicians, remarking, "This will make it unnecessary for you to obtain information from books or well-meaning but uninformed friends." With the rationale "A well-informed mother is a happy mother," the hospital urged the women to attend its Mothers' Classes, education that reinforced the practices and the authority of the patient's physician. Yet still, the physician remained unquestionably in charge because "after all, he is the final judge as to how you should regulate your life."[48]

This new relationship had no place for the strictly autocratic physician in whose presence the mother was expected to be acquiescent. Under these changed circumstances, doctors needed to cultivate their patients, be aware of their patients' personalities and needs. As early as 1950, Spock explained to other physicians what they needed to do when faced with a nervous new mother. It was, Spock noted in an article that originally appeared in the medical journal *Pediatrics*, and that was reprinted in the popular magazine *Consumer Reports*, "the physician's long-term job . . . to help [the mother] acquire confidence in herself, and a sense of balance with her child. In all his contacts the physician should be uncritical, friendly, reassuring, to avoid giving her new cause of uneasiness."[49] Parents were told too that "personal compatibility, as well as medical knowledge" was important in selecting a physician.[50] Women were urged to interview several health-care providers before selecting the physician for their child. During the interview, what was important was not just what the doctors said, but how they said it, as manuals explained: "You should be able to sense if this person is competent, caring, and considerate. The right person to provide health care for your baby is some-one whose style and philosophy are compatible with yours."[51] This is a very different picture from that presented by Hanrahan and Wood a few decades earlier.

Though the definition of scientific motherhood was changing over the decades of mid-century, and despite the diversity among child-care advisors, there were still several very critical components that were consistently pro-moted. First of all was the primacy of the medical practitioner. Whether it was the authoritarian style of Sackett or the chatty style of Spock or some-where in between, all the doctors, psychologists, and other educators agreed that the doctor had the final word in child care. By doctor, they meant a per-son whom the mother would use for well-child checkups, immunizations, and the multiplicity of questions that arise in raising a child. Books and articles based on contemporary science and medicine should be a back-up system only, except if dire circumstances kept a mother from her physician. Psychol-ogy was increasingly employed to explain the reasons why mothers should do thus and so. Moreover, intense mothering remained a hallmark of scien-tific motherhood for decades, whether it was Spock's diligently watching for readiness or Sackett's rigid schedules. And, most interestingly, all claimed that their directions were based not only on their experiences but also the experi-ences of their patients. Even Sackett, the authoritarian, justified his instruc-tions with the note that they were based on "customs practiced by mothers of great experience, and have been followed by the mothers of more than fif-teen hundred babies under my care in the last dozen years."[52]

How much influence mothers had in the development of this era's ver-sion of scientific motherhood is more difficult to document. In Sackett's case, for example, it could very well be that the doctor gave directions that the mothers were to follow, that is, top-down instruction. What of the other di-rection? Did physicians listen to mothers and change their advice accordingly? The rhetoric of the manuals intimates that doctors did incorporate into their advice practices they heard from their patients. Some mothers told doctors what they didn't like and what didn't work, even taking advisors to task for their ideas. In other instances, mothers were so pleased with what they had read or been told that they praised the advisor to the skies. In such cases, we can track the impact that mothers had on the scope and content of scientific motherhood of the period.

In the same time period, hospitalized childbirth was undergoing dra-matic change. Though the institutionalization of Jackson's rooming-in may best be characterized as "fits and starts," the move toward prepared childbirth proceeded more quickly. The two names most commonly associated with this crusade, the British Grantly Dick-Read and the French Fernand Lamaze, were medical practitioners who sought to engage women more directly in the childbirth experience. American women learned of Dick-Read's approach from his book *Childbirth Without Fear* and through his personal visits to the United States.[53] It was *Thank You, Dr. Lamaze*, written by an admiring disciple, that popularized the Lamaze approach in America.[54] Both Dick-Read and Lamaze stressed the importance of women's active, aware participation in the birth process. With both programs, women could expect physicians to listen to and respond to their concerns more than with routinely anesthetized births. The growth and popularity of the prepared childbirth movement were impelled by tens of thousands of women demanding that they participate in decisions about their childbirth procedures.

Many women in the United States who read about Dick-Read's method felt encouraged to write him with their thanks and with their problems.[55] Their letters came from large cities and small towns, many giving details of their births. A few claimed that Dick-Read, a man, could not know the pain of childbirth, and insisted that they would take anesthesia in any case. These women related horror stories of protracted and painful labor and were pleased to report that with anesthetized delivery they would wake up with peace of mind. Many, many more letters, however, thanked Dick-Read for his procedure, which enabled them to give birth with relative ease and little discomfort and which facilitated a speedier recuperation. Though termed "natural childbirth," Dick-Read's "childbirth without fear" did not reject the physician. Therefore, many women wrote him asking for recommendations of physicians in their area of the U.S. who practiced the Dick-Read method. Typical was Mrs. L.S., who wrote in 1947 from the Bronx, New York:

> Almost as far back as I can remember I associated childbirth with excruciating pain. As a child I over heard [*sic*] my mother's detailed description of the agonizing process. And I've been hearing similar stories ever since from friends and relatives. As a result I have a deep-rooted fear of childbirth.
>
> I'm 26 and have been married for 6 years. I love children and probably would have had a baby by now if I could find a doctor like you. I believe I am pregnant now.
>
> Will you help me? Will you recommend a doctor in New York who believes in your theories?
>
> Please help me.[56]

Here we have a woman who fervently believes in the new, "modern" physician-directed childbirth. Reading Dick-Read's book gave her the courage to challenge the local system, at least to the extent of seeking a compatible physician. Others found in Dick-Read's writing the courage to challenge the medical system more directly. M.I. already had one child when she wrote Dick-Read in 1947, but she needed Dick-Read's book to give her the strength to act on her sense of the situation. As she joyfully told the doctor, "I have just finished your book *Childbirth Without Fear* and know that there is the answer to the many questions I have asked. With only instinct to guide me and confronted with doctors who talk 'facts' to me I had no leg to stand on. Now I do! I can't tell you what it meant to me to read your book and know that there really is a path open to me heading to the end I *know* is right—happy, content pregnancies and lovely births for my children (which I hope will be many)."[57] M.I. and others sensed that there were problems with contemporary medicalized childbirth, but they needed the validation of a medical practitioner, even a controversial one such as Dick-Read, to give themselves the confidence and the credibility to insist on what they believed they needed. In so doing, these women forced a change in the way that childbirth was conducted in U.S. hospitals over the second half of the twentieth century.

Mothers had similar effects on child-care practices and the shape of scientific motherhood, though since these are more private, in the home, they are more difficult to document. There is much evidence to show that some child-care experts, some very influential child-care experts, actually did listen to mothers and learn from their experiences. Certainly, Benjamin Spock, the iconic child-care advisor of the period, did so.

The focus on Spock and his readers should not be misinterpreted. Spock was, of course, not the only proponent of this transformed scientific motherhood. By the 1960s, though, he had gained iconic stature. His book sold incredibly well, his magazine columns were widely read. Mothers did not have to seek him out; they were given copies of his book by their doctors and by their hospitals. Despite its own famous booklets, such as *Infant Care* and *The Child from One to Six,* even the Children's Bureau fed the popularity of Spock. In responding to queries from concerned mothers, the Bureau's staff was just as likely to recommend Spock. Representative is a 1964 response to the question from a concerned mother regarding pacifiers and thumb sucking that included "an excerpt on this from the book *Baby and Child Care*, by Dr. Benjamin Spock," with the explanation, "We think this will help to answer your questions."[58] Because of Spock's position as the primary expert on modern children we can analyze his writings and the responses of his readers in order to achieve an understanding of mothering practices in the mid-twentieth century and the influence of mothers on the shape of scientific motherhood.

In the first edition of *The Common Sense Book of Baby and Child Care*, in the section "Special Problems," Spock had advised, "If the family can afford to place the Mongolian [Down syndrome] baby in a special home, it is usually recommended that this be done right after birth. Then the parents will not become too wrapped up in a child who will never develop very far."[59] In 1956, the mother of such a child wrote from Roanoke, Virginia, after hearing that Spock was revising his book. She made one request: "that you do not make the outlook for Mongoloid children so hopeless. I will never forget my feeling when I read your brief sentence about them. I am glad that my child was four years old then, and I would not give her up as hopeless."[60]

Spock defended his position with the explanation that "a great majority [of these children] develop with discouraging slowness and that if placement in a nursing home or school is going to prove inevitable it's better for the suggestion to come from the professional person rather than be left to the parents who become very guilty thinking about it."[61] By the 1957 edition of *Baby and Child Care*, he had significantly enlarged and altered the section to read, in part: "Some doctors recommend to parents who can afford it that the baby be cared for in a private nursing home from birth, so that they will not become overattached to a child who is not likely to develop far. . . . This may be the better plan in some families, not in others. I think parents should take their time in coming to a decision and that if they are in doubt, it is helpful to get counsel from a family social agency or a psychiatrist."[62] It is not clear whether this revision was a direct result of the letter from Virginia, but it is likely.

Spock did not just accept mothers' input correspondence; he also solicited it. In his first column in the *Ladies' Home Journal*, in July 1954, Spock discussed his ambivalence about the use of pacifiers and admitted that he consciously decided not to include the topic in his book because, as he explained to *LHJ* readers, "I was afraid to." He feared that if he recommended pacifiers and mothers followed his advice, they would face attacks from those vehemently opposed to them. He also feared that if he recommended pacifiers, then other doctors would "think my book so unreliable they would advise parents not to use it."[63] In the *LHJ* article he admitted that there were times and situations for a pacifier, that much maligned device that many people consider "unhygienic, germ-laden, habit-forming, tooth-deforming, disgusting." He detailed cases from his practice in which pacifiers solved a problem and he ended the column with an invitation to mothers to write him with their experiences. And write him they did. It is amazing the number of letters mothers sent to Spock, triggered by this one article alone. Though the readers of the *Ladies' Home Journal* cannot be considered a representative sample of mothers in the mid-twentieth century (they were more likely than the general population to be white, educated, middle- and upper-middle-class), still their stories present us with a wide range of reactions that document the ways in which mothers negotiated between scientific and medical expertise in the form of the physician and the circumstances of their everyday life.

Mothers clearly had come to a point where they expected child-care manuals to answer a broad spectrum of questions, and they were annoyed that Spock was no help to them on the issue of pacifiers. The reaction of V.S. of Brooklyn, New York, was typical of the disappointment with his book as well as gratitude for the tone of Spock's article. She explained, "When we first gave it [a pacifier] to her [their daughter] we ran to your book to see what you had to say. We were very disappointed when you avoided the question. When I saw your article it pleased me immensely."[64] Such mothers were surprised that Spock had not discussed pacifiers in his book but that did not discourage them from using the device to calm their children.

Frequently mothers mentioned that they were leery of pacifiers, that all they heard about pacifiers was negative, but when they acquiesced they were pleased with the results, and particularly pleased that Spock validated their experiences. J.S. of Milwaukee found that her second daughter's first three months were very difficult. She thought about using a pacifier, but was concerned because everything she read and heard about it was negative. She trusted Spock, however, and so, "trying to find an answer to my problem, I looked through your book but could find no answer on such a problem." Finally, she made her own decision. "So I gave up all my dislikes for the 'darn thing' (I never liked the looks of a pacifier sticking out of a baby's mouth)," she reported, "and gave her one. Wondrous! Miracle of miracles! It worked! My trouble had ended."[65] Mothers found that they had to defy the standards of their communities or even of their own physicians. Thus, they found Spock's support of pacifiers heartening. It reinforced their confidence in their own abilities and common sense. "Since I used pacifiers for both my children despite the utter disgust of friends and relatives," W.C.K. of Chicago confided in Spock, "I am somewhat more than casually impressed by the success I had." She had an additional obstacle to overcome, her doctor. As she sheepishly explained, "Incidently [*sic*], I used them behind my own doctor's back. He frowned on the very idea."[66]

Some who found solace with pacifiers urged Spock to include his remarks in the next edition of his book. They knew that this could be awkward, since pacifiers were not easily accepted by many physicians or by society in general at this time. Writing from Boise, Idaho, J. and J. S. suggested a subterfuge: "We don't think that you would stir up too much controversy in your book if you made a few general factual statements about these pacifiers. You might index it under some such title as, 'Treatment for Sleepless Parents.'"[67] They and others also continued the idea of sister-to-sister advice, though modified for the world of the mid-twentieth century, that is, they pressed Spock to use their experiences to instruct others. "P.S. Should you wish to do so, you may quote any portion or portions of this letter—for the benefit of others," wrote W.W.M., giving Spock permission to use her letter.[68]

Many letter writers rejoiced that a medical expert like Spock ratified their experiences. His acceptance of pacifiers not only reassured them about the validity of the devices but it also enhanced their sense of competence. Even mothers with professional training appreciated Spock's endorsement, as A.M.P.'s telling letter revealed: "I am a graduate nurse and therefore did receive much ridicule from relatives and friends [for using a pacifier]. Since I could see how beneficial the pacifier proved I continued to use it. . . . Now I know that an authority has the same opinion as mine."[69] Approval from such an expert was to be savored and used to defend a mother's position, especially in light of vociferous opposition. Spock's article provided "expert" evidence that some mothers then used to justify their practices. As N.H. of Buffalo explained to the doctor: "I have just finished reading your article in the July issue of the 'Ladies Home Journal,' and wanted to let you know I thought it was wonderful. I am going to save it to show all my aunts, my sister and my mother who think that pacifiers are discusting [*sic*]."[70]

The Eisenhower era, the growth of suburbia, the baby boom, the return to domesticity: all are associated with the postwar decades, when we retreated into the sanctuary of the home after the trauma of the Depression and World War II. Yet, as historians have been increasingly documenting, in this period lay the seeds for the activism of the 1960s and 1970s, the slow emergence of a national civil rights movement and of the nascent women's movement. So too we can see in this period the genesis of a redefinition of scientific motherhood. In ratifying mothers' ideas about childbirth and child care, Dick-Read, Spock, and others sanctioned women's beliefs and reinforced women's confidence and, in effect, empowered them to question other authority figures. Doing so shifted mothers' relationships to experts and the spirit of scientific motherhood. Scientific and medical expertise remained the final authority in child care, but women were emboldened to push their doctors, to demand that they participate in decision making about their children's lives. By the last third of the twentieth century, the ideology of scientific motherhood moved away from the picture of women who unquestionably assented to the directions of medical and scientific experts. In practice, women no longer unilaterally and without reservation accepted the advice they read and heard. However, though they could disagree with the physician in certain particulars, the idea of medical and scientific expertise remained the critical component of modern motherhood, of scientific motherhood. Mothers did not expect to raise their children alone; they did not reject the advances of contemporary scientific and medical expertise; they appreciated when they could point to medical and scientific experts who supported their practices. In the subsequent decades, mothers increasingly demanded an integral role in decision making about their children's lives, while they embraced contemporary medicine and science. Rather than being subservient to an autocratic health-care practitioner, women worked with experts and used their expertise to shape their mothering practices for the health and welfare of their families.

CHAPTER 6

"Use it to guide, not to dictate"

MOTHERHOOD IN THE LATE TWENTIETH CENTURY

*W*hat did a late-twentieth-century mother do when faced with a coughing child at two in the morning? One worried woman called her physician and explained to him, "I was reading Spock, and Spock says if a child with croup does this, this, and that, I ought to call my doctor. So I'm calling." Her physician, Dr. Lawrence Elfman, in Madison, Wisconsin, considered this an appropriate and practicable use of child-care books. Not that books should replace the physician, but that "parents can look up their questions and then decide whether or not they need to talk to the doctor."[1] Evidently physicians became enamored with the educated mother because they appreciated that better educated patients were more compliant patients and led to improved outcomes. Recognizing that they had only a limited amount of time to spend with each mother, they accepted assistance in this area, especially when they selected the education and it matched the specifics of their practices.[2] The struggle to remove authoritarian physicians, but importantly not medicine and science, from the center of child-care advice and to insert mothers as active participants in decision making about their families' health was not a simple change. It resulted from a complex of social and medical developments that encompassed women pushing against contemporary medical practices and a changing medical system pulling women more deeply into health care.

Two movements exemplify how the relationship between mothers and experts and expertise in the last quarter of the twentieth century had shifted from the earlier dyad of subservient mother and authoritarian physician—La Leche League and the Boston Women's Health Book Collective, with its publication of *Our Bodies, Ourselves* and later *Ourselves and Our Children.*

These movements consciously or unconsciously built on the efforts of women who earlier fought to alter the authoritarian medical system they faced. The prepared childbirth movement and doctors such as Benjamin Spock not only gave women the confidence to challenge their physicians and the medical system they saw around them, but they also fostered the production of alternative sources of medical and scientific information. As a consequence, mothers were not restricted to one person or one institution to answer their questions about child care and child health. They could and did seek solutions in a host of venues. Yet, this very multiplicity presented additional problems. Who should be considered the experts? How does a mother evaluate the many sources available? How can a mother be sure that the advice she follows is the best, the most appropriate, the most healthful for her family?

One dramatic example of mothers' "pushing" back into the decision-making arena of child care is La Leche League, which was established in 1956 in Franklin Park, Illinois, by a group of women drawn together through their common experience of maternal nursing.[3] Most commentators focus on the League's primary objective—to encourage every mother to breast-feed her infants. In this light, the League defied contemporary mid-twentieth-century medical practice. The founding mothers saw in worst case scenarios that physicians and hospitals encouraged bottle feeding and even in best case scenarios that the medical system did not encourage breast feeding. The image of La Leche is of a group of women insisting on their knowledge, their maternal instincts, about the best child-care practices and railing against a disinterested or outright hostile medical profession. They rejected common medical guidance, which sanctioned bottle feeding. In this romanticized view, some feminist scholars see La Leche League and its sister organizations in other parts of the world as a proto-feminist health movement refusing to accept the dictates of the masculine, highly scientific medical system. The point often missed in these analyses is that La Leche league was *not* rejecting medical advice. True, these mothers did not believe that doctors were necessarily the best sources for advice on breast feeding and they did elevate the role of experienced nursing mothers in instructing new mothers about the techniques, and the trials and tribulations of maternal lactation. Yet, from the very beginning of the organization they also reminded the public and their members that doctors considered "breast is best." La Leche justified its stance both with traditional arguments for maternal nursing and with medical arguments drawn from contemporary scientific literature, actively soliciting the support of physicians who promoted breast feeding.

The origins of the League are well known. In July 1956, Mary White and Marian Tompson were attending a Christian Family Movement (CFM, formerly the Catholic Family Movement) picnic. They were sitting under a tree, breast-feeding: White had breast-fed all of her six children except the first; for Tompson this was her first breast-fed child, though she had three older children. They watched other mothers scramble around keeping baby bottles chilled and then worrying about warming them. These other women often remarked that they would have liked to breast-feed but. . . . When White and Tompson considered what made it possible for them to nurse their children, they realized that they had both enjoyed the confidence of Dr. Gregory White, the husband of Mary White. White had had difficulties breast-feeding her first child, but with subsequent children she read all she could find and with the support of her husband, she was able to nurse them. Tompson also had wanted to breast-feed, but when she birthed in the hospital, she was told that she had insufficient milk and so she bottle-fed her children. However, during her fourth pregnancy, she read Dick-Read's book, *Childbirth Without Fear*. She was determined to follow his procedure but she could find no hospital willing to allow it. She and her husband were friends of the Whites and Dr. White agreed to attend her in a Dick-Read style home birth and to support her efforts to breast-feed.

Through their study and their connection with White's husband, both Tompson and White understood the medical and scientific rationales for breast feeding; they were not rejecting science and medicine. But they did see that most medical practitioners and medical institutions were not organized to help women nurse their children. They believed that the best support for a nursing mother, or a woman who wanted to nurse, was learning from other mothers who had similar experiences. From these roots grew the La Leche meetings, at which mothers discuss their experiences, problems, and solutions. If they encounter difficulties, there are more experienced mothers to aid them. This sister-to-sister network, while valorizing the experiences of women, does not deny the significance of scientific and medical knowledge. Individual medical practitioners may not be the best providers of advice on lactation, but the scientific and medical information that exists is valid and significant. The activities of La Leche League helped to push the medical profession and United States culture to accommodate breast feeding. In so doing, it did not deny the importance of medical and scientific advice but used it for a different end. La Leche League emphasized the "naturalness" of breast feeding, but the League began with the support of a physician, it has always had medical practitioners on its advisory board, and it utilizes medical and scientific evidence to support its stands. Thus, the League is not a rejection of medical authority but a directed use of medical evidence.

A somewhat different challenge to medical dominance appeared with *Our Bodies, Ourselves*. The genesis of the book is similar to that of La Leche League. Though the founding mothers came not from the CFM but from the ranks of the women's liberation movement in Boston, these early advocates too earnestly wanted to enable women to make their own decisions. Initially, the Boston Women's Health Course Collective, as they named the group, intended to prepare course material for women's health classes in the Boston area. The introduction to the 1971 edition of *Our Bodies, Ourselves* explains:

> The impetus for this course grew out of a workshop on "women and their bodies" at a women's conference at Emmanuel College in Boston, May 1969. After that, several of us developed a questionnaire about women's feelings about their bodies and their relationship to doctors. We discovered there were no "good" doctors and we had to learn for ourselves. We talked about our own experience and we shared our own knowledge. We went to books and to medically trained people for more information.

Then the Collective taught courses at which other "sisters added their experiences, questions, fears, feelings, excitement." From these "dynamic" experiences and carefully evaluated contemporary medical and scientific knowledge, the course papers were revised and enlarged. The Collective found a small press, the New England Free Press, which published the essays so that the material could be "shared, not only with women in Boston, but with women across the country."[4] The book quickly sold out its first printing and was reprinted by the press. Its popularity persuaded Simon and Schuster to publish a significantly enlarged trade press edition in 1973.

The Boston Women's Health Book Collective has continued to revise and expand *Our Bodies, Ourselves* and has added to the series with *Ourselves, Growing Older* and, most critically for mothers, *Ourselves and Our Children*.[5] The latter is not a how-to book, like Holt or Spock. Rather, it aims to *"empower"* parents, but particularly mothers, so that "you can get the very best help for yourself, your child, your family,"[6] pointing out various lay and professional sources and explaining how to negotiate among them. Again, as in *Our Bodies, Ourselves* the authors do not dismiss medical professionals or contemporary medical and scientific knowledge. They warn of "the mystique of professionalism," in which the "true nature and importance of the professionals' knowledge and skills become inflated, so that they are seen as more powerful, more expert, more broadly knowledgeable than they either are or should be." Such a situation, they caution, can "create a syndrome in which the client's strengths and intelligence are downplayed, and the power imbalance between professional and client is increased."[7]

The women of both the Boston Women's Health Book Collective and La Leche League came to recognize the validity and significance of their own experiences. Yet, this did not lead them to repudiate scientific and medical expertise. They did, however, reject the idea of an authoritarian practitioner and insisted that women were capable of evaluating this information for themselves. They affirmed that women could and should be actively involved in weighing evidence and making decisions. Groups such as La Leche League and the Boston Women's Health Book Collective as well as personal and organized efforts to have hospitals and physicians accept the notion of prepared childbirth helped to validate women's personal and familial health-care experiences and to alter the balance of relationships within contemporary medical practice. They pushed for a more equal partnership between medical practitioners and patients.

The trend toward a more cooperative relationship becomes clearer in the last decades of the twentieth century as the theme of partnership, albeit an unequal partnership, is reiterated in physician-authored literature as well. Physicians continued to encourage patients to bring their questions to the doctor's office, anticipating queries about physical symptoms, child development, and the like. But now, physicians approached nonprofessional advice somewhat differently. Rather than dismissing it out of hand, as had Wood and Hanrahan, they are more likely to explain, "Of course, you will receive much good help from your friends, relatives and neighbors, but usually they lack the experience to recognize something as being extremely rare or unusual."[8] Patients needed to get "actual facts" and in order to realize that, physician-authors urged women to "quiz them." That is, medical practitioners now embraced the involvement of the inquiring and educated patient. Physicians had determined that appropriately educated patients facilitated their medical practice because "we received fewer phone calls from patients who know how they are doing." Not that the physicians expected this education to make patients equal partners in the decision-making process about their children's care. After all, they reassured the mothers, "You must remember that we have had considerable experience in 'worrying' about many more things than you may possible be aware of. So do not worry unnecessarily. You have 'hired' experts to worry for you, when and IF any worrying really needs to be done."[9] As Dr. Henry Harris wrote in his foreword to the popular *What to Expect the First Year*: "Read it. Enjoy it. You can rely on it. . . . It won't replace your pediatrician, but it will make his or her life easier."[10] The doctors valued the educated mother while retaining their role as final arbiter.

A host of professional and social factors influenced this shift in the ideology of scientific motherhood from the physician as the sole authority to a partnership of mother and doctor. Through the twentieth century, infant morbidity and mortality rates fell sharply. Advances such as antibiotics and polio vaccines changed the content of medical practice. Thus the physician's practice began to deal less with acute disease episodes, in which the doctor's medical expertise was unquestioned. Instead, practitioners more often saw patients for well-child checkups and preventative examinations and chronic or long-term conditions. Reducing the need for immediate decision making allowed mothers space to study an issue from multiple perspectives and alternative sources, sources that were growing exponentially. Media analysts Susan J. Douglas and Meredith W. Michaels estimate that in the early 1970s at the most four or five new books were published each year on motherhood. Slowly numbers increased. By 1988, there were more than forty new books and by 1995, more than sixty. Between 1970 and 2000, over eight hundred books on motherhood had been published. Similar growth was apparent in magazine publishing also. For example, in 1970, *McCall's*, a popular women's magazine, produced no regular columns on motherhood. Two decades later, it published one column by a child therapist, one column by a pediatrician (who was also a mother of five), and another column to which mothers sent essays. We see the identical evolution in *Redbook*, another women's magazine. In 1970, there was one column for the expectant mother in every other monthly issue. By the beginning of 1992, the magazine devoted a whole section to "You & Your Child," which included from four to six articles ranging from children's health, through childrearing trends, to conflicts with teen-agers.[11]

In addition to the booming market in traditional sources, such as books, newspapers, and magazines available in bookstores and libraries across the country, there were also the radio and television doctors and, by the late 1980s and 1990s, the spread of the World Wide Web. Some of these websites were established by manufacturers and publishers, in a sense as a helpful extension of their promotional campaigns. Johnson & Johnson, maker of baby shampoos, powders, nursing pads, and other child-related products, sponsors a website that advertises the company's book *Johnson's Mother and Baby*, written by two doctors. It includes sections of the "Learning Place," with information on pregnancy, child development, and the like, and "Resources," with a drop-down menu to newsletters and other "Helpful Links." Hospitals, clinics, and university extension departments also include child care and child health in their websites. The Mayo Clinic's site provides information in a section titled "Children's health." Parents have established other websites. One, AOL's Moms Online, was initiated by a mother in Port Townsend, Washington, who found "herself cut off from interaction with adults while she took care of her baby." The website enables mothers to interact with others in similar situations, providing access to "parenting tips, resources, essays, craft ideas, polls, and a daily trivia game."[12] Other nonprofessional websites were launched under the auspices of academic or medical organizations. The Berkeley Parents Network website

> contains thousands of pages of recommendations and advice from the Berkeley Parents Network, a parent-to-parent advice newsletter for the community of parents in the Berkeley, California area. Formerly called "UCB Parents", the network is run by a group of volunteer parents in their "spare" time. We send out 10-12 email newsletters each week to over 10,000 local parents. We've been doing it since 1993. Many busy parents have taken the time to enlighten and inform us with their suggestions, their wisdom, and their experience, archived here for all who need it. Please help yourself and use it in the spirit of sharing![13]

Google words and phrases such as mothering, child health, or toilet training, and you will get literally millions of websites. Of course, some of them will be off the subject. "Toilet training" results in 1,700,000 possibilities, including toilet training your cat.[14] But others deal more directly with the subject, such as commercial pages for various toilet-training products and books, pages mounted by health-care practitioners and health-care organizations, and more personal stories of toilet-training experiences. Benjamin Spock died in 1998, but his name and advice live in both his books and a website established in 2005 (DrSpock.com), which combines Spock's writings, sometimes revised by current practitioners, and new essays, as well as message boards, consumer alerts, and other material of interest to mothers.

All these alternative sources did not necessarily replace the physician. Child-care advisors continued to promote the importance of scientific and medical expertise, usually personified in the doctor but not limited to an exclusive or authoritarian role for the male doctor. Illustrative of this trend was *Mother's Medicine*, written by Nancy Moore Thurmond. In its Preface, Pat Boone, the singer, and his wife, Shirley, championed the book because, as they explained, "Nancy goes to the Bible as her final authority and quite often quotes from it."[15] Thurmond laced her advice with biblical quotations and proverbs and often reminded readers that motherhood is a "sacred ministry." The Scriptural premise of the book was unusual for a manual in the period. But, in other respects, the book was typical because at the same time, Thurmond consistently referred mothers to their doctors for advice on virtually every aspect of infant and child care. She told mothers, "The best friend a mother has is her child's pediatrician, the family physician, or the pediatric nurse practitioner." She took this relationship very seriously, explaining that "I often feel as if an appointment with the pediatrician is not so much a chance to check up on Junior as an appointment to check up on how I am developing and growing as a mother."[16] Thurmond's book is written with the partnership of doctor and mother assumed,[17] and this partnership, she insisted, is expected to continue from infancy through the later years of childhood:

> As your child grows, the doctor will be able to give you sound advice and good counsel if, for example, your son has perpetual low grades and low interest in school, or if your daughter is having trouble making friends in her peer group. . . .
>
> The guidance of your pediatrician can be a positive factor and a tremendous influence in shaping the direction your child will go as he begins his journey in life.

She admonished her readers to "use [the pediatrician] to the best of his and your ability."[18] And many mothers did continue to view physicians as essential elements in healthful childrearing.[19]

However, their status as essential elements did not mean that women wanted or even accepted authoritarian physicians on the earlier model of scientific motherhood. No longer did women necessarily assume that health-care practitioners had all the answers and that they, the patients, were dependent on them and their ideas. In the late twentieth century, women were demanding to be more involved and many physicians responded. Now, physicians needed to be certain that mothers were comfortable with them in other, less dramatic situations as well. A 1984 study of La Leche League mothers points to this emerging aspect of medical practice very specifically. The authors advise that doctors need to understand not only what mothers are doing but also why, in order to provide needed health care. For example, typically in the United States at the time, breast-fed infants were weaned at about ten months or when the child began to walk. Many League mothers, however, practiced unrestricted breast feeding with weaning occurring much later. If physicians did not recognize this fact, they could easily alienate their patients. The study's authors warned of the dangers of such insensitivity: "The physician, who often may fail to explore the benefits of breast-feeding beyond its nutritional role, is not immune to cultural norms and may give subtle messages to the mother to wean the infant at an early age. Any perceived pressure and/or lack of support from the physician only places additional stress on the mother and can destroy the physician-patient relationship."[20] They cautioned physicians to "pay close attention to the many aspects of the trend as they emerge."[21]

Physicians felt pushed and slowly accepted the involvement of mothers in the decision-making process. Feminist criticism caused even Spock to modify his views in the 1970s. Before, he had insisted that mothers belong in the home and that women's highest calling was motherhood. He now backed off from these claims and began to assert that child care was the responsibility of both parents, for example, and that mothers might have careers outside the home.[22] In the same period, Dick-Read and Lamaze encouraged women to be more actively involved in the childbirth process and in decisions shaping their childbirth experiences, promoting a culture of assertive women who demanded greater involvement in child-care decisions as well. Moreover, indicative of the general distrust of experts in American society in the 1970s, the women's health movement challenged the medical establishment and medical authority.

Doctors recognized that this new relationship had economic and health consequences. The editors of *Mayo Clinic Complete Book of Pregnancy & Baby's First Year* proudly announced that they had extensively interviewed expectant and new parents about what they needed in a book.[23] Dr. Frances Drew found that by the early 1990s, doctors were "responding (in many cases grudgingly) to the increasing independence of women so that a partnership is established in which both parties profit from the circumstance that the well-informed patient is healthier, recovers faster, and is more gratifying to treat."[24] Studies disclosed that patients wanted information, but they also wanted more time with their physicians and they wanted to ask their questions in a relaxed environment. Health-care practitioners became aware that a mother was now more likely to "shop around" for a physician whose personality and perspectives on health and health care meshed with hers. Health-care providers saw this happening in obstetrics. Women who knew what they wanted in terms of labor and delivery would not merely accept their doctors' ideas. They would seek out the environment they preferred, even to the extent of "traveling 20, 30, or 40 miles to another couple of hospitals, for the precise reason that they feel they are receiving in those hospitals the kind of care that will involve the husband and give them the kind of deliveries they want."[25] True, not all patients were in a position to be so selective. Poor and working-class mothers who attended clinics often were seen by the available practitioner. Patients who were members of Health Maintenance Organizations could choose from only a select list of physician members. Still, many mothers, even those in HMOs, could and did search for a compatible doctor. Physicians understood that "determining patients' attitudes is key to any marketing plan—whether you want to maintain your practice at its current level or want to attract new patients and increase the size of your practice."[26] One health maintenance organization even advertises, "Moms love doctors who listen." Reminding mothers that "no one knows your family better than you," the group concludes that "hearing you makes it easier for us to care for you"—an unequivocal sign of promotion of partnership on the part of modern health-care systems.[27] Drs. Brunworth and Rigden noticed that with the use of their patient education handouts "patients [were] going out of their way to transfer to a practice noted for this approach."[28] In other words, it behooved health-care practitioners financially to promote this new relationship.

Physicians were influenced also by legal issues. As our society became more litigious, patient education could act as a legal protection. This was a major selling point for a series of informational pamphlets entitled *Beginnings*. Each copy of the publication included an education record form for the patient that, the advertising copy reminded physicians, provided "patients complete written information about their care, *and charting that you did so.*" This form, the promoters claimed, "has proven helpful in avoiding lawsuits."[29] The American Academy of Pediatrics stressed the importance of keeping the lines of communication open between parents and physicians, suggesting that the doctor should "educate" and "should aim to develop a relationship based on trust, honesty, concern, commitment, and reassurance," as one way of deflecting potential malpractice cases.[30]

Altered hospital routines also displayed the effects of these push–pull efforts that served to shift the relationship between mother and health-care provider. Women pushed for prepared childbirth, for example. Moreover, as the birth rate declined in the last third of the twentieth century, hospitals became ever more eager to attract increasingly scarce consumers. They did so by offering services patients demanded, such as rooming-in, birthing rooms, and the like. In other cases, health-care practitioners' attempts to improve health care had unintended consequences that encouraged mothers beyond medical expectations. Take, for example, the Expectant Parent Program in

Bedford County, Pennsylvania, in the 1970s.[31] Bedford County was basically rural and "medically understaffed." Mental health professionals in the region were "concerned with the increased incidence of childhood problems related to poor or misguided parenting skills and the problems of poor medical care delivery." In conjunction with the local medical society, these mental health professionals designed a six-module course that began with conception and gestation, and stretched through to principles of child development from birth to age three. As hoped for, mothers reported less apprehension about their impending childbirth and parenthood at the end of the class. But the mothers were not simply students; they took what they had learned in the course and demanded changes in the hospital. They insisted that fathers be present during delivery and labor, a change to which the hospital agreed; they requested and got Lamaze classes to augment the Expectant Parent Course. Once again, the women were not passive learners. They accepted the importance of medical and scientific expertise; they learned from it and used that knowledge to force changes in their relationship to the experts.

Similarly, structural changes in hospitals helped to shift the roles of mothers and experts. Throughout the last quarter of the twentieth century, hospitals increasingly emphasized their outpatient services with a concomitant decrease in inpatient services. Conditions that in the 1920s necessitated hospital stays are today more and more often treated outside the institution or with significantly shorter hospital stays. Historian Rosemary Stevens estimates that hospitals of the 1920s were "centers of the young," characterized by tonsillectomies, appendectomies, deliveries, pneumonia, injuries, poisonings, and asthma. By the 1990s, many of these were handled on an outpatient basis (more than one-third of hospital funds came from outpatient procedures), in the doctor's office, or at home. This change in venue, of course, also signaled a change in treatment, treatment that demanded proportionally more care by the watchful mother at home than by medical professionals in an institution. And the hospital architecture itself was compelling. As semiprivate rooms replaced wards, and then as private rooms replaced semiprivate rooms, patients found themselves isolated in single rooms. At the same time, nursing stations became dominated by technology, critical technology to be sure, but technology that took nurses away from the bedside more and more. In such a situation, "patients' families provide additional eyes, ears, and legs for individual patients" and "many hospitals encourage family members to stay with patients around the clock."[32] In other words, both inside and outside the hospital, the mother was expected to be more directly occupied in the caretaking, even in cases of illness. True, she is typically following the directions of the physician, but as the "eyes, ears, and legs" she is also more intimately involved in evaluating the patient, enabling her to balance more evenly her relationship with the medical practitioner.

Toward the end of the twentieth century, advice manuals and advisors appear to have reached a consensus. The educated mother, the mother aware of modern scientific and medical knowledge, was a critical component in healthful child care. Accordingly, few doubted that medical and scientific expertise should and did intervene directly in the daily lives of mothers. Where they differed was in degree. On one end of the spectrum were those who insisted that books, radio, television, the internet were adjuncts to medical practitioners, not replacements. In his *Pregnancy, Birth, and Family Planning* in 1973, Alan F. Guttmacher, M.D., cautioned even the most well read of mothers to maintain a close relationship with their physicians, reminding them, "Even if you are the best informed of the new mothers in your community, it does not relieve you of the privilege and necessity of visiting and consulting your pediatrician. In obstetrics and pediatrics, books should never be substituted for a doctor, they should be used only to supplement his care and wisdom."[33] Others, however, were much less dogmatic. Acknowledging that "it can be frustrating to be unsure of the many questions and problems that arise in the first few months of an infant's life, such as: 'Why is he crying? What are we doing wrong? Will we spoil him if we pick him up every time he cries?'" Joyce L. Kieffer, R.N., promised her readers that "time, practice and patience will gradually provide the answers to these and many other questions. So will a good book or two on child care and a good pediatrician or family doctor."[34] What individual advisors as well as health organizations such as La Leche League and the Boston Women's Health Book Collective all agreed on was the necessity of authoritative information to insure healthful childrearing.

To some extent, this counsel reflected the reality and practical considerations of motherhood during this period. Literature on child care flourished. Hospitals, medical centers, social service agencies, and schools held classes to instruct prospective mothers and fathers. As the internet grew, websites were developed by formal and informal groups of mothers, along with commercial websites launched by manufacturers of child-care products and magazine publishers. All purported to hold the answers to healthful, modern child care. To be a good mother, now, demanded a knowledge of medicine, psychology, nutrition, the social sciences, *and* the ability to evaluate emerging new information. With such competition, few medical practitioners were in a position to be authoritarian, though they still needed to be authoritative.

As the medical and social cultures of the United States were changing, mothers faced a different world than their mothers did.[35] In this different world mothers continued to reach out to each other for advice and solace, as the example of the internet and the number of books published by women about their mothering experiences demonstrates. But there was also a new tone to these sources. Previously, nineteenth-century authors such as Palmer were highly didactic, as well as somewhat romantic about mothers and mothering, while early-twentieth-century authors such as Ruth William Thompson wrote in a more objective style. By the late twentieth century, women clearly felt comfortable expressing less romanticized, less "soft-focus" perspectives on motherhood and instead delighted in detailing the trials and tribulations of maternity, often with a note of humor but sometimes full of desperation as well. So we have reporters determined to "tell the 'real' truth" about motherhood. Alice Petlock Pauser's column was typical, focusing on the weeks following her return home from the hospital with a new baby. First came her recognition of the situation: "It isn't bad enough that you are exhausted and that none of your clothes fit; it's that feeling you get when you walk in the door at home and finally realize that the baby really does come with you." Then comes her definition of modern motherhood: "Books were enlightening to say the least, and I was determined to follow them to the letter. It was through this diligent effort that I began entering the real world of motherhood."[36] In this world, women expected childrearing to be difficult and at times frustrating. But they also accepted the notion that the information was out there to help them and, most significantly, that it was their responsibility to find and utilize that information.

One of the earliest books of this genre was Jane Lazarre's *The Mother Knot*.[37] Lazarre aimed to replace the romanticized myth of the placid, all-knowing mother with what she believed was a more realistic image of a sometimes agitated, sometimes overly emotional, even an unloving mother. She put herself in that category. After her few weeks at home, when her mother-in-law, who had been helping her care for the infant, was ready to leave, Lazarre was desperate:

> I felt I never should have had a baby. If anyone had told me what it would be like, I might have saved my life in time. . . . I would never be a good mother. . . . The experts were right, I thought. Babies are born to be placid, contented creatures. It is only the bad mother repressing her unfair resentment, holding the baby too tightly, too loosely, too often, too rarely, letting him cry, picking him up too soon,

feeding him too much, too little, suffocating him with her love or not loving him enough—it is only the bad mother who is to blame.[38]

She read and read and read—all she could about child care and childrearing—only to discover that her baby, unlike those in the books, did not fall asleep after nursing. What was wrong? The books told her that her son should be sleeping through the night at six months of age; hers was not. In attempting to get him to sleep, she needed to be careful not to overidentify with her son; Bruno Bettelheim warned that if she did overidentify, the result could be an autistic child. Lazarre's story of her infant's bedtime illustrates how mothers of the late twentieth century tried to incorporate scientific and medical expertise into their child care, while at the same time balancing their emotions.

> For three weeks we had clung to our determination that he [her son] could be trained to sleep eight hours at a stretch. Listening to him cry out the prescribed twenty minutes advised by Dr. Spock, clutching the pillow into my sweaty palms, my head pounding with his screams, I tried to lie still so as to drive out the image of the withdrawn, vanquished, perhaps even autistic child I expected to find in the crib in the morning. . . .
>
> . . . Sometimes, not able to bear it, I would take him out of his crib, resigned to spending the hour between three and four a.m. walking him into slumber. But as soon as I lifted him out of the bed, he would smile, dry-eyed and evidently unharmed; he was obviously ready to play.
>
> . . . One night Benjamin woke up five times. He was nine months old. He was not sick and didn't appear to be teething. Two pediatricians had told me that almost every child sleeps through the night by six months.
>
> "But, of course," I said sarcastically as I tossed in bed, holding one, two, three pillows over my ears. "Not Benjamin."
>
> Five times I gave in and fed him a bottle. The third, fourth and fifth times, he pushed the bottle away, not hungry, no longer crying, in fact smiling at me as we sat there together, staring at each other in the middle of the night. His obvious contentment at having me instead of his crib beneath him so infuriated me that, calmly, I put him down in his crib and went back to bed, where to the music of his miserable cries, enjoying every second of his pain, I fell in to a deep sleep. I do not know how long he cried. But after that he slept through the night.[39]

Lazarre, while admitting her failings as a mother, was also writing about the difficulties of balancing "expert advice" and experience. She too was not rejecting experts but found that she could not follow all their directives.

Other authors simply dismissed experts and insisted that it was time for mothers to regain a sense of their own value. Sonia Taitz even subtitled her book *Reclaiming Motherhood from the Experts*. She noted the "paradox in buying a book about motherhood that tells you to go easy on those motherhood books." But despite her subtitle, she did not banish scientific and medical experts and expertise. She was grateful to T. Berry Brazelton, "who reassured me that cold-turkeying the pacifier or bottle was (as I suspected) a rather cruel thing to force a child to do. And Louise Bates Ames and Francis Ilg, countering the Mother-can-never-be-replaced line, [who] assured me that baby-sitters can and should be sought out for relief." Most critically, Taitz realized that with the plethora of advice available "there are always experts who suit your line of thought, gadgets and tapes that buoy you up." It was not a question of looking for advice, it was a question of selecting the appropriate advice and not "surrender[ing] your mind to them."[40] The solution for mothers like Lazarre and Taitz was not to return to some romanticized vision of a natural or instinctive maternal faculty. Rather, it was the more difficult task of carefully considering and selecting from the broad range of experts and expertise available to them, to decide for themselves what was the most beneficial and most helpful in their situations for the health of their families.

An article in the *New York Times Magazine* in 1999 epitomized the dilemma mothers faced, confronted with wildly different advice informed by differing philosophies and shaped by technological and commercial interests.[41] "Two Experts Do Battle over Potty Training" pitted the stringent training recommended by John Rosemond, a family psychologist, syndicated columnist, and author of many parenting advice books, against that advocated by T. Berry Brazelton, a leading pediatrician and at this time professor emeritus of pediatrics at Harvard Medical School. Since the 1960s, Brazelton, along with Spock, had been instructing mothers in a flexible approach to toilet training. It was counterproductive, they argued, to force toilet training. All that would do is set up a power struggle between mother and child and potentially injure the child psychologically. When children are ready to be potty trained, they will use the toilet, the doctors instructed. This was quite a switch from Holt and Watson, who expected the child out of diapers in the first year, if not the first months of life. There is some evidence that mothers took the advice of Spock and Brazelton; certainly, practices mirrored their recommendations. In 1957, at the age of eighteen months, 92 percent of U.S. children were toilet-trained. By the end of the 1990s, at the age of twenty-four months, only 4 percent were toilet-trained. Studies show that a majority of children, 60 percent, were diaper-free by thirty-six months while 2 percent remained in diapers at the age of four years. Late toilet training became practical because of technological advances. A multibillion-dollar industry of training pants and oversized disposable diapers designed for children over the age of two relieved the mother of laundry problems and modern washers and dryers took some of the drudgery out of the use of cloth diapers.

Rosemond contended that such behavior was "a slap to the intelligence of a human being that one would allow him to continue soiling and wetting himself past age 2." The psychologist complained that delayed toilet training was inspired by "Freudian mumbo jumbo" and criticized Brazelton for serving as a consultant to Pampers, a popular disposable diaper manufacturer, and for appearing in its advertising. In advocating a return to more traditional methods of childrearing, Rosemond designed a simple routine for training a child in a few days, and for a mere seventy-five dollars, rather than the many dollars parents spend for years on cloth diapers, disposable diapers, or diaper service. As he advised mothers: "You stay home from work with your child for a few days, . . . you let the child walk around the house naked all day long." You put a potty or child's toilet in the room where the child spends a majority of the time, moving it when required from room to room. Once in a while, you remind the child to use the potty. He explained that "children at this age do not like urine and feces running down their legs. When they have an accident, they stop and start to howl, and the mother comes along and says, 'Well, you forgot to use the toilet.' She puts him on the toilet, wipes him off, speaks reassuringly to him. And within three days, or five days, he is doing it on his own." The seventy-five dollars, by the way, is to clean the carpet.

No mother could confuse these two methods and the author concluded that mothers are pragmatic: they use "whatever works." Still, how to decide between these two opposing views? How to determine what works? Such was the dilemma of the modern mother. And toilet training was only one aspect of childrearing and child health. For virtually every facet of infant and child care, advisors could be found in publications, in doctors' offices, and on the internet with various, and at times conflicting, suggestions, rationales, and opinions. Heidi Murkoff, coauthor of the popular *What to Expect* series, succinctly summed up the problem: "Information can be empowering, but too much information or conflicting information can leave you feeling insecure, and it makes you reluctant to use your own judgment."[42]

The *What to Expect* books illustrate the conundrum of late-twentieth-century child-care advice and the complicated relationships between mothers and medical and scientific experts. Murkoff's rationale for these books was simple. In contemporary society, the amount of advice thrown at mothers was daunting, but women should not "burn their parenting books, cancel subscriptions to parenting magazines, [and] operate on instinct and common sense." No, mothers needed all the help they could get for this difficult task of childrearing, but they needed to put the information into perspective. "Use it to guide, not to dictate. To augment your instincts, not supplant them. To build your confidence, not tear it down,"[43] Murkoff counseled.

In writing their books, Murkoff and her coauthors represented themselves as "experts" thanks to their experiences and to their research.[44] They interspersed their text with questions and comments that mothers might ask themselves. "My baby is awake more during the day now and I'm not sure—and I don't think he is either—how many naps he needs." "My son puts everything in his mouth. Now that he plays on the floor so much, I have less control over what goes in. What's safe and what isn't?" The book answered questions and described practices in a down-to-earth style that reads easily, while admitting the confusion evident in many child-care issues. For instance, on the question of when to introduce the infant to solid foods, the text notes that the mother's mother says one thing, the pediatrician says another, and a well-meaning friend supplies yet a different age for solid food with different reasons. The book concluded that "recent research indicates that an infant's individual development, rather than arbitrary age parameters, should be the deciding factor."[45] So, the mother should listen to her baby. Yet, the text warned, if the mother selected the wrong time, the future eating habits of her child may be undermined. So, the mother should watch the child *and* "consult the doctor."[46] In the book, what seemed a simple and straightforward approach to ameliorate confusion, served to compound the chaos—an illustration of the difficulties faced by late-twentieth-century mothers who were trying to raise their children healthfully.

Along with their friendly support, Murkoff and her coauthors stressed the authority of medical practitioners and the importance of regular medical advice; they outlined both the routines of regular medical checkups, which they insisted on, and the indications for calling the physician. In pointing out the importance of selecting the "Right Physician" (the authors' term), the authors remind mothers that you will "want someone you feel comfortable and compatible with. Someone you wouldn't hesitate to waken at two a.m. when your nine-month-old's fever hits a new high, someone you wouldn't be embarrassed to ask about your six-month-old's sudden fascination with his genitals, someone you would feel free to question when you aren't sure an antibiotic that's been prescribed is necessary."[47]

Just as earlier mothers had eagerly embraced what Spock said and how he said it, mothers in the late twentieth century have made the *What to Expect* series best sellers. That does not mean, however, that women unilaterally and automatically accepted what they read in the books. The questioning of authoritative, if not authoritarian, sources that was increasingly apparent following World War II was also evident in the later period. Mothers reported both loving and hating the *What to Expect* series. Jennifer Reese was delighted to find *What to Expect When You Are Expecting* when she had just learned that she was pregnant. This was an unplanned pregnancy and she had had quite a bit to drink at least twice before she knew of the conception. Many child-care and pregnancy advice books warned mothers of the dangers of alcohol consumption when pregnant, which could result in the birth of a child with fetal alcohol syndrome. Reese was scared. *What to Expect* reassured her, noting that there was no evidence that a few drinks early in the pregnancy proved a danger to the developing embryo. Relieved, Reese promptly bought the book. Later, though she continued to value much of the information in *What to Expect*, the tone and some of its advice began to grate on her. She considered some of the prose "icky" and was bothered particularly by the advice on dieting and exercise, which she found to be "control-freak suggestions."[48]

As was typical in earlier eras, mothers picked what they wanted and needed from books such as *What to Expect the First Year*. Sociologist Susan Walzer found in her study of twenty-five heterosexual couples from upstate New York, that almost three-quarters of the mothers had read the book. Though limited in size, Walzer's sample was fairly broad. Economically it represented a wide spectrum, with 40 percent from poor and working-class households. But racially it was relatively homogeneous; all the informants but one were white. These mothers referred to *What to Expect the First Year* as a previous generation had turned to Spock, likening it to their "Bible" and using terms such as "practical" and "nonjudgmental." Some of these mothers, like Reese, found that the book's advice did not necessarily reflect their lives, but that did not preclude their appreciation of it. As one of her informants told Walzer: "Like to read *What to Expect*. Although I don't think they're too accurate. . . . So your baby should be doing this and the other thing. And never give him any white sugar. Don't give him any cookies. Make sure they're muffins made from fruit juice. Yeah, okay. I'll just pop off in the kitchen and make some muffins."[49] Clearly this mother did not feel it necessary to follow all the dietary suggestions of Murkoff and her coauthors, and yet she did "like to read" the book. As with other forms of scientific motherhood, mothers did not accept all the advice they read; they were pragmatic in their choices.

The sales of books and magazines, the number of websites and the number of hits, all attest to the fact that this mother and thousands like her read books and searched the internet. They also visited their doctors and clinics. Most critically, they did not feel comfortable or capable of relying on "instinct" or "innate knowledge." They knew they needed assistance in their child care and childrearing, assistance from experts. But that did not mean they needed or wanted to accept that assistance blindly. Faced with a vast array of advisors and advice, of experts and expertise, they selected what worked best in their lives, what resonated with their beliefs and values. While rejection of the authoritarian medical practitioner was typical in the late twentieth century, appreciation of the importance of scientific and medical experts and expertise was equally common.

Conclusion

"I WANTED TO DO IT RIGHT"

$\mathcal{B}$y the time her daughter was fifteen months old, J.W., an early-twenty-first-century mother, had a number of childcare books on her shelf. She read them but at times found them "confusing" because they contradicted each other. She also got advice from neighbors, the mail carrier, and even total strangers, who would tell her what to do and what not to do. They insisted, without being asked, that it was too cold outside for the baby, or that the baby was too young to be taken out. J.W.'s natal family was a thousand miles away and so she did not have a mother nearby to query. She doubted that she would have listened to her mother's advice anyway because they have such different ideas about childrearing. J.W.'s mother had raised four children on a strict schedule; J.W. had a more "baby-centric" perspective. She read widely, mostly doctor-authored books, and had found those that agreed with her view and these, therefore, gave her confidence in her own childrearing. However, she was very clear that she did not follow their advice verbatim. Rather, she followed them in the "spirit" of their writings. When faced with a crying child, J.W. did not let the baby cry herself out, as her mother would have done. Instead, she waited six to seven minutes, as her books suggested, and then, if the baby had not calmed down, J.W. would go in to comfort her. Understanding the importance of close physical contact between her and the baby in the first few months of life, J.W. carried the baby in a sling much of the time, even while washing dishes, folding clothes, and vacuuming. Yet, she did not believe that this need for contact extended into letting the baby sleep in a "family bed."[1] J.W. did not depend on a single source to decide how she would raise her child; she read the literature, she listened to the advice, and made her choices.

In contemporary scientific motherhood, modern mothers like J.W. continue to be responsible for the health and well-being of their families, and they expect to learn from current scientific and medical literature, to evaluate the mass of books and advice available, and discuss options with their chosen physician or nurse-practitioner. This partnership does not insist on unquestioning allegiance to a health-care provider; there is no authoritarian physician on the scene. In many ways, this partnership concept makes the ideology of scientific motherhood much more demanding today than formerly as women must select from the host of advice before them. J.W., a middle-class, professional woman, is fortunate that she has the time, the economic resources, and the education to make her decisions thoughtfully.

Today the idea that we need scientific and medical information to raise our families healthfully and appropriately is so prevalent that popular authors take it as a given and popular culture plays with the image for humorous effect. Articles on motherhood catch the attention of readers with pictures of mothers buried in books. The sketch of a woman carrying a baby on one arm, several books under the other arm, while reading intently yet another book on child care, headed a 1963 article, "Plight of the Brand-New Parent," in the *New York Times Magazine*. With some updating of her clothes, the picture could still be used today and with the same caption: "She leaves the hospital with her baby, three books on child care and, too often, a sense of panic."[2] Other mothers are portrayed as avoiding this "panic" by simply turning their child over to professionals. A 1999 *New Yorker* cartoon (fig. C.1) shows a mother standing beside her baby's cradle, informing a visitor, "We're planning on sending him away to be reared by experts."[3]

Cultural expectations mirror this vision of education for motherhood. So much so that movies and television use the image of the mother summoning scientific and medical expertise for comic ends. *Mad about You* was a popular television sit-com of the late 1990s, still in syndication on cable television. An episode originally broadcast in 1998 employs comedy to demonstrate how some mothers embrace medical and scientific expertise in their everyday lives. Paul (played by Paul Reiser) and Jamie (played by Helen Hunt) are parents trying to get their infant daughter, Mabel, to sleep through the night. Jamie is convinced that Mabel must "learn to go to sleep on her own" so that she "learns to comfort herself." The method that they use is a popular one based on Dr. Richard Ferber's book *Solve Your Child's Sleep Problems*, though Ferber is not named specifically in the program. With the Ferber method, the child is put to bed and if she cries, the parents are to wait a specified interval, typically five minutes, before checking on her. If she is still

"*We're planning on sending him away to be reared by experts.*"

FIGURE C.1. New mother with friends. *Source: New Yorker,* 2 August 1999. © The New Yorker Collection 1999 Barbara Smaller from cartoonbank.com. All Rights Reserved.

crying after five minutes, then a parent goes into the room to comfort the child, soothing her by voice alone, not picking her up or rocking her. Once she calms down, but before she falls asleep, the parent walks out. If the child starts to cry again, then the wait interval is extended. This pattern of crying followed by verbal calming continues with ever extended wait intervals until the infant learns to fall asleep on her own. Jamie insists that this is what they must do with Mabel. They put Mabel in her crib, close the bedroom door, and wait. Paul has misgivings, but Jamie is so confident that he supports the process. When Mabel's crying wears on Jamie and she starts to question what they are doing, Paul strengthens her resolve to stick to the plan. Most telling is what Paul says to calm Mabel when he creeps into her room at the end of the first interval: "We love you, we love you very much. The only reason we are outside is that a sadistic man from Columbia University said we have to." Though Paul and later Jamie start to doubt the wisdom of this method, they decide it is medically and scientifically sanctioned and they reluctantly follow it.

Other instances from popular culture are more subtle and thus illustrate in a more matter-of-fact tone just how far scientific motherhood had been normalized in United States society. Take, for example, the 1987 Hollywood film *Baby Boom*, starring Diane Keaton as J. S. Wiatt, a high-powered, unmarried executive in New York City. Wiatt "inherits" a baby, Elizabeth. Like *Bachelor Mother* nearly five decades earlier, this film is an example of the "fish-out-of-water" plot in which a child is thrust onto a totally unprepared woman, a career woman with no domestic aspirations. In the 1930s, a man brought a book, brought science, to the novice mother. Now in the late twentieth century, an independent woman gets her own book, which is exactly what Wiatt does. When she has a problem with the child, she pulls out a book, which appears to be *Dr. Spock's Baby and Child Care*, checks the index, and follows the instructions. What is significant is just how much child care is identified with scientific and medical authority. In these examples, mothers do not call upon other mothers when they face decisions about their child care; they expect to and they do take their lead from scientific and medical experts.

The question remains: by the twenty-first century, how were women using scientific and medical advice? Were they dependent on scientific and medical authorities to direct their child care? In other words, does the image of scientific motherhood presented in the media represent mothers' lived experience? Some of the evidence is indirect. The sales of an ever growing number of child-care books continue to increase every year. More and more specialized magazines appear on the market tailored for the modern mother. Clearly women are buying these sources. The number of websites devoted to scientifically and medically informed child care also continues to multiply. Carol Weston and J.W. talk about the books they read and the physician advice they follow. They embrace the benefits of modern science and medicine, while maintaining a cautious outlook. Others, such as author Muffy Mead-Ferro, in *Confessions of a Slacker Mom*, bemoan the torrent of advice that threatens to drown the modern mother and remind mothers of the importance of maternal instinct, that is, "if you are one of those fundamentally decent persons, the parent who loves their kid."[4] Mead-Ferro looks back to a halcyon era when, she believes, mothers had an easier time because they were not faced with "the glut of child-rearing news articles, books, and equipment that we modern-day mothers have to contend with."[5] Yet, she too accepts that "modern science has made more than one or two discoveries during the past decades that have added some insight to the way we raise our offspring or that even corrected the misguided notions of an earlier generation as they tried to do their best by their kids."[6]

And there is a significant correlation between the spread of scientific motherhood and a decline in the infant and child mortality and morbidity rates.[7] For children under one year of age, the death rate in 1900 was 162.4; that is, of each 1,000 live births, mothers could expect to lose more than 160 children before their first birthday. Throughout the twentieth century, this figure consistently fell: in 1910, to 131.8; in 1920, to 92.3; in 1930, to 69.0; in 1940, to 54.9; in 1950, to 33.0; in 1960, to 27.0; and, by 1970, the number had dropped to 21.4. Some of this decline was a direct result of medical breakthroughs, such as the discovery of sulfa drugs in the 1930s and the development of antibiotics beginning in the 1940s, which turned previously feared diseases such as pneumonia and tuberculosis into treatable conditions. One disease, diphtheria, demonstrates the power of modern medicine. Its death rate dropped from 40.3 per 1,000 cases in 1900 to 21.1 in 1910, and 1.1 by 1940, with the development and dissemination of, first, the diphtheria antitoxin in the 1890s and 1900s, then the general acceptance of the diphtheria toxin-antitoxin in the 1920s. Declines such as these, well publicized in the media, added to the aura of "doctor as hero" and affirmed the important role of modern science and medicine in child health and welfare.

In the same period, women were increasingly and directly exposed to education in scientific motherhood with a consequent appreciation for the benefits of modern science and medicine. As noted earlier, the growing production of child-care literature in magazine and book form coincided with rising rates of literacy and increasing school attendance from the late nineteenth century onward, facilitating women's maternal education. By the twentieth century, we can document women's exposure to more formal modes of instruction also: prenatal care and hospitalized childbirth. Before the turn of the previous century, the overwhelming majority of babies were not born in hospitals. However, hospitalized childbirth became increasingly popular through the century, rising to 55.8 percent of total births in 1940 and to 96.6 percent in 1960. Due to our segregated society and income differentials, African American women were less likely to birth in hospitals than Euro-American women, but the gap slowly closed and by the 1970s, over 98 percent of black women gave birth in hospitals. In this controlled setting mothers learned from physicians, nurses, and other health-care practitioners about modern methods and the importance of medical supervision of child care. Weeks and even months before their hospital stay, women visited physicians and clinics and attended classes that taught them the need for medical and scientific advice. Towards the end of the twentieth century, the practice of prenatal care became more common: by 1980, over three-quarters of mothers began such care in the first trimester of their pregnancy and by 2000, over 80 percent. True, this figure differed by race and national origin. In 2001, for Euro-Americans it stood at 88.5 percent; for African Americans, 74.5 percent, and for Hispanics, 75.7 percent. But the numbers have been rising. Even more crucial, the number of women who did not receive care until the last trimester declined from 6.1 percent in 1900 to 3.7 percent in 2001, while the number who received no care at all dropped from 2.0 percent in 1900 to 1.1 percent in 2001. This is indicative of women's ongoing interest in the benefits of contemporary scientific and medical knowledge, an interest that has been facilitated by the expansion of Medicaid for pregnant women in the late 1980s. This government-financed program has provided prenatal care to poor women who otherwise lack the health insurance or the financial resources necessary to obtain this health care.[8] As researcher Margaret K. Nelson discovered, women who attend childbirth classes are more likely to "become more accepting of the preferred medical model."[9]

Correlation and coincidence do not mean causality. We cannot say that scientific and medical advances and mothers' education in and of themselves were the sole determinants of improved statistics and changes in child care over the past 150 years. For instance, study after study in the twentieth century documented a connection between mortality rates and race and ethnicity. Typically, rates were lower among Jewish immigrants and greater for French Canadians; the rates among African Americans usually lagged behind Euro-Americans. Other studies document a connection between family income and health status. Not surprisingly, Children's Bureau studies of the 1910s, for example, disclosed that families headed by fathers with incomes of less than $50 per family member had an infant mortality rate of 22 percent; and when fathers earned more than $400 per family member, the rate dropped to 6 percent.[10] Medical expenditures also varied by race, in part due to the segregation intrinsic to much of our medical system, especially earlier in last century. During the Depression, African American families spent approximately two-fifths as much as white working-class families on physicians, but about the same amount on drugs. Similarly, many African Americans found hospitals and other health-care institutions closed to them. As more employment carried health insurance benefits in the second half of the twentieth century, medical expenditures rose across classes and races, though significant differentials remained. By 1973, 68 percent of laborers had health-care insurance, while this number stood at 72 percent for salaried workers.[11]

At the same time, other radical social transformations directly and indirectly affected the health of children and families. There were close connections between some medical and scientific advances and dramatic developments such as the widespread implementation of the pasteurization of milk, which protected children from contamination of this major source of nutrition. As scientists and physicians learned more about bacteriology and immunology, we gained a greater understanding of the spread of infectious diseases and their treatment and prevention. As the science of nutrition evolved with a greater appreciation for the role of micronutrients, such as vitamins and minerals, health-care workers could construct diets that enhanced the physical growth and development of children. Some scientific and medical influences were more diffuse. The introduction of the automobile in the early twentieth century meant that physicians could more easily and more quickly get to their patients in need, and patients could more rapidly get to medical care when they needed it. It also meant that there were fewer and fewer horse-drawn vehicles. Fewer horses resulted in less manure and less dirt, which in turn made it easier to keep clothes and households cleaner. Similarly, the construction of massive urban water systems through the nineteenth and early twentieth centuries brought clean water into homes. Numerous other examples—the impact of electricity and new electrical appliances such as washing machines and refrigerators, the building of municipal sewer systems, and the like—do not detract from the significance of scientifically and medically informed motherhood, but rather show that there is no simple one-to-one correspondence.

Similarly, many mothers of today, as in previous generations, find themselves seeking out other experiences and sources that they integrate with scientific and medical counsel. As a result of shrinking family size through the twentieth century, fewer women had experience with the child care of younger siblings. In 1950 there were over 100 children born per 1,000 women in the United States; by 1970, this number was down to less than 90, and by 2001 it stood at 65.3, a nearly 50 percent drop in five decades.[12] Smaller families resulted in less opportunity for girls to learn child care at home. In addition, in our highly mobile society, young mothers were less likely to live near their mothers and other experienced female relatives. Susan Hassebrock definitely felt this lack and was grateful to her friend Lisa, who reminded her during a particularly trying weekend that, yes, it was difficult it was to keep up with a child but "that's why your second and third kids turn out better. You learn on your first."[13] Tracey, a character in the syndicated comic strip *For Better or for Worse*, also felt that she lacked critical knowledge based on experience. In 1997, she was pregnant and complained to a friend who had several older children that "I've taken every book out of the library on birth and baby care an' Gord [her husband] and I have started classes, so I guess we are start-ing to feel like parents, but . . . Elly, what's it REALLY like?!!"[14] Modern par-ents read books and attended classes, but they also realized that something was missing in all this education. In another memoir, a mother, Christina Kline, remembered stacking books on the bedside table "in a pile like re-search for a term paper."[15] She did not dismiss this mass of information, but, like Tracey, she sought and appreciated a broader framework. She found that child-care books, hospital and clinic classes, mothers, and even strangers on the street offered suggestions and she diligently tried to digest and balance this cacophony of advice because she wanted to be a good mother, a modern mother: "I wanted to do it right."[16]

By the late twentieth century, physicians too expressed growing appre-ciation for maternal experience in child care. As a young intern, Claire McCarthy nervously faced her first pediatric patient, grievously aware of her own inexperience. Her first case was a three-month-old baby, Jessica, whose mother explained that "every time I feed her, she pukes." McCarthy asked what she considered the "usual medical questions" and could not determine what was wrong. Then, the mother noted that "my friend's baby did the same thing as Jessica, the throwing up, I mean. . . . She mixed some rice cereal in with his formula—not a lot, just a little to make it heavier in his stomach. Worked real well. Could I try that?" Though the doctor had not heard of this plan before, she concluded that it would do no harm and so she agreed. When the infant returned for her next regular checkup, she had stopped the vomit-ing that had worried the mother.[17] For several more years while in training, McCarthy continued to see Jessica and her mother. Not infrequently, the nov-ice physician would have little idea about the problems she faced with Jes-sica, the mother would offer a suggestion with which McCarthy would concur, and the situation would be resolved. At other times, McCarthy was the prob-lem solver. In her memoir, McCarthy is grateful to the mother because "she taught me so much." At the same time, the mother was grateful to the doc-tor. She needed the affirmation from McCarthy, a physician, to assure her that she was caring for her children healthfully and appropriately.[18]

This partnership between mother and physician, each learning from the other, is now the idealized form of modern motherhood. Authoritarian phy-sicians are fading from the equation, often replaced by doctors who enthusi-astically support, or at least accept, the self-motivated patients who seek out information for themselves. Now, especially, with all the resources that pa-tients can reach easily through the internet, physicians recognize that health-care providers do not hold exclusive access to the information patients need to make decisions. On the one hand, as Dr. David Teitel, a pediatric cardiologist from the University of California, explains, an informed patient can be a boon: "It's a phenomenally powerful thing when you're not just sitting down and drawing pictures about the plumbing."[19] In other cases, patients use the internet and alternative sources to uncover experimental procedures or drugs, alerting their physicians to previously unknown options. Most contemporary physicians find this advantageous. A 2002 survey by the Pew Internet Project found that 73 million people, or over 62 percent of internet users in this country, used the web for health information, 6 million on a typical day. Queried about their most recent search, 37 percent reported talking with their physician about what they found. Most significantly, of these, 79 percent reported that their practitioners were interested in what they found; only 13 percent reported that their doctor was "not too interested" or "not interested at all."[20]

However, there is also an "on the other hand," which makes some physicians nervous. Dr. Richard Rockefeller, of Health Commons Institute, a non-profit organization that encourages the use of computerized information tools in clinical settings, explains a downside for some doctors, who find their educational role supplanted by alternative sources. As he notes: "It's hard for physicians because once you get the [patient] education out of the way, you can get to more depth of humanity, and a lot of physicians have never had discussions like that before."[21] The modern educated mother places the physician in a new role, one for which many physicians are unprepared. Other commentators echo the concerns voiced by physicians of earlier generations, such as Brennemann, namely that an educated patient makes their job more difficult because the patient believes she knows more than the doctor. They also warn that with the wealth of information easily available today, patients can have difficulty differentiating the valuable from the erroneous and even downright dangerous.

Some physicians fear that mothers will use this material to challenge medical autonomy. The web, especially, has empowered mothers and enhanced the ability of parents to learn from each other as well as experts and to use their knowledge to question commonly accepted medical practices, such as childhood immunization and circumcision, or to implement procedures healthcare providers question. The Feingold Diet is one example of the latter. In the 1960s, Dr. Ben F. Feingold, a pediatrician in Kaiser-Permanente Medical Center in San Francisco, developed a carefully constructed dietary program that he believed improved the behavior of hyperactive children. By the early 1970s, he was announcing his results at medical meetings and in 1974 published his findings in a widely sold book, *Why Your Child Is Hyperactive*, which also attracted media attention. His diet proved popular in many families, despite its continued controversial status in medical circles. This would be considered by many in the health-care profession as an instance of mothers' rejection of accepted medical and scientific expertise. However, these parents were not rejecting science and medicine but rather reaching out and studying information for themselves. They were not blindly following the advice of experts, but rather they were evaluating that counsel and justifying its use with scientific and medical data, in the same way that La Leche employed contemporary medical science to bolster its claims for the significance of breast feeding. In modern scientific motherhood, physicians and other health-care providers are finding that they cannot just dismiss objections to their advice but must answer them with considered scientific and medical justification.[22]

The shift in the tone of child-care advice is evident when we look at directions for infant bathing over the years. In the twentieth century, infant bathing remained an important aspect of physician-authored manuals. Though the details of their advice changed (from no soap to soap, from temperature-specific water to water "comfortably warm" to mother's elbow or wrist), the tone continued the same for most of the century. Mothers were given step-by-step directions that they were to follow because that was what the doctor said; mothers were expected simply to comply with the physician's instructions. The pendulum began to swing back toward the end of the twentieth and into the twenty-first century. A prime illustration of the return to an earlier era in which mothers were told not only what to do but why they should do it is Robert Needlman's *Dr. Spock's Baby Basics*, published in 2003, under the auspices of the Dr. Spock Company. The name of the series highlights the significant shift in the relationship between mothers and physicians: "Take Charge Parenting Guides for a New Generation." Infant bathing in this book is included in a chapter on "Hygiene," thus placing bathing within a larger issue, something the earlier books rarely did. In this chapter, the section on "Newborns" opens with "The best reason to pay special attention to a newborn's hygiene is to lower the risk of infection." Needlman discusses germs and the immune system before providing hints for sponge and tub baths. In this case, the author gives the reader a rationale for the practices that follow, a critical change from just a few decades earlier.

During the modern period, dramatic cures and their confidence in physicians led mothers to believe that they needed scientific and medical experts and expertise to raise their children healthfully and appropriately and convinced mothers to turn more frequently to medical advice about a broad array of child-care questions. The impetus for scientific motherhood lay initially in the concerns for child and maternal health and well-being. As we have seen, Catherine Beecher's mid-nineteenth-century scientific motherhood was more a hope and an expectation based on the promises of scientific discoveries in physics, biology, and physiology. By late that century, medicine and science had developed specific treatments for some diseases, the discoveries of bacteriology offered explanations for disease causation, and the breakthroughs in nutrition provided a new understanding of the role of diet in health. Using the principles of scientific motherhood, promoters promised, mothers would raise healthier and happier families. By the end of the nineteenth century, they could point to dramatic examples. The childhood of Blanche Beal Lowe is a graphic illustration of the impact of modern medicine. Lowe was born in 1892 and for the first several years of her life lived on a farm in rural Kansas. Her family had a photograph taken a year before her birth, which showed her four older siblings. Her mother told her that in 1891 another student in one of the brothers' classes came down with whooping cough. Immediately, their parents insisted on having their children photographed. The family wanted a memorial in case their children contracted the disease and died. As it turned out, the children were sick with whooping cough, but the local physician, Dr. McIlhenny, came out to the farm and "pulled them through." The grateful family believed that all the children survived due to the efforts of the doctor. A few years later, the neighborhood faced diphtheria, an equally fearsome childhood illness. Again, the doctor came and again the ill children survived. However, just when they thought all was well, Blanche herself contracted diphtheria.

> Dr. McIlhenny said I was so sick nothing could save me unless it might be the new antitoxin he'd read about in the medical journal. No doctor in Sumner County had used it, he said, but if Papa and Mama wanted him to try. . . .
>
> So that's what he did. The medicine worked like a miracle, and next morning they were all thanking God for the miracle of medicine and for the doctor who wasn't afraid to use it.[23]

Cases like this indicate why mothers increasingly turned to science and medicine in raising their children: modern science offered miracles. If a mother was worried about her children, she would look to a scientifically and medically informed expert, most often a physician, to tell her what to do. Scientific motherhood promoted a vision of medical and scientific progress, which could reassure a concerned mother.

Examples from more recent history confirm the continuing influence of medical pronouncements on maternal practices. A half a century earlier, child-care advisors were ambivalent about the baby's sleeping position, maintaining that the "babies who seem to sleep more comfortably on their stomach should be allowed to do so."[24] By the end of the last century, however, controversy over Sudden Infant Death Syndrome (SIDS) significantly altered this reassuring counsel. SIDS is the unexpected death of an apparently healthy infant, most often at night and most commonly in infants aged two to four months. Its cause is unknown but researchers note a correlation between the occurrence of SIDS and sleeping position: there is a significantly higher incidence of SIDS in children who sleep on their stomachs. This has led to the recommendation that infants be placed on their backs to sleep. Surveys show that mothers have heeded this advice. Previously, 70 percent of infants slept on their stomachs; now, 70 percent sleep on their backs.[25] Again, concern for the physical health of her children leads a mother to follow the directions of experts. Connections between lowered child mortality and morbidity and the advances in science and medicine strengthened the lure of scientific motherhood.

In other cases, it is less clear that change in practice resulted strictly from scientifically and medically informed advice. We know that ideas about toilet training have changed significantly over the twentieth century. In the beginning of the century, physicians advised that mothers start to train their children at a few months, or in extreme cases, a few weeks. By the Spock era, the advice was much less stringent, suggesting that the mother wait until the child was ready for the toilet, even to age two or three or more. Mothers' memoirs and letters show that women did change their toilet-training practices over the century and that their changes generally reflected the advice they were given. What is more difficult to evaluate is why mothers moved from strict regulation of the child's bodily processes to a more laissez-faire approach. Some mothers were undoubtedly influenced by Spock's Freudian-informed advice and later Brazelton's, but others may have been equally affected by the significant time constraints involved in very early training; others by the ready accessibility of efficient washing machines and later disposable diapers; and still others by the availability of rubber and plastic pants, which protected furniture and rugs. As one observer noted: "Perhaps these technological innovations have influenced the behavior of mothers more than the theories of Freudian psychologists. Most probably mothers would not have

adopted the advice of psychologists if it were not for the technological im-
provements."[26] We cannot easily separate the theoretical considerations from
the technological and pragmatic.

The example of toilet training also shows how interest in expert advice on child care moved from a focus on physical care and physical health
to psychological care and questions of behavior. In the mid-nineteenth century, medical advice manuals and the like devoted most of their attention to
childhood illnesses and infant care that directly concerned health. Many, many
pages were devoted to the topic of infant feeding because high rates of infant mortality were blamed on poor or erroneous modes of feeding. Well into
the twentieth century, physicians who specialized in the care of children spent
most of their efforts in this area, their interest fueled by humanitarian concerns for child welfare as well as their own financial and professional well-
being.[27] Their success in treating dramatic cases, such as diphtheria, their
dedicated cultivation of the area of infant feeding, and continuing medical
breakthroughs, such as the development of antibiotics in the mid-twentieth
century, gave physicians credibility and a platform for dealing with a wider
and wider range of child-care questions, from infant bathing to sleep patterns
to thumb sucking. Other scientific and medical professionals also added their
voices to the mix. Mothers heard from advisors ranging from doctors to nurses
to psychologists to psychiatrists to nutritionists and others who touted their
scientific and medical credentials. All claimed that their counsel was sanctioned by the latest, most modern scientific and medical discoveries and that
the good mother, the modern mother, would follow their directions diligently.
As the multitude of counselors has continued to grow throughout the twentieth century, mothers have faced a dizzying array of advice.

By the turn of the twenty-first century physicians' views on the ideology of scientific motherhood had come full circle. A hundred and fifty years
earlier, doctors had prompted women to use science and medicine to inform
their mothering practices. Women could learn from doctors, either their own
or through physician-authored publications. Whether medical practitioners
believed that women were actually making independent, medically informed
decisions is less certain and less significant. What is significant is the idealization of modern motherhood, of scientific motherhood, as shaped by contemporary scientific and medical knowledge, which women could read and
digest for themselves. Professional, medical, scientific, and cultural changes
at the turn of the twentieth century modified the ideology of scientific motherhood. Very soon, mothers and their ignorance were blamed for high rates
of infant mortality and morbidity. Physicians depicted mothers as incapable

of evaluating scientific and medical information for themselves. Now, they needed doctors to tell them how to carry out their maternal tasks; in other words, they required an authoritarian physician to direct their mothering. Mothers' experiences indicate that women were concerned about their abilities to handle child care healthfully and appropriately in the rapidly changing twentieth-century world and they increasingly looked to medical and scientific professionals to answers questions about the health and welfare of their families.

Factors internal and external to medicine continued to shift the expert-mother relationship throughout the twentieth century. By the turn of the twenty-first century, the power dynamic was represented more as a partnership. Not an equal partnership, it is true, but one that increasingly recognized that mothers needed to be directly involved in decision making about their children's lives and welfare, from decisions about immunization and circumcision to thumb sucking and discipline. Physicians and other scientific and medical professionals could no longer, nor should they, expect blind obedience to their directions. Most significantly, mothers could and should be informed and empowered patients. What remains, however, is the conviction that mothers need scientific and medical experts and expertise to aid them in child care, the same conviction that founded the ideology of scientific motherhood in the nineteenth century. Today's partnership of mother and expert remains true to this foundation.

We need to ensure that scientific and medical professionals and mothers have the resources necessary to learn from each other. In the world of modern medicine, with information available from a wide range of sources, just gathering all the materials and sifting the substantial from the fraudulent can be daunting. As Amy Alliana, program director of the National Women's Health Network, notes, "It is an overwhelming task for women, and consumers in general, to be able to sort through the information they find and make decisions."[28] J.W.'s example makes clear that even when a mother is making less than life-threatening decisions about her child, the task of deciding how to rear your child is intense and time-consuming.

The short life of Tyler Walrond in New York City in 1997 documents the problems even mothers committed to following modern child-care advice can have when they lack the educational and financial resources of J.W. Tabitha Walrond was nineteen years old when Tyler, her son, was born. She was poor and her health care was covered by Medicaid. Through her prenatal classes and hospital stay, she was convinced of the importance of breast-feeding her son. Two weeks after Tyler's birth, Walrond returned for her postnatal checkup. Though she brought her son with her to the clinic, her physician did not examine Tyler; the clinic insisted that he could not be seen until he had his own Medicaid card. The infant slowly lost weight, while the family applied for a Social Security card for him and obtained an official birth certificate, both of which they were told were required to obtain a Medicaid card. On 27 August 1997, Tyler died; two weeks later, his Medicaid card arrived; and a month later, Walrond was charged with criminally negligent homicide. She was accused of failing to feed him properly and consequently starving him to death. Toward the end of his life, some family members had become concerned that Tyler looked too thin and urged Walrond to supplement her breast milk with infant formula. She refused and kept repeating, "The doctor said, only my breast, only my breast." Moreover, her lawyers insisted that Walrond had not been warned that earlier breast reduction surgery could compromise her ability to successfully breast-feed and lactation experts testified at the trial that nursing mothers who see their children every day may not see even extreme weight losses until the infant is weighed by a physician. Most telling, the psychiatrist who examined her explained that Walrond lacked the skills to negotiate the barriers of the health-care system. Two years later, Walrond was convicted and sentenced to five years' probation, a victim of insufficient direction and an unresponsive health-care system.[29]

As the experience of Walrond illustrates, we must be careful not to romanticize this modern partnership of mother and physician; it has created a new clinical world for both patient and doctor, a world in which there are no simple rules or procedures. Cooperation between mothers and experts should be our goal. But it will not be easy to attain. It requires respect for the knowledge of scientific and medical experts, and for the knowledge of mothers. It requires physicians and other advisors in child health and child care to be sensitive to differing needs of the mothers who consult with them, to use their expertise to aid and direct, not order. It requires mothers to reach out critically for information and advice, to actively engage with health-care providers in making decisions about their children's health and well-being. And today, this partnership is not limited to mothers and scientific and medical professionals. Though mothers remain the primary caretakers of children, fathers and grandparents, too, are increasingly involved with direct child care. Their roles should be more specifically acknowledged and integrated into our system. Crucially, in order for both practitioners and caretakers to realize their roles to the fullest requires a supportive social and cultural network. We need to insure that the education of our health-care providers is comprehensive not only in content but in tone. We need to think more about educating them to be responsive to a wide variety of patients, who have different backgrounds and different education. Mothers must be given the opportunities to question and to learn for themselves, for their opinions and observations to be heard. Modern mothers are not challenging scientific and medical authority, though they are challenging medical authoritarianism. This partnership is not a rejection of science and medicine, but an involvement in it. For this shared process to be successful, we need a comprehensive, accessible, affordable health-care system that is well funded and scrupulously maintained.

We must be honest. To respect the voices of mothers and the health needs of millions of children in our country requires a radical change in our health-care system. Today, under financial constraints and nonmedical oversight, doctors, nurses, and other health-care providers are obliged to more efficiently process patients through the system, leaving less and less time for the necessary conversations between them and mothers and other care givers. Pressures on parents make it difficult for mothers and others to find the time to acquire and digest the information they need from the confusing array of contemporary sources. Most critically, such a health-care system cannot be seen simply as an add-on. It can only be sustained within the larger social complex that admits society's responsibility for child welfare and acknowledges that health is not merely a question of access to medical services but also requires sufficient housing, adequate wages, safer neighborhoods, and better schools. Such a massive transformation will not be easy.

Recognizing these problems, however, does not stop us from doing all we can to ameliorate the situation now. Modern scientific motherhood that values the intelligence, commitment, and integrity of all participants provides us with the blueprint for healthful and improved child care. We have the blueprint; now we need to build the health-care system to attain it.

NOTES

Introduction

1. *Parents' Magazine*, November 1938, 77.
2. Charles E. Rosenberg, "Health in the Home: A Tradition of Print and Practice," in *Right Living: An Anglo-American Tradition of Self-Help Medicine and Hygiene*, ed. Charles E. Rosenberg (Baltimore: Johns Hopkins University Press, 2003), 11.
3. *The Maternal Physician; A Treatise on the Nurture and Management of Infants, from the Birth until Two Years Old. Being the Result of Sixteen Years' Experience in the Nursery. Illustrated by Extracts from the Most Approved Medical Authors. By an American Matron*, fac. of 2nd ed. (1818; New York: Arno Press and the *New York Times*, 1972). Among her unstated reasons for publishing was probably her financial need. For more on Tyler, see Marilyn S. Blackwell, "The Republican Vision of Mary Palmer Tyler," *Journal of the Early Republic* 12 (1992): 11–35; Kathleen Brown, "The Maternal Physician," in Rosenberg, *Right Living*, 88–111.
4. Linda Kerber, "The Republican Mother: Women and the Enlightenment—an American Perspective," *American Quarterly* 28, no. 2 (1976): 187–205; Linda K. Kerber, "The Republican Mother and the Woman Citizen: Contradictions and Choices in Revolutionary America," in *Women's America: Refocusing the Past*, ed. Linda K. Kerber and Jane Sherron DeHart (New York: Oxford University Press, 2000), 112–20.
5. Brown, "The Maternal Physician."
6. Ruth Bloch, "American Feminine Ideals in Transition: The Rise of the Moral Mother, 1785–1815," *Feminist Studies* 4 (1978):100–126; Nancy F. Cott, "Notes toward an Interpretation of Antebellum Childrearing," *Psychohistory Review* 6, no. 4 (1978): 4–20.
7. John S. C. Abbott, *The Mother at Home; or, The Principles of Maternal Duty* (New York: American Tract Society, 1833), 177–182.
8. Kathryn Kish Sklar, *Catharine Beecher: A Study in American Domesticity* (New York: W. W. Norton, 1973), 154.

9. Catharine E. Beecher and Harriet Beecher Stowe, *The American Woman's Home*, ed. Nicole Tonkovich (1869; New Brunswick: Rutgers University Press, 2002).

10. "Mrs. Kate Hunnibee's Diary," *Hearth and Home* 1 (1869): 108.

11. Beecher and Stowe, *The American Woman's Home*.

12. Ibid., 204.

13. Peter N. Stearns, *Anxious Parents: A History of Modern Childrearing in America* (New York: New York University Press, 2003), 45–46.

14. Elizabeth M. R. Lomax, *Science and Patterns of Child Care* (San Francisco: W. H. Freeman, 1978); Andrea Meditch, "In the Nation's Interest: Child Care Prescriptions, 1890–1930" (Ph.D. diss., University of Texas at Austin, 1981); Paul Starr, *The Social Transformation of American Medicine* (New York: Basic Books, 1982); Nancy Tomes, *The Gospel of Germs: Men, Women, and the Microbe in American Life* (Cambridge, MA: Harvard University Press, 1998).

15. Alexandra Minna Stern, "Better Babies Contests at the Indiana State Fair: Child Health, Scientific Motherhood, and Eugenics in the Midwest, 1920–1935," in *Formative Years: Children's Health in the United States, 1880–2000*, ed. Alexandra Minna Stern (Ann Arbor: University of Michigan Press, 2002), 121–52.

16. Ruth Schwartz Cowan, *More Work for Mother: The Ironies of Household Technology from the Open Hearth to the Microwave* (New York: Basic Books, 1983); Susan Strasser, *Never Done: A History of American Housework* (New York: Pantheon, 1982).

17. Sydney A. Halpern, *American Pediatrics: The Social Dynamics of Professionalism, 1880–1980* (Berkeley: University of California Press, 1988); Manfred J. Wasserman, "The Emergence of Modern Child Health Care: Pediatrics, Public Health, and the Federal Government" (Ph.D. diss., Catholic University of America, 1981).

18. Ann Hulbert, *Raising America: Experts, Parents, and a Century of Advice about Children* (New York: Knopf, 2003), documents the philosophies of three pairs of leading experts of the twentieth century: L. Emmett Holt and G. Stanley Hall; John Broadus Watson and Arnold Gesell; and Benjamin Spock and Bruno Bettelheim. She focuses less on how their philosophies were received and more on the changes in mothers' roles in childrearing.

19. Meditch, "In the Nation's Interest."

20. For an example of this in another arena, a response that Abel and Reifel term "strategy of resistance," see Emily K. Abel and Nancy Reifel, "Interactions between Public Health Nurses and Clients on American Indian Reservations during the 1930s," *Social History of Medicine* 9, no. 1 (1996): 89–108.

21. W. Nicholas Lackey, "Pediatric Practice in the Small Towns and Country," *Pediatrics* 25 (1913): 367–74.

22. *Perfect Motherhood* relies heavily, though not exclusively, on sources used by and left by literate mothers, which often means middle-class, primarily Euro-Americans. It is this group that was setting the standards to which the majority of mothers in the U.S. aspired. I will be careful to point out differences among mothers, differences that emerge between racial and ethnic groups, between rural and urban, between middle class and working class. These differences will serve to heighten our understanding of how the specific material and cultural

conditions of mothers influenced their acceptance, rejection, and modification of the basic tenets of scientific motherhood. See also Stearns, *Anxious Parents*, esp. 7–8.

CHAPTER 1   *"Follow the lead of physicians"*

1. "Narcissa Prentiss Whitman," in *Pacific Northwest Women, 1815–1925: Lives, Memories, and Writings,* ed. Jean M. Ward and Elaine A. Maveety (Corvalis: Oregon State University Press, 1995), 143–50.

2. Doctor-directed infant and child care in the nineteenth century was sometimes presented in books on diseases of infants and children and more frequently in home medical manuals focused on women's health.

3. John D. West, M.D., *Maidenhood and Motherhood; or, Ten Phases of Woman's Life* (Detroit: Rominger & Rayner, 1888), 25.

4. Ibid., 26–27.

5. John Brisben Walker, "Motherhood as a Profession," *Cosmopolitan* 25 (1898): 89–93.

6. Abraham Jacobi, quoted in Russell Viner, "Abraham Jacobi and the Origin of Scientific Pediatrics in America," in *Formative Year: Children's Health in the United States, 1880–2000,* ed. Alexandra Minna Stern and Howard Markel (Ann Arbor: University of Michigan Press, 2002), 36.

7. John Harley Warner, "Science in Medicine," *Osiris,* 2nd series, 1 (1985): 37–58.

8. Andrew McClary, "Germs Are Everywhere: The Germ Threat as Seen in Magazine Articles, 1890–1920," *Journal of American Culture* 3 (Spring 1980): 33–46; Nancy Tomes, *The Gospel of Germs: Men, Women, and the Microbe in American Life* (Cambridge, MA: Harvard University Press, 1998); Matthew D. Whalen and Mary F. Tobin, "Periodicals and the Popularization of Science in America, 1860–1910," *Journal of American Culture* 3 (Spring 1980): 195–203.

9. See, for example, Francis Tweddell, *A Mother's Guide; A Manual for the Guidance of Mothers and Nurses* (New York: J. Dougherty, 1911).

10. Rima D. Apple, *Mothers and Medicine: A Social History of Infant Feeding* (Madison: University of Wisconsin Press, 1987), passim.

11. Louise E. Hogan, *How to Feed Children; A Manual for Mothers, Nurses, and Physicians,* 8th ed. (Philadelphia: J. B. Lippincott, 1906).

12. Peter C. English, "'Not Miniature Men and Women': Abraham Jacobi's Vision of a New Medical Specialty a Century Ago," in *Children and Health Care: Moral and Social Issues,* ed. Loretta M. Kopelman and John C. Moskop (Boston: Kluwer, 1989), 259.

13. Stephen Tracy, *The Mother and Her Offspring* (New York: Harper, 1853).

14. Ibid.

15. Ibid.

16. Jerome Walker, *The First Baby: His Trials and the Trials of His Parents* (New York: Brown & Derby, 1881), 7. For more on Walker, see Janet Golden, *A Social History of Wet Nursing in America: From Breast to Bottle* (New York: Cambridge University Press, 1996), 64–67.

17. Walker, *The First Baby*, 7, 185, 12.
18. Edward Hazen Parker, *The Handbook for Mothers: A Guide in the Care of Young Children* (Chicago: Belfords, Clarke, 1880), vi.
19. Prudence B. Sauer, *Maternity: A Book for Every Wife and Mother* (Chicago: L. P. Miller, 1887).
20. J. P. Crozer Griffith, *The Care of the Baby: A Manual for Mothers and Nurses, Containing Practical Directions for the Management of Infancy and Childhood in Health and Disease* (Philadelphia: W. B. Saunders, 1888), 17. Similar sentiments were repeated in the 1915 and 1923 editions.
21. Ibid., 19.
22. "The Doctor's Talk with Mothers: Feeding Children," *Home Science* 21 (1904): 36–40, 21.
23. Jay Mechling, "Advice to Historians on Advice to Mothers," *Journal of Social History* 9 (1975): 44–63.
24. Though the shifting definitions of literacy make this number difficult to pin down, what is significant for this argument is the undeniable downward trend of illiteracy.
25. U.S. Department of Commerce, "Historical Statistics of the United States: Colonial Times to 1970, Part 1" (Washington, DC: U.S. Bureau of the Census, 1975), Tables Series H 433–41, Series H 598–601, and Series H 64–68.
26. Selma Harju Steinberg, *Reformer in the Marketplace: Edward W. Bok and the Ladies' Home Journal, 1889–1916* (Baton Rouge: Louisiana State University Press, 1979).
27. Lucy White Palmer, "The Coming Guest," *Babyhood* 2 (1886): 312–13.
28. Ada E. Hazell, "Timely Hints about Baby," *Ladies' Home Journal* 5, no. 4 (1888): 5.
29. Jack's Wife, "Mother's Corner," *Ladies' Home Journal* 5 (1888): 5.
30. Frau Bertha, "The Training of Mothers," *Babyhood* 1 (1885): 182.
31. Helen Watterson Moody, "The True Meaning of Motherhood," *Ladies' Home Journal* 16, no. 6 (1899): 12.
32. Romaine Douglas Taylor, "Pioneer Child Rearing Practices on the Kansas Frontier" (Ed.D. diss., University of Kansas, 1990), 54.
33. Millicent Washburn Shinn, *The Biography of a Baby* (Reading, MA: Addison-Wesley, 1900; repr. 1985), 51.
34. H., "Worms Once More," *Babyhood* 1, no. 6 (1885): 181.
35. Judith Walzer Leavitt, *Brought to Bed: Childbearing in America: 1750–1950* (New York: Oxford University Press, 1986).
36. S., "Science versus Colic," *Babyhood* 10, no. 116 (1894): 244.
37. Harriet S. Blaine Beale, ed., *Letters of Mrs. James G. Blaine*, vol. 1 (New York: Duffield, 1908), 55.
38. A true lover of babies, "A Sound Opinion as to the 'Autocrat,'" *Babyhood* 12, no. 19 (1886).
39. J.P., "General Information Wanted," *Babyhood* 10, no. 10 (1894).
40. "Prairie Croquet," in *To All Inquiring Friends: Letters, Diaries, and Essays from North Dakota, 1880–1910*, ed. Elizabeth Hampsten (Grand Forks, ND: Department of English, University of North Dakota, 1980).

41. Clifford Dale Whitman, "Private Journal of Mary Ann Owen Sims," *Arkansas History Quarterly* 35 (1976). See also Hazell, "Timely Hints about Baby"; Elizabeth Duncan Putnam, "Diary of Mrs. Joseph Duncan (Elizabeth Caldwell Smith)," *Journal of the Illinois State Historical Society* 21 (April 1928).

42. Elizabeth Cady Stanton, *Eighty Years and More: Reminiscences, 1815–1897* (New York: Schocken, 1971), esp.112–13.

43. Ibid., esp.114–15.

44. See, for example, Carol Kammen, ed., "The Letters of Calista Hall," *New York History* 63 (April 1982): esp.218. Also, numerous letters to editors of women's magazines and child-care journals asked for recommendations for books. See, for example, "Letters to the Editor," *Babyhood* 4 (1887–88); J.P., "General Information Wanted."

45. Putnam, "Diary of Mrs. Joseph Duncan," 31. See also Julia Grant, *Raising Baby by the Book: The Education of American Mothers* (New Haven: Yale University Press, 1998), 24–32.

46. L.McD., "The Practical Side of Mothers' Meetings," *Babyhood* 11, no. 125 (1895). For more examples of mothers' clubs at the turn of the century, see E. G. Peckham, "The Milwaukee Mother's Club," *Babyhood* 5 (1889); Willametta Preston, "A School of Mothers," *American Motherhood* 38 (1914).

47. Records of the Lowell House Mothers' Club, 1900–1944, New Haven Colony Historical Society.

48. Mrs. J. M. Mulligan, "The Trials of a Baby," *American Agriculturist* 47 (1890).

49. Mamma, "A Baby Dislikes Cereals," *Babyhood* 2, no. 20 (1886).

50. A grateful reader, "Babyhood: Its Friends and Foes," *Babyhood* 11, no. 121 (1894).

51. A country physician, "Babyhood's Missionary Work," *Babyhood* 11, no. 122 (1895); R.C.F., "A Country Mother's Comprehensive Request," *Babyhood* 11, no. 124 (1895).

52. A. P. Carter, "Don't Waste," *Babyhood* 10, no. 116 (1894).

53. See, for example, a Brooklyn reader, "Questions of Feeding: Gradual Increase in Quantity; Lime and Barley Water," *Babyhood* 14 (1898).

54. A new reader, "Nursery Problems," *Babyhood* 12 (1896).

55. F.B.S., "Various Points of Diet," *Babyhood* 10 (1894).

56. E.V.D., "Pasteurization," *Babyhood* 9 (1893).

57. See, for example, L.B.V., "The Perplexities of Bottle-Feeding," *Babyhood* 2, no. 13 (1885); Mother, "The Experiences of Twins," *Babyhood* 2 (1885); N.N., "Excessive Amount of Food; The Functions of Lime Water," *Babyhood* 11, no. 129 (1895).

58. See, for example, (Mrs.) Jenness Miller, *Mother and Babe* (Washington, DC: Jenness Miller, 1894); (Mrs.) Hannah Whitall Smith, *The Science of Motherhood* (New York: Fleming H. Revell, 1894).

59. Palmetta Goldsmith, "How to Bathe the Baby," *American Agriculturist* 48 (1889).

60. Julia L. Munger, "How to Bathe Baby," *Babyhood* 11, no. 121 (1894).

61. For a sample of these suggestions, see various issues of *Babyhood*, especially those of the 1890s. The *American Agriculturalist* of the 1880s had many such articles.

62. A mother, "Feeding the Baby," *Farm, Stock, and Home* 14 (1898).
63. "Mothers and the Nursery," *Herald of Health* 41 (1891).
64. Bell, "Mother's Council," *Ladies' Home Journal* 9, no. 2 (1892).
65. Betty Allen, "A Baby in Three-Room Flat," *Ladies' Home Journal* 31, no. 10 (1914). For other examples, see Mrs. Horace P. Cook, "Weaning the Baby," *American Motherhood* 38 (1914); Rosamond E., "Mother's Council: Preparing and Keeping Babies' Food," *Ladies' Home Journal* 7, no. 12 (1890).
66. "A 'Symposium' on Constipation," *Babyhood* 2, no. 14 (1886). For other examples, see A.B., "Another Word on Hernia and Its Treatment," *Babyhood* 11, no. 131 (1895); Mrs. J. F. Duncan, "The Case of Rubber Nipples," *Babyhood* 10, no. 119 (1894); E.S., "A Despairing Wail Concerning Nipples," *Babyhood* 10, no. 116 (1894); M.W.F., "The Other Side of the Trouble with 'Nipples,'" *Babyhood* 10, no. 118 (1894); R.D.R., "A Probable Case of Hernia," *Babyhood* 11, no. 122 (1895). Janet Golden has an extensive analysis of another such lengthy series; see Golden, *A Social History of Wet Nursing in America*, 159–72.
67. Busy Mother, "About the Measles," *Farm, Stock, and Home* 13, no. 1 (1897).
68. A. L. Toland, "Ginger Cake as Medicine," *Babyhood* 10, no. 120 (1894).
69. X.Y.Z., "A Plea for Mutual Confidence between Physician and Patient," *Babyhood* 11, no. 124 (1895).
70. A.F.B.K., "Physician and Patient," *Babyhood* 11, no. 126 (1895).
71. For more on this point as expressed in a limited geographic region, see Sylvia D. Hoffert, *Private Matters: American Attitudes toward Childbearing and Infant Nurture in the Urban North, 1800–1860* (Urbana: University of Illinois Press, 1989).

CHAPTER 2   *"Mamma's scientific—she knows all the laws"*

1. *The Forecast: A Magazine of Home Efficiency* 9 (1915): 391.
2. Marjorie A. [Mrs. Hugh] Brown, *Lady in Boomtown: Miners and Manners on the Nevada Frontier* (Palo Alto, CA: American West Publishing, 1968), 79–80.
3. For other examples of home remedies and self-reliance, see James C. Mohr, ed., *The Cormany Diaries: A Northern Family in the Civil War* (Pittsburgh: University of Pittsburgh Press, 1982); Romaine Douglas Taylor, "Pioneer Child Rearing Practices on the Kansas Frontier" (Ed.D. diss., University of Kansas, 1990).
4. Holt (1855–1924) was one of the foremost leaders in child health in the decades before and after the turn of the twentieth century. From 1889 to 1923 he headed New York Babies Hospital. His *The Diseases of Infancy and Children*, first published in 1897, was for decades considered the standard text in pediatrics.
5. L. Emmett Holt, *The Care and Feeding of Children: A Catechism for the Use of Mothers and Children's Nurses* (New York: D. Appleton, 1894), 15–16.
6. Richard M. Smith, *The Baby's First Two Years* (Boston: Houghton Mifflin, 1915), 15.
7. For more on the professional development of the specialty of pediatrics, see Sydney A. Halpern, *American Pediatrics: The Social Dynamics of Professionalism, 1880–1980* (Berkeley: University of California Press, 1988).
8. Rima D. Apple, *Vitamania: Vitamins in American Culture* (New Brunswick, NJ:

Rutgers University Press, 1996); Nancy Tomes, *The Gospel of Germs: Men, Women, and the Microbe in American Life* (Cambridge, MA: Harvard University Press, 1998).

9. Halpern, *American Pediatrics;* Paul Starr, *The Social Transformation of American Medicine* (New York: Basic Books, 1982); Rosemary Stevens, *American Medicine and the Public Interest* (Berkeley: University of California Press, 1998).

10. Roger H. Dennett, M.D., *The Healthy Baby: The Care and Feeding of Infants in Sickness and in Health* (New York: Macmillan, 1912), vii.

11. Smith, *The Baby's First Two Years*, 8–9.

12. John Spargo, *The Bitter Cry of Children* (New York: Macmillan, 1907), 27–28.

13. C.-E.A. Winslow, *The Public Health Nurse: How She Helps to Keep the Babies Well*, Pub. No. 47 (Washington, DC: U.S. Children's Bureau, 1918), quoted in Robert Hamlett Bremner, *Children and Youth in America: A Documentary History*, vol. 2, part 7 (Cambridge, MA: Harvard University Press, 1970–74).

14. Julia Grant, *Raising Baby by the Book: The Education of American Mothers* (New Haven: Yale University Press, 1998), 70–112.

15. Some of these agencies provided certified milk, that is, unpasteurized milk produced under highly controlled situations and tested frequently to insure a low level of bacterial contamination. Others dispensed pasteurized milk. See Rima D. Apple, *Mothers and Medicine: A Social History of Infant Feeding* (Madison, WI: University of Wisconsin Press, 1987); Richard A. Meckel, *Save the Babies: American Public Health Reform and the Prevention of Infant Mortality, 1850–1929* (Baltimore, MD: Johns Hopkins University Press, 1990) for more on the various processes employed.

16. Several decades later the activities of this private organization were adopted by the San Francisco Department of Public Health, including its Well Baby Centers and Hospital-based Postnatal Care for Mothers.

17. Philip Van Ingen, "Editorial: The Present-Day Position of the 'Milk Station,'" *Archives of Pediatrics* 29 (1912): 721–23. See also S. Josephine Baker, "The Infants' Milk Stations: Their Relation to the Pediatric Clinics and to the Private Physician," *Archives of Pediatrics* 31 (1914): 165–70.

18. Sidonie M. Gruenberg, Chairman, *Parent Education: Types, Content, Method; Report of the Subcommittee on Types of Parent Education, Content and Method* (New York: Century, 1932).

19. Sandra Lee Barney, "Maternalism and Promotion of Scientific Medicine during the Industrial Transformation of Appalachia, 1880–1930," *NWSA Journal* 11, no. 3 (1999): 80–81.

20. Anne Meis Knupfer, *Toward a Tenderer Humanity and a Nobler Womanhood: African American Women's Clubs in Turn-of-the-Century Chicago* (New York: New York University Press, 1996), 13, 100.

21. Quoted in Sonya Michel, *Children's Interests, Mothers' Rights: The Shaping of America's Child Care Policy* (New Haven: Yale University Press, 1999), 88.

22. John M. Connolly, "Some Results of the Work of the Committee on Milk and Baby Hygiene in Behalf of Babies," *Boston Medical and Surgical Journal* 162, no. 5 (1910): 127–31.

23. S. Josephine Baker, *Fighting for Life* (1939; repr., Huntington, NY: R. E. Krieger,

1980), passim; Charles Herrman, "Editorial: Instructing Mothers and Older Girls in the Care of Babies," *Archives of Pediatrics* 25 (1908): 617–18.

24. Department of Health, City of Chicago, "Report for 1922," (1922); H. E. Kleinschmidt, "Little Mothers' Leagues: A Long-Distance View," *Journal of Social Hygiene* 12 (1926): 129–36.

25. Elizabeth Toon, "Selling the Public on Public Health: The Commonwealth and Milbank Health Demonstrations and the Meaning of Community Health Education," in *Philanthropic Foundations: New Scholarship, New Possibilities,* ed. Ellen Condliffe Lagemann (Bloomington: Indiana University Press, 1999), 119–30; Estella Ford Warner and Geddes Smith, *Children of the Covered Wagon: Report of the Commonwealth Fund Child Health Demonstration in Marion County, Oregon, 1925–1929* (New York: Commonwealth Fund, Division of Publications, 1930).

26. See, for example, Grant, *Raising Baby by the Book;* Knupfer, *Toward a Tenderer Humanity and a Nobler Womanhood*; Susan L. Smith, *Sick and Tired of Being Sick and Tired: Black Women's Health Activism in America, 1890–1950* (Philadelphia: University of Pennsylvania Press, 1995).

27. "Best Babies Are Blow to Science; Some Babies, Too!" *Milwaukee Sentinel,* 18 May 1916.

28. Ellen Swallow Richards, "The Social Significance of the Home Economics Movement," *Journal of Home Economics* 3, no. 2 (1911): 117–25.

29. University of Wisconsin Catalog of Home Economics, 1913–14, located at the University of Wisconsin Steenbock Archives, series 10/0/1, box 1. See also Rima D. Apple, *The Challenge of Constantly Changing Times: From Home Economics to Human Ecology at the University of Wisconsin–Madison, 1903–2003* (Madison, WI: Parallel Press, University of Wisconsin–Madison Libraries, 2003).

30. Caroline L. Hunt, *The Life of Ellen H. Richards* (Boston: Whitcomb & Barrows, 1912).

31. On the broadening of outlook and advantages in rural areas of the United States in this period, see Apple, *The Challenge of Constantly Changing Times;* Marilyn Irvin Holt, *Linoleum, Better Babies and the Modern Farm Woman, 1890–1930* (Albuquerque: University of New Mexico Press, 1995).

32. Molly Ladd-Taylor, *Mother-Work: Women, Child Welfare, and the State, 1890–1930* (Urbana: University of Illinois Press, 1994), 76–77.

33. Molly Ladd-Taylor, *Raising a Baby the Government Way: Mothers' Letters to the Children's Bureau, 1915–1932* (New Brunswick, NJ: Rutgers University Press, 1986), 22–23. See also Ladd-Taylor, *Mother-Work;* Nancy Pottisham Weiss, "Mother, the Invention of Necessity: *Baby and Child Care*," *American Quarterly* 29 (1977): 519–46; Nancy Pottisham Weiss, "The Mother-Child Dyad Revisited: Perceptions of Mothers and Children in Twentieth Century Child-Rearing Manuals," *Journal of Social Issues* 34, no. 2 (1978): 29–45.

34. Reformers bridled at the limitations of an agency that could do no more than conduct studies and publish brochures. Of course, the staff of the Bureau did do more. As letters flooded into the Bureau from concerned mothers all over the country, staff members would respond with advice, even with money. They also contacted local agencies to provide additional assistance to mothers in need. Much of this they did from their own resources because the Bureau's finances were

always limited and their mandate restricted. For examples of the Bureau's work, see Emily K. Abel, "Correspondence between Julia C. Lathrop, Chief of the Children's Bureau, and a Working-Class Woman, 1914–1915," *Journal of Women's History* 5, no. 1 (1993): 79–88; Ladd-Taylor, *Raising a Baby the Government Way;* Kriste Lindenmeyer, *"A Right to Childhood": The U.S. Children's Bureau and Child Welfare, 1912–1946* (Urbana: University of Illinois Press, 1997).

35. *Babyhood* 9, no. 103 (1893): xii.

36. The nurse was Elizabeth Robinson Scovil; the physician, Josephine Hemenway Kenyon. For more on their columns and the booklets they provided mothers, see Apple, *Mothers and Medicine*, esp. chapters 6 and 7. In 1910 in a more targeted move, Dr. Emelyn Coolidge established the "Young Mother's Register" in the *Ladies' Home Journal*. Within one year over five hundred mothers registered; they sent monthly reports to Coolidge and questions that the doctor promised to answer personally. By 1912, Coolidge proudly announced, "The young mother is fast becoming educated, being no longer satisfied to follow the advice of well-meaning but inexperienced neighbors, but preferring to turn to a higher authority for help in solving nursery problems." Emelyn Lincoln Coolidge, "The Young Mother's Guide," *Ladies' Home Journal* 28, no. 1 (1911): 37; Coolidge, "The Young Mother's Guide," *Ladies' Home Journal* 29, no. 1 (1912): 65; Salme Harju Steinberg, *Reformer in the Marketplace: Edward W. Bok and the Ladies' Home Journal, 1889–1916* (Baton Rouge: Louisiana State University Press, 1979), 36. Similar articles and correspondence columns appear in other journals, such as *Babyhood, Mother's Friend, Home Science,* and *Farmer's Wife*. In this case, and increasingly, that higher authority was the scientific or medical expert.

37. Mrs. R.M., "A Word of Appreciation," *American Motherhood* 38 (1914): 38.

38. Mrs. O.K., "A Wise Mother," *American Motherhood* 39 (1914): 49.

39. A trained mother, "Maternal Instinct Run Riot," *Good Housekeeping* 52 (1911): 245–47.

40. Harriet Hubbard, "The Up-to-Date Homemaker," *The Forecast* 7 (1914): 305; Ellen Key, *The Renaissance of Motherhood*, trans. Anna E. B. Fries (New York: G. P. Putnam's Sons, 1914); Jane Stewart, "Is the Mother Ready for the Baby? Training Versus 'Instinct' and 'Experience,'" *Ladies' Home Journal* 30, no. 2 (1913): 76.

41. Ruth Freeman, "Put Yourself in Baby's Place," *Hearth and Home* 4, no. 50 (14 Dec. 1872): 913.

42. Ellen Battelle Dietrick, "A Scientifically Trained Baby," *New England Kitchen Magazine [Home Science]* 2 (1895): 179–80. For additional examples, see Coolidge, "The Young Mother's Guide," 1911; Anna Virginia Miller, "Food for Children," *American Kitchen [Home Science]* 11 (1899): 42–46; Helen Watterson Moody, "The True Meaning of Motherhood," *Ladies' Home Journal* 16, no. 6 (1899): 12.

43. Hannah Whitall (Mrs.) Smith, *The Science of Motherhood* (New York: Fleming H. Revell, 1894), 6.

44. Viviana A. Zelizer, *Pricing the Priceless Child: The Changing Social Value of Children* (New York: Basic Books, 1985), 31–32.

45. Camillo Frederick Mueller, "Prenatal and Child Clinics" (M.D. diss., University of Wisconsin, 1928), 12.
46. Mrs. W. R. Hollowell, "Why the Young Doctor Is to Be Trusted," *Progressive Farmer* 31 (1916): 1154.

CHAPTER 3   *"Follow my directions exactly"*

1. American Association of University Women, San Francisco Branch, Baby Hygiene Committee records, 1909–64, MS51, courtesy of the California Historical Society.
2. Frank Howard Richardson, *Simplifying Motherhood* (New York: Putnam, 1925), 9–10.
3. Harold C. Tooker, "Infant Feeding," *Hygeia* 16 (1938): 406–7. See also Della Thompson Lutes, "Motherhood What We Make of It: A Really Good Mother Is a Practical Trained Mother," *Farmer's Wife* 25 (1922): 185, 203.
4. For interesting cross-cultural comparisons, see Katherine Arnup, *Education for Motherhood: Advice for Mothers in Twentieth-Century Canada* (Toronto: University of Toronto Press, 1994); Denyse Baillargeon, "Care of Mothers and Infants in Montreal between the Wars: The Visiting Nurses of Metropolitan Life, Les Gouttes de Lait, and Assistance Maternelle," in *Caring and Curing: Historical Perspectives on Women and Healing in Canada*, ed. Dianne Dodd and Deborah Gorham (Ottawa: University of Ottawa Press, 1994), 163–81; Linda Bryder, *Not Just Weighing Babies: Plunket in Auckland, 1908–1998* (Auckland: Pyramid Press, 1998); Cynthia R. Comacchio, *Nations Are Built of Babies: Saving Ontario's Mothers and Children, 1900–1940* (Montreal: McGill's-Queen's University Press, 1993); Alisa Klaus, *Every Child a Lion: The Origins of Maternal and Infant Health Policy in the United States and France, 1890–1920* (Ithaca: Cornell University Press, 1993); Hilary Marland, "The Medicalization of Motherhood: Doctors and Infant Welfare in the Netherlands, 1910–1930," in *Women and Children First: International Maternal and Infant Welfare, 1870–1945*, ed. Valeria Fildes, Lara Marks, and Hilary Marland (New York: Routledge, 1992); Jay Mechling, "Advice to Historians on Advice to Mothers," *Journal of Social History* 9 (1975): 44–63; Richard A. Meckel, *Save the Babies: American Public Health Reform and the Prevention of Infant Mortality, 1850–1929* (Baltimore, MD: Johns Hopkins University Press, 1990); Philippa Mein Smith, *Mothers and King Baby: Infant Survival and Welfare in an Imperial World: Australia, 1880–1950* (Houndmill, Basingstoke, Hampshire: Macmillan Press, 1997); Sachlav Stoler-Liss, "'Mothers Birth the Nation': The Social Construction of Zionist Motherhood in Wartime Israeli Parents' Manuals," *NSHIM: A Journal of Jewish Women's Studies and Gender Issues* (2003): 104–18.
5. Joseph Brennemann, "Vis Medicatrix Naturae in Pediatrics," *American Journal of Diseases of Children* 40 (1930): 5–6. McCollum was E.V. McCollum, a nutrition researcher at Johns Hopkins University, who frequently published articles in the popular press about the importance of proper diet; Gesell was Arnold Gesell, a psychologist and pediatrician, also widely published in the popular press.
6. Isaac A. Abt, *Baby Doctor* (New York: Whittlesey, 1944), 3. Abt (1867–1955)

was a highly influential pediatrician based in Chicago. He was the first president of the American Academy of Pediatrics (1930–31).

7. Ibid., 290–91.

8. Sydney A. Halpern, *American Pediatrics: The Social Dynamics of Professionalism, 1880–1980* (Berkeley: University of California Press, 1988); Paul Starr, *The Social Transformation of American Medicine* (New York: Basic Books, 1982); Rosemary Stevens, *American Medicine and the Public Interest* (Berkeley: University of California Press, 1998).

9. Elizabeth MacDonald, "Our Babies: X. A Talk with the Doctor," *Modern Priscilla*, August 1920, 40.

10. Whiteis and Anthony, *Instructions for Expectant Mothers and the Care of Infants* (Iowa City: 1932), 2. I wish to thank Toby Appel for sending me a photocopy of this pamphlet.

11. Ibid., back cover.

12. [Frank O. Wood], *Instructions for Expectant Mothers* ([Hartford, CT]: 1935). Though no author is given on the pamphlet, internal evidence points to Frank O. Wood, M.D., of Hartford, CT. A copy of this pamphlet is located in files of the American College of Obstetricians and Gynecologists, Washington, DC. I would like to thank Susan Rishworth, archivist there, for her help in locating this material.

13. William M. Hanrahan, *General Instructions to Prospective Mothers* (Chicago, IL: Stewart Printing, 1927). The photocopy given to me by D. O. Carey, D.D.S., 26 March 1981. It was given to his mother in 1932 when his older brother was born.

14. Judith Walzer Leavitt, *Brought to Bed: Childbearing in America: 1750–1950* (New York: Oxford University Press, 1986).

15. "American Academy of Pediatrics: 8th Annual Meeting, June 1938: Roundtable Discussion of Nursing Care in the Newborn Infant," *Journal of Pediatrics* 13 (1938): 434–44, quotation on p. 440. See also Irma Gladys Fuehr, "Hospital Baby," *Hygeia* 17 (1939): 189–90; Velma West Sykes, "Baby's Bath," *Hygeia* 3 (1925): 269–70.

16. William J. Corcoran, "The Baby That Cries at Night," *Hygeia* 7 (1929): 359–61.

17. Benjamin Harris, "'Give Me a Dozen Healthy Infants…': John B. Watson's Popular Advice on Childrearing, Women, and the Family," in *In the Shadow of the Past: Psychology Portrays the Sexes,* ed. Miriam Lewin (New York: Columbia University Press, 1984), 126–53.

18. Elizabeth Thankful Bailey, "Your Healthy Baby: Acquiring Regular Habits," *Woman's World*, June 1930, 29; Philip M. Stimson, "Putting Baby on a Schedule," *Hygeia*, March 1928, 131–32.

19. Emma E. Walker, M.D., "Enemies of the Baby: III—Habits," *Good Housekeeping* 44, no. 5 (1907): 602–3.

20. Francis Tweddell, *A Mother's Guide; A Manual for the Guidance of Mothers and Nurses* (New York: J. Dougherty, 1911), 132–33.

21. This advice was typical in the period. See, for example, Richardson, *Simplifying Motherhood*, which advocates stool training as early as the third or fourth week, 48–50.

22. Roger H. Dennett, M.D., *Healthy Baby; The Care and Feeding of Infants in Sickness and in Health* (New York: Macmillan, 1912). For other examples of pre-Watsonian behaviorism, see L. Emmett Holt, *The Care and Feeding of Children: A Catechism for the Use of Mothers and Children's Nurses* (New York: D. Appleton, 1894).

23. Sidonie M. Gruenberg, Chairman, *Parent Education: Types, Content, Method; Report of the Subcommittee on Types of Parent Education, Content and Method* (New York: Century, 1932).

24. Martha M. Eliot and Lillian R. Freedman, "Four Years of the EMIC Program," *Yale Journal of Biology and Medicine* 19 (1947): 621–35; Louise Sheddan and Helen M. Culp, "Mothers' Classes for Service Men's Wives," *Public Health Nursing* 36 (1944): 97–99.

25. Rima D. Apple, "Liberal Arts or Vocation Training? Home Economics Education for Girls," in *Rethinking Home Economics: Women and the History of a Profession*, ed. Sarah Stage and Virginia B. Vincenti (Ithaca, NY: Cornell University Press, 1997), 79–95.

26. Alma L. Binzel, "For the Homemaker: Making Children Worth While," *Journal of Home Economics* 11 (January 1919): 28.

27. For a case study of this transformation, see Rima D. Apple, *The Challenge of Constantly Changing Times: From Home Economics to Human Ecology at the University of Wisconsin–Madison, 1903–2003* (Madison, WI: Parallel Press, University of Wisconsin–Madison Libraries, 2003).

28. Juliette Low formed the first Girl Guide units in America in 1912, in 1913 she worked for the establishment of a national organization, and in 1915 it became known as the Girl Scouts of America.

29. The Girl Scouts also produced another publication, a journal entitled *The American Girl*. It was not included in this study for several reasons. First, the publication was not required reading for Girl Scouts and in its early years it reached only a relatively small number of Scouts. Second, by the mid-1920s, though the magazine continued under the auspices of the Girl Scout organization, it was conducted as a separate *commercial* publication, its subscription was voluntary, and it was not tied as closely to Girl Scout activities.

30. *75 Years of Girl Scouting* (New York: Girl Scouts of the U.S.A., 1986), 10.

31. W. J. Hoxie, *How Girls Can Help Their Country* (New York: Knickerbocker Press, 1913, 1914), 86–89, 130.

32. *Scouting for Girls: Official Handbook of the Girl Scouts* (New York: Girl Scouts, Inc., 1920), 1.

33. Ibid., 25.

34. Ibid., 105.

35. *Girl Scout Handbook* (New York: Girl Scouts, Inc., 1929), 294.

36. *Girl Scout Programs and Activities* (New York: Girl Scouts, Inc., 1938), 247.

37. G. P. Earnshaw, *Baby's Outfit*, 4th rev. ed. (Newton, MA: Earnshaw Publications, 1933), 3–4.

38. Ibid., 7.

39. Viviana A. Zelizer, *Pricing the Priceless Child: The Changing Social Value of Children* (New York: Basic Books, 1985). New York City statistics are on pp. 29–30.

40. Helen M. Dart, "Maternity and Child Care in Selected Rural Areas of Mississippi," in *Child Care in Rural America* (1921; New York: Arno Press, 1972), 42.

41. Ibid., 44.

42. Viola I. Paradise, *Maternity Care and the Welfare of Young Children in a Homesteading County in Montana, Rural Child Welfare Series No. 3, Bureau Publication No. 34* (Washington, DC: U.S. Department of Labor, Children's Bureau, 1919).

43. Ibid., 73.

44. Ibid., 80–81.

45. See also Frances Sage Bradley and Margaretta A. Williamson, *Rural Children in Selected Counties of North Carolina, Rural Child Welfare Series No. 2, Bureau Publication No. 33* (Washington, DC: U.S. Department of Labor, Children's Bureau, 1918); Florence Brown Sherbon and Elizabeth Moore, *Maternity and Infant Care in Two Rural Counties of Wisconsin, Bureau Publication No. 46, U.S. Department of Labor, Children's Bureau* (Washington, DC: Government Printing Office, 1919). For a similar study conducted two decades later during the Depression, see Margaret Jarman Hagood, *Mothers of the South: Portraiture of the White Tenant Farm Woman* (1939; repr., New York: W. W. Norton, 1977).

46. John E. Anderson, *The Young Child in the Home: A Survey of 3000 American Families: Report of the Committee on Infant and Preschool Child* (New York City: Appleton-Century, 1936). See also Anderson, "The Clientele of a Parental Education Program," *Social and Society* 26 (1927): 178–84; Ruth W. Washburn and Marian C. Putnam, "A Study of Child Care in the First Two Years of Life," *Journal of Pediatrics* 2 (1933): 517–36.

47. Anderson, *The Young Child in the Home*, 73–84.

48. Anderson's tables do not have a category for general physician. We might assume that the category "pediatrician" was intended to encompass all medical doctors. However, the text notes in passing "the absence of pediatricians in rural areas"; this phrase suggests that "pediatricians" refers to medical specialists only.

49. Narrative Report, Catherine McLethie, R.N., Shawno County, August 1942, Wisconsin Bureau of Maternal & Child Health Series 2253, box 13, folder 13, "Wisconsin. Bureau of Maternal & Child Health, Programs & Demonstrations, 1922–1961" (Madison, WI: State Historical Society).

50. For more on rural health care during the Depression, see Lynn Curry, *Modern Mothers in the Heartland: Gender, Health, and Progress in Illinois, 1900–1930* (Columbus: Ohio State University Press, 1999); Michael R. Grey, *New Deal Medicine: The Rural Health Programs of the Farm Security Administration* (Baltimore, MD: Johns Hopkins University Press, 1999).

CHAPTER 4   *"The modern way"*

1. Ruth Williams Thompson, *Training My Babies* (Boston: Gorham Press, 1929).

2. Ibid., 16. For another interesting example of this genre, see Maud Wilde, *The Business of Being a Mother (Manual of Child Training)* (Los Angeles, CA: The author, 1926).

3. For women's lives in the period, see Susan M. Hartmann, *The Home Front and*

Beyond: American Women in the 1940s (Boston: Twayne, 1982); Susan Ware, *Holding Their Own: American Women in the 1930s* (Boston: Twayne, 1982).

4. Thompson, *Training My Babies*, 21–22.

5. Ibid., 23–25.

6. For another example of the steps mothers could take to train their children, see Grace Langdon, "Toilet Training," *Parents Magazine* 6 (1931): 19, 50–51.

7. Mrs. L.J.R. to Grace Abbott, 4 November 1923, letter and the agency's response from Ethel M. Watters, M.D., dated 9 November 1923, are located in Records of the Children's Bureau, Central File, Record Group 102 (hereafter cited as Rec. CB), 1921–28, folder 4–5–3–0, National Archives, Washington, DC. Watters suggested that Mrs. L.J.R. continue with the diet schedule, remarking that today's doctors were recommending more vegetables than earlier, an implication that the doctor Mrs. L.J.R. visited was behind the times.

8. The letters and carbon copies of the responses of Bureau staff are housed in Rec. CB. Historians Nancy Weiss, Molly Ladd-Taylor, and Ralph La Rossa, among others, have studied the collection for insights into the lives of parents in the interwar period. Weiss estimates that as many as 125,000 were received in a single year; La Rossa puts the total number of letters at 400,000. The overwhelming majority were sent by mothers. La Rossa estimates about 5–10 percent were posted by fathers but my survey of the collection suggests that his estimate is overly optimistic. For more on the collection, see Ralph La Rossa, *The Modernization of Fatherhood: A Social and Political History* (Chicago: University of Chicago Press, 1997); Molly Ladd-Taylor, *Raising a Baby the Government Way: Mothers' Letters to the Children's Bureau, 1915–1932* (New Brunswick, NJ: Rutgers University Press, 1986); Nancy Pottisham Weiss, "Mother, the Invention of Necessity: *Baby and Child Care*," *American Quarterly* 29 (1977): 519–46; Weiss, "The Mother-Child Dyad Revisited: Perceptions of Mothers and Children in Twentieth Century Child-Rearing Manuals," *Journal of Social Issues* 34, no. 2 (1978): 29–45.

9. Jacquelyn S. Litt, *Medicalized Motherhood: Perspectives from the Lives of African-American and Jewish Women* (New Brunswick, NJ: Rutgers University Press, 2000). See also Litt, "American Medicine and Divided Motherhood: Three Case Studies from the 1930s and 1940s," *Sociological Quarterly* 38 (1997): 285–302; Litt, "Mothering, Medicalization, and Jewish Identity, 1928–1940," *Gender & Society* 10, no. 2 (1996): 185–98. Another similar, interesting study is Alice Goldstein, Susan Cotts Watkins, and Ann Rosen Spector, "Childhood Health-Care Practices among Italians and Jews in the United States, 1910–1940," *Health Transition Review* 4 (1994): 45–62.

10. Litt, *Medicalized Motherhood*, 13. Neil M. Cowan and Ruth Schwartz Cowan, *Our Parents' Lives: The Americanization of Eastern European Jews* (New York: Basic Books, 1989), substantiates Litt's analysis.

11. Litt, *Medicalized Motherhood*, 52.

12. Ibid., 55–56.

13. Ibid., 60–81.

14. Ibid., 296–97.

15. Carolyn Leonard Carson, "'and the Results Shows Promise . . . ': Physicians,

Childbirth, and Southern Black Migrant Women, 1916–1930: Pittsburgh as a Case Study," *Journal of American Ethnic History* 14 (1994): 32–64.

16. Narrative Report, Monroe and Jackson Counties, 22 April 1938, Camp Douglass Route, Wisconsin Bureau of Maternal & Child Health, Programs & Demonstrations, Wisconsin Historical Society Archives (hereafter cited as WBM&CH), Series 2253, box 13, folder 3.

17. Narrative Report, Constance E. Carmody, R.N., Marathon County, June 1940, WBM&CH, Series 2253, box 12, folder 7.

18. Florence Brown Sherbon and Elizabeth Moore, *Maternity and Infant Care in Two Rural Counties of Wisconsin, Bureau Publication No. 46, U.S. Department of Labor, Children's Bureau* (Washington: Government Printing Office, 1919), 42.

19. Narrative Report, Monroe and Jackson Counties, Nov. 1937, and Narrative Report, (Miss) Marie Skog, Demonstration Nurse, Monroe and Jackson Counties, December 1937, both in WBM&CH, Series 2253, box 13, folder 3.

20. Quoted in Ann Hulbert, *Raising America: Experts, Parents, and a Century of Advice About Children* (New York: Knopf, 2003), 183.

21. Estelle Mulqueen Reilly, *Common Sense for Mothers on Bringing Up Your Children from Babyhood to Adolescence* (New York: Funk & Wagnalls, 1935), 1–2. Reilly sent a prepublication copy of her book to the Children's Bureau, asking for the staff's opinion. As she explained in her cover letter, the book "contains much of what I've learned under the guidance of the best doctors and nurses, about how to bring up my own family of three boys and four girls." Letter from Reilly to Katherine Lenroot, dated 28 January 1935, Rec. CB, 1933–36, folder 4–8–0.

22. May C. Whitaker, *Mothercraft: A Primer for Parents* (Cleveland, OH: Judson, 1926), 65–67.

23. Ibid., 17–19.

24. A.E.F., 24 May 1918 letter to the Children's Bureau and the Bureau's reply, dated 29 May 1918, Rec. CB, 1914–20, folder 4–4–0.

25. Quoted in Eleanor Arnold, ed., *Voices of American Homemakers* (Bloomington: Indiana University Press, 1985), 103.

26. Lenore Pelham Friedrich, "I Had a Baby," *Atlantic Monthly* 163 (1939): 461–65.

27. Kathleen Norris, *The Fun of Being a Mother* (Garden City, NY: Doubleday, Page, 1927), 12.

28. Mrs. H.A.C., letter dated 23 July 1915, with reply by Mrs. Max West, Rec. CB, 1914–20, folder 4–4.

29. Mrs. J.S., letter dated 6 May 1929, and agency's reply, Rec. CB, 1929–32, folder 4–8–1–1.

30. Mrs. H.L., letter dated 22 November 1938, and the agency's reply, dated 1 December 1938, Rec. CB, 1937–40, folder 4–1–2–1.

31. Quoted in Deborah Fink, *Agrarian Women: Wives and Mothers in Rural Nebraska, 1880–1940* (Chapel Hill: University of North Carolina Press, 1992), 161.

32. Doris W. McCray, "A Housewife Looks at the Committee on Foods," *Hygeia* 13 (1935): 446–50, 77.

33. Summary Report, 31 July 1942, Dr. [Marie] Wittler, Center held at Marshall, WI, WM&CH, box 4, file: Dane County (Center Narratives).

34. Mrs. M.G.P., letter dated 28 November 1927, with reply, Rec. CB, 1921–28, folder 4–5– 3.

35. Mrs. E.L.H., letter dated 17 July 1930, Rec. CB, 1929–32, folder 4–8–1–2–4.

36. Mrs. E.O.T., letter dated 21 September 1925, Rec. CB, 1925–28, folder 4–5–3–0.

37. Mrs. B.R.N., letter dated 14 August 1928, Rec. CB, 1925–28, folder 4–5–3–2.

38. Mrs. H.M., letter dated 11 January 1939, Rec. CB, 1937–40, folder 4–8–0.

39. Narrative Report, Sadie Engesether, R.N., Polk and Burnett Counties, May 1937, WBM&CH, Series 2253, box 13, folder 8.

40. Narrative Report, Monroe and Jackson Counties, 9 June 1938, Fairchild, WBM&CH, Series 2253, box 13, folder 3.

41. Narrative Report, [Lelia J. Johnson, R.N.], [Jackson County], October [1939], WBM&CH, Series 2253, box 12, folder 8.

42. Narrative Report, Mildred Cook, R.N., Brown-Kewaunee County, October 1936, WBM&CH, Series 2253, box 11, folder 11.

43. Narrative Report, Kathryn Lynch, R.N., Marathon County, January 1940, WBM&CH, Series 2253, box 12, folder 17.

44. Mrs. V.K., letter dated 15 August 1939, Rec. CB, 1937–40, folder 4–1–3–1.

45. Mrs. M.B., letter dated 28 January 1926, Rec. CB, 1925–28, folder 4–5–3–2. Spelling and grammar in the original.

46. Mrs. M.B.W., letter dated 21 May 1915, Rec. CB, 1914–20, folder 4–5–3–2. Spelling and grammar in the original.

47. J.B., "My $100 Baby," *Cosmopolitan* 108, no. 6 (1940): 54–55, 88.

48. Mary Breckinridge, *Wide Neighborhoods: A Story of the Frontier Nursing Service* (New York: Harper & Brothers, 1952), 61.

49. Mrs. R.E.D., "Letters Worth Reading," *Farmer's Wife* 28, no. 355 (1925).

50. I. L. Smith, "We Modern Parents," *Atlantic Monthly* 152 (1933): 94–99.

51. Narrative Report, Dr. Bessie Mae Beach, Dane County, DeForest, WBM&CH, Series 2253, box 6, folder 15.

52. R.W.B., "Infant Feeding," *Hygeia* 7 (1929): 934.

53. Clementine Wheeler, "Jig-Time Formula," *Parents Magazine* 2, no. 3 (1947): 165– 67.

54. Narrative Reports, Nathalie Voge, Marinette County, July 1942, WBM&CH, Series 2253, box 13, folder 1.

55. Judith Walzer Leavitt, *Brought to Bed: Childbearing in America: 1750–1950* (New York: Oxford University Press, 1986); Rosemary Stevens, *In Sickness and in Wealth: American Hospitals in the Twentieth Century*, expansion of 1989 edition with new preface (Baltimore, MD: Johns Hopkins University Press, 1999).

56. Department of Pediatrics, *Information for the Mother Following Delivery of the Baby* (New York City: Lenox Hill Hospital, [1944]). The booklet is undated but contains the statistics and formula for a child born in 1944.

57. Lois Huntington, "Schedule for a New Baby's Mother," *Parents Magazine*, September 1942, 24–25, 61.

58. Sarah K. Hepburn, "Caring for the New Baby," *Parents Magazine*, December 1935, 21, 95.

CHAPTER 5   *"Now I know that an authority has the same opinion as mine"*

1. Benjamin Spock, *The Common Sense Book of Baby and Child Care* (New York: Duell, Sloan and Pearce, 1946).
2. Niles Newton, *The Family Book of Child Care* (New York: Harper and Brothers, 1957).
3. L. Emmett Holt, Jr., *The Good Housekeeping Book of Baby and Child Care* (New York: Popular Library, 1957).
4. "Bringing Up Baby on Books . . . Revolution and Counterrevolution in Child Care," *Newsweek*, 16 May 1955, 64–68.
5. Gretchen Krueger, "Death Be Not Proud: Children, Families, and Cancer in Postwar America," *Bulletin of the History of Medicine* 78 (2004): 836–63. For more on mother-blaming, see Molly Ladd-Taylor and Lauri Umansky, *"Bad" Mothers: The Politics of Blame in Twentieth-Century America* (New York: New York University Press, 1998). For more on the hope of contemporary science and medicine, see Allan M. Brandt and Martha Gardner, "The Golden Age of Medicine?," in *Medicine in the Twentieth Century,* ed. Roger Cooter and John Pickstone (Amsterdam: Harwood Academic Publishers, 2000), 21–37; Paul Starr, *The Social Transformation of American Medicine* (New York: Basic Books, 1982).
6. Katherine Burns, "The 2 Weeks after the First 10 Days," *American Home*, September 1940, 38, 54.
7. S.R., personal communication, 3 July 2001; Edith Appleton, "Bathing and Feeding the Baby," *Hygiea* 23 (1945): 594–97.
8. See Edith B. Jackson, "Mothers and Babies Together," *Parents Magazine*, October 1947, 18–19, 146–49, for a good example of Jackson's own descriptions of the routines and her rationale for instituting them.
9. Sara Lee Silberman, "Pioneering in Family-Centered Maternity and Infant Care: Edith B. Jackson and the Yale Rooming-in Research Project," *Bulletin of the History of Medicine* 64 (1990): 262–87.
10. Marilyn Parks Davis, "The 'Rooming in' Plan," *Hygiea* 26 (1948): 784–85, 827–28. See also "Babies Are Welcome Here," *Woman's Home Companion* 76 (January 1949): 116–19; Rhoda Hanson, "You Can Nurse Your Baby," *Parents Magazine* 23, no. 5 (1948): 23, 136.
11. Jackson, "Mothers and Babies Together," 148.
12. Henry L. Barnet, "A Note on Experiences with a Rooming-in Arrangement for Newborn Infants in a Small Hospital," *Journal of Pediatrics* 31 (1947): 49–53, quotation on p. 51. See also Herbert Thoms, *Training for Childbirth: A Program of Natural Childbirth with Rooming-In* (New York: McGraw-Hill, 1950).
13. Though Jackson's rooming-in plan garnered widespread praise, the realities of the postwar baby boom, which flooded hospital obstetrical wards and overwhelmed critically short-handed nursing staff, limited the number of hospitals that could attempt to implement it. It was not until the 1970s that other, more open rooming-in plans were established in hospitals throughout the United States.
14. Arnold Gesell and Frances L. Ilg, *Infant and Child in the Culture of Today: The Guidance of Development in Home and Nursery School* (New York: Harper & Brothers, 1943).

15. C. Anderson Aldrich and Mary M. Aldrich, *Babies Are Human Beings: An Interpretation of Growth* (New York: Macmillan, 1938).

16. Dorothy V. Whipple, M.D., *Our American Babies: The Art of Baby Care* (New York: M. Barrows 1943), viii. For another book in this genre, see Evelyn Barkins, *The Doctor Has a Baby* (New York: Creative Age Press, 1947), in which the doctor is actually the father, but the text is written from the perspective of the doctor's wife, a mother of three.

17. Whipple, *Our American Babies*, viii.

18. Ibid., 108.

19. Lynn Z. Bloom, *Doctor Spock: Biography of a Conservative Radical* (Indianapolis: Bobbs-Merrill, 1972); Margaret Talbot, "A Spock-Marked Generation," *New York Times Magazine*, 3 January 1999.

20. Bloom, *Doctor Spock*, 104.

21. Quoted ibid., 107.

22. Spock, *The Common Sense Book of Baby and Child Care*, 1.

23. Walter W. Sackett, Jr., *Bringing Up Babies: A Family Doctor's Practical Approach to Child Care* (New York: Harper & Row, 1962), xvii–xviii.

24. Ibid., 5.

25. Ibid., 64.

26. Ibid.

27. Mrs. S.M., letter dated 18 September 1945, with reply from Katherine Bains, Rec. CB, 1945–48, folder 4–8–6–4.

28. For a contemporary perspective on *Infant Care*, see Robert M. Yoder, "Were You Boiled as a Baby?," *Saturday Evening Post* 232 (1959): 25, 67–68.

29. For more on the transition from strict regimentation to a more permissive practice in this period, see William M. Tuttle, Jr., "America's Children in an Era of War, Hot and Cold: The Holocaust, the Bomb, and Childrearing in the 1940s," in *Rethinking Cold War Culture*, ed. Peter J. Kuznick and James Gilbert (Washington, DC: Smithsonian Institution Press, 2001), 14–34.

30. Spock, *The Common Sense Book of Baby and Child Care*, 3. My emphasis.

31. Benjamin Spock, John Reinhart, and Wayne Miller, *A Baby's First Year* (New York: Pocket Books, 1956).

32. Benjamin Spock, *Dr. Benjamin Spock's Baby and Child Care* (New York: Pocket Books, 1957), 150.

33. Examples of Dr. Hirshberg's pads may be found in the Archives of the Hartford (Connecticut) Medical Society. I thank archivist Diane Neumann for helping me locate these.

34. See, for example, Rima D. Apple, *Mothers and Medicine: A Social History of Infant Feeding* (Madison: University of Wisconsin Press, 1987), 121–22.

35. Isaac A. Abt, *Baby Doctor* (New York: Whittlesey, 1944), 294.

36. Spock, *The Common Sense Book of Baby and Child Care*, 1.

37. Mrs. M.J.W. of Fort Lewis, WA, letter dated 13 July 1954, Benjamin Spock Archives, Special Collections Research Library, Syracuse University (hereafter cited as Spock Archives), box 2, folder: July 1954.

38. Mrs. K.B.B., Stanford University, CA, letter dated 20 May 1949, Spock Archives, box 1, folder 19.

39. Mrs. R.D.S., Concord, CA, letter dated 10 October 1954, Spock Archives, box 2, folder: September 1954.

40. Mrs. H.W., Rolla, MO, letter dated 4 August 1954, Spock Archives, box 2, folder: August 1954. Mrs. H.W.'s husband was stationed at Fort Leonard Wood.

41. P.C., Butte, MT, letter dated 22 November 1954, Spock Archives, box 2, folder: Nov. 1954.

42. Mrs. W.S.B., Long Beach, CA, letter dated 19 July 1954, Spock Archives, box 2, folder: July 1954.

43. Mrs. T. T., Flemington, NJ, letter 25 Oct. 1954, Spock Archives, box 2, folder: Oct. 1954.

44. Holt, *The Good Housekeeping Book of Baby and Child Care*, xix. Emphasis in the original.

45. Herman N. Bundesen, M.D., *The Baby Manual: A Practical Guide from Early Pregnancy through the Second Year of Life* (New York: Simon and Schuster, 1944), 1.

46. Harry R. Litchfield and Leon H. Dembo, *A Pediatric Manual for Mothers* (New York: Grune & Stratton, 1951), 1. Emphasis in the original.

47. Dr. Edward Glaber, quoted in "Michigan's Expectant Parents' Classes Point the Way," *The Mother* 13, no. 4 (1952): 14–15.

48. "Information for Expectant Mothers," (Chicago: Chicago Lying-In Hospital and Dispensary, 1958), 11–12.

49. Benjamin Spock, "Baby vs. Sleep," *Consumer Reports*, (Jan. 1950): 28–30.

50. Niles Anne Newton, introduction to *Pregnancy, Birth, and the Newborn Baby: A Publication for Parents*, ed. Boston Children's Medical Center (Boston: Seymour Lawrence, 1972), 39.

51. Penny Simkin, Janet Whalley, and Anne Keppler, *Pregnancy, Childbirth, and the Newborn: The Complete Guide* (New York: Simon & Schuster, 1992[?]), 13.

52. Sackett, *Bringing Up Babies*, 3.

53. Grantly Dick-Read, *Childbirth Without Fear: The Principles of Natural Childbirth* (New York: Harper, 1944).

54. Marjorie Karmel, *Thank You, Dr. Lamaze: A Mother's Experience in Painless Childbirth* (Philadelphia: Lippincott, 1959).

55. Mary Thomas, ed., *Post-War Mothers: Childbirth Letters to Grantly Dick-Read, 1946–1956* (Rochester, NY: University of Rochester Press, 1997) contains a selection of letters from the Dick-Read Collection at the Contemporary Medical Archives Center at the Wellcome Library for the History and Understanding of Medicine, London, UK (hereafter cited as Dick-Read Archives]). There is a significantly greater collection at the Wellcome.

56. Mrs. L.S., Bronx, NY, letter dated 22 April 1947, Dick-Read Archives, box 48, folder D124.

57. M.I. (Mrs. C.G.I.), letter dated 9 September 1947, Dick-Read Archives, box 46, folder 106. Stress in the original.

58. Lena S. Hayman, to Mrs. R.S., letter dated 28 August 1964, CB Rec., 1963–66, folder 4–12–6–3–5.

59. Spock, *The Common Sense Book of Baby and Child Care*, 502–3.

60. Mrs. B.J.T., Roanoke, VA, letter dated 20 August 1956, Spock Archives, box 3, folder: August 1956.

61. Spock's reply to Mrs. B.J.T, Spock Archives, box 3, folder: September 1956.
62. Spock, *Dr. Benjamin Spock's Baby and Child Care*, 593.
63. Benjamin Spock, "Dr. Spock Talks with Mothers," *Ladies' Home Journal* 71, no. 7 (1954): 42–43. Many of these columns were collected and enlarged in Benjamin Spock, *Dr. Spock Talks with Mothers: Growth and Guidance* (Boston: Houghton Mifflin, 1961).
64. V.S., Brooklyn, NY, letter dated 2 August 1954, Spock Archives, box 2, folder: August 1954.
65. Mrs. J.S., Milwaukee, WI, letter dated 17 July 1954, Spock Archives, box 2, folder: July 1954.
66. Mrs. W.C.K., Chicago, IL, letter dated 19 July 1954, Spock Archives, box 2, folder: July 1954.
67. J. and J.S., Boise, ID, letter dated 8 August 1954, Spock Archives, box 2, folder: August 1954.
68. Mrs. W.W.M., Jr., Lima, MT, letter dated 20 July 1954, Spock Archives, box 2, folder: July 1954. See also T.M.Z. (Mrs. M. J. Z.), Islip Terrace, NY, letter dated 23 July 1954, Spock Archives, box 2, folder: July 1954.
69. A.M.P., no address given, letter dated 19 July 1954, Spock Archives, box 2, folder: July 1954.
70. Mrs. N.H., Buffalo, NY, letter dated 28 July 1954, Spock Archives, box 2, folder: July 1954.

CHAPTER 6   *"Use it to guide, not to dictate"*

1. Quoted in Carr-Eising, "Parenting by the Book," *Capital Times*, 29 June 1993.
2. See, for example, the hospital standards promulgated by the American Academy of Pediatrics, Committee on Fetus and Newborn, *Standards and Recommendations for Hospital Care of Newborn Infants*, 6th ed. (Evanston, IL: Academy, 1977).
3. There is a huge literature on the League and its history. Some of the most recent publications include Linda M. Blum, *At the Breast: Ideologies of Breastfeeding and Motherhood in the Contemporary United States* (Boston: Beacon Press, 1999); Julie Dejager Ward, *La Leche League: At the Crossroads of Medicine, Feminism, and Religion* (Chapel Hill: University of North Carolina Press, 2000). On similar developments in another context, see Kerreen M. Reiger, *Our Bodies, Our Babies: The Forgotten Women's Movement* (Melbourne: Melbourne University Press, 2001).
4. Boston Women's Health Book Collective, *Our Bodies, Ourselves: A Course by and for Women* (Boston: New England Free Press, 1971), 1. Much has been written about the origins of the Boston Women's Health Book Collective. See, for example, Wendy Kline, "'Please Include This in Your Book': Readers Respond to *Our Bodies, Ourselves*," *Bulletin of the History of Medicine* 79 (2005): 81–110.
5. Boston Women's Health Book Collective, *Ourselves and Our Children* (New York: Random House, 1978).
6. Ibid., 232. Emphasis in the original.

7. Ibid., 231.
8. Laurence G. Roth, Louis E. Green, and John T. Chua, "Advice to the . . . Prenatal Patients" (Batavia, NY: Genesee Medical Specialists Center, 1974), 45.
9. Ibid., 20.
10. Henry Harris, "Foreword: 'A Word from the Doctor,'" in *What to Expect the First Year*, by Arlene Eisenberg, Heidi E. Murkoff, and Sandee E. Hathaway (New York: Workman, 1989, 1996), xxii.
11. Susan J. Douglas and Meredith W. Michaels, *The Mommy Myth: The Idealization of Motherhood and How It Has Undermined Women* (New York: Free Press, 2004), 229–30, 8–9.
12. "Moms on AOL Trade Parenting Tips," *Capital Times*, 28 March 1997; "Mothers Connect Online with Other Moms," *Capital Times*, 12 September 1996.
13. Berkeley Parents Network Web site, http://parents.berkeley.edu/ (accessed 15 March 2005).
14. Accessed 15 March 2005.
15. Pat Boone and Shirley Boone, preface to *Mother's Medicine*, by Nancy Moore Thurmond (New York: William Morrow, 1979), 13.
16. Nancy Moore Thurmond, *Mother's Medicine* (New York: William Morrow, 1979), 161.
17. She recognized that not all mothers have access to a private physician. In these cases she recommended that mothers visit a nearby clinic for the benefits of medical attention. But the majority of the book assumed that the mother has carefully selected a pediatrician, whom she sees regularly.
18. Thurmond, *Mother's Medicine*, 163–64.
19. See, for example, Sara Harkness et al., "Ask the Doctor: The Negotiation of Cultural Models in American Parent-Pediatrician Discourse," in *Parents' Cultural Belief Systems*, ed. Sara Harkness (New York: Guilford Press, 1996), 289–90.
20. Thomas A. Cable and Lee A. Rothenberger, "Breast-Feeding Behavioral Patterns among La Leche League Mothers: A Descriptive Study," *Pediatrics* 73, no. 6 (1984): 835.
21. Ibid., 830.
22. Judith Martin, "Dr. Spock Confesses to Errors," *State Journal*, 3 October 1971.
23. Robert V. Johnson, ed., *Mayo Clinic Complete Book of Pregnancy and Baby's First Year* (New York: William Morrow, 1994), xi.
24. Frances Drew, "You, Your Doctors, and the Health Care System," in *Every Woman's Health*, ed. D. S. Thompson and Helene MacLean (New York: Simon & Schuster, 1993), 528.
25. Dr. C. H. Kempe, commenting on Betsy Lozoff, "The Effects of Hospital Routines on the Mother-Newborn Relationship," in *Child Advocacy and Pediatrics, 8th Ross Roundtable on Critical Approaches to Common Pediatric Problems* (Columbus, OH: Ross Laboratories, 1978), 67. See also Dianne Hales, "Getting Along with Your Child's Doctor," *Working Mother*, October 1992, 132; Katherine Karlsrud and Dodi Schultz, "Choosing Your Baby's Doctor," *Parents Magazine*, 19 February 1985, 174.
26. Morton Lebow and Laurie Hall, "How Do Patients Rate Your Practice?" *Contemporary OB/GYN*, September 1988, 19–20, 22–23, 27, 30.

27. Dean Health system advertisement, *Capital Times* (Madison, WI), 17 August 2005.

28. David Brunworth and Scott Rigden, *Patient Education for the Family: Practical Patient Aids for Health Care Professionals* (Hagerstown, MD: Harper & Row, 1979).

29. Quotation from a promotional brochure for Diane McClurg Sanders, *Beginnings: A Practical Guide through Your Pregnancy* (Seattle, WA: Practice Development, [1989]), a series of pamphlets available for physicians to purchase for their patients. Among the other benefits touted for the series were "improved patient compliance and outcomes," "increase[d] patient referrals to your practice," and "a marketing tool for your obstetrics service." Brochure located in the Archives of the Library of the American College of Obstetrics and Gynecology.

30. Task Force on Medical Liability, American Academy of Pediatrics, *An Introduction to Medical Liability for Pediatricians*, 2nd ed. (1985), 11.

31. E. Rick Beebe, "Expectant Parent Classes," *The Family Coordinator* 27, no. 1 (1978): 55–58.

32. Rosemary Stevens, *In Sickness and in Wealth: American Hospitals in the Twentieth Century*, expansion of 1989 edition with new preface (Baltimore, MD: Johns Hopkins University Press, 1999), xvii–xix.

33. Alan F. Guttmacher, *Pregnancy, Birth, and Family Planning: A Guide for Expectant Parents in the 1970's* (New York: New American Library, 1973), 389.

34. Joyce L. Kieffer, *To Have...To Hold...: A Parents' Guide to Childbirth and Early Parenting* (Harrisburg, PA: Training Resource Associates, 1981), 63.

35. Helena Znaniecki Lopata, *Occupation: Housewife* (New York: Oxford University Press, 1971), 182–223.

36. Alice Petlock Pauser, "Memoirs of a Very Pregnant First-Time Mother," *Capital Times*, 6 November 1984.

37. Jane Lazarre, *The Mother Knot* (New York: Dell, 1976).

38. Ibid., 51–52.

39. Ibid., 96–98.

40. Sonia Taitz, *Mothering Heights: Reclaiming Motherhood from the Experts* (New York: William Morrow, 1992), 215–16.

41. Erica Goode, "Two Experts Do Battle over Potty Training," *New York Times Magazine*, 12 January 1999.

42. Samantha Critchell, "Parenting Author Didn't Expect Such Renown," *Wisconsin State Journal*, 9 May 2004.

43. Heidi Murkoff, "The Real Parenting Expert Is—You," *Newsweek*, Fall-Winter 2000, 20–21.

44. The original *What to Expect When You Are Expecting* was written by Heidi E. Murkoff and her mother, Arlene Eisenberg. They are joined in *What to Expect the First Year* by Murkoff's sister-in-law, Sandee Hathaway. Since Eisenberg's death, Murkoff and Hathaway have continued the series.

45. Arlene Eisenberg, Heidi E. Murkoff, and Sandee E. Hathaway, *What to Expect the First Year* (New York: Workman, 1989, 1996), 202.

46. Ibid., 203.

47. Ibid., 25.

48. Jennifer Reese, "Expecting the Worst," in *Mothers Who Think*, ed. Camille Peri and Kate Moss (New York: Washington Square Press, Pocket Books, 1999), 155–59.

49. Susan Walzer, *Thinking About the Baby: Gender and Transitions into Parenthood* (Philadelphia: Temple University Press, 1998), 37–41.

Conclusion   *"I wanted to do it right"*

1. Family bed, also referred to as co-sleeping, involves the baby and young child sleeping with the parents. Today it is more typical that a child has his or her own room, or at least his or her own crib. Recently, the idea of the family bed has been popularized in the United States primarily by advocates of attachment parenting.

2. Frances Bauer, "Plight of the Brand-New Parent," *New York Times Magazine*, 7 April 1963, 132.

3. *New Yorker* cartoon, 2 August 1999.

4. Muffy Mead-Ferro, *Confessions of a Slacker Mom* (Cambridge, MA: Da Capo Lifelong, 2004), 131.

5. Ibid., 134.

6. Ibid., 136.

7. Figures from U.S. Department of Commerce, Historical Statistics, Series B 149–166 and Series B 181–192, "Historical Statistics of the United States: Colonial Times to 1970, Part 1," (Washington, DC: U.S. Bureau of the Census, 1975).

8. U.S. Department of Health and Human Services, "Special Reports from the National Vital Statistics Reports" (Washington, DC: Centers for Disease Control and Prevention, 2004), 14; U.S. Department of Health and Human Services, "Vital Statistics of the United States, 1993," (Washington, DC: Centers for Disease Control and Prevention, 1999), Table 1–1.

9. Margaret K. Nelson, "The Effect of Childbirth Preparation on Women of Different Social Classes," *Journal of Health and Social Behavior* 23, no. 4 (1982): 350.

10. David I. MacLeod, *The Age of the Child: Children in America, 1890–1920* (New York: Twayne, 1998), 32–74.

11. Clair Brown, *American Standards of Living, 1918–1988* (Cambridge, MA: Blackwell, 1994), 140–43, 233–37, 320–26, 419–24.

12. U.S. Department of Commerce, "Historical Statistics of the United States: Colonial Times to 1970, Part 1," Table B 20–27; U.S. Department of Health and Human Services, "Special Reports from the National Vital Statistics Reports" (Washington, DC: Centers for Disease Control and Prevention, 2004), 15.

13. Susan Hassebrock, *The First 12 Months of Motherhood* (Los Angeles: Lowell House, 1996), 207.

14. Lynn Johnston, "For Better or for Worse" (Madison, WI: *Capital Times*, 1997).

15. Christina Baker Kline, ed., introduction to *Child of Mine: Writers Talk about the First Year of Motherhood* (New York: Hyperion, 1997), 1–2.

16. Ibid., 5.

17. Claire McCarthy, *Learning How the Heart Beats: The Making of a Pediatrician* (New York: Viking, 1995), 141–43.

18. Ibid., 146–48.
19. Quoted in Katie Hafner, "Can the Internet Cure the Common Cold?" *New York Times*, 9 July 1998.
20. "Vital decisions: How Internet users decide what information to trust when they or their loved ones are sick," http://www.pewinternet.org/pdfs/PIP_Vital_Decisions_May2002.pdf (accessed 16 May 2005).
21. Quoted in Hafner, "Can the Internet Cure the Common Cold?"
22. An example of this tension between parents and physicians is the question of the extent of treatment for newborns with birth defects and/or very low birth weight. For a recent analysis of the historically shifting relationships of parents and health care practitioners in this arena, published by an internist at Columbia University, see Barron H. Lerner, "Playing God with Birth Defects in the Nursery," *New York Times*, 14 June 2005.
23. Blanche Beal Lowe, "Growing up in Kansas," *Kansas History* 8 (1985): 36–53.
24. U.S. Department of Health, Education, and Welfare, Children's Bureau, *Infant Care*, Publication No. 8 (Washington, DC: U.S. Printing Office, 1951), 100.
25. "Change Noted in Infant Sleeping Practices," *NICHD News Notes*, October 1995.
26. Beatrice B. Whiting, "Folk Wisdom and Child Rearing," *Merrill-Palmer Quarterly* 20 (1974): 12–13. See also Jane E. Brody, "How to Keep Toilet Training from Being a Power Struggle," *New York Times*, 3 August 1999.
27. Rima D. Apple, *Mothers and Medicine: A Social History of Infant Feeding* (Madison, WI: University of Wisconsin Press, 1987), passim.
28. Quoted in Sheryl Gay Stolberg, "The Big Decisions? They're All Yours," *New York Times*, 25 June 2000. See also Gina Kolata, "Women Want Control, Just Not All the Time," *New York Times*, 22 June 1997; Jan Hoffman, "Awash in Information, Patients Face a Lonely, Uncertain Road," *New York Times*, 14 August 2005.
29. Quotation from Nina Bernstein, "Trial Begins for Mother in Breast-Fed Infant's Starvation Death," *New York Times*, 28 April 1999. Also Nina Bernstein, "Mother Charged with Starving Baby Tells of Frantic Effort to Save Him," *New York Times*, 19 May 1999; Nina Bernstein, "Mother Convicted in Infant's Starvation Death Gets 5 Years' Probation," *New York Times*, 9 September 1999; Nina Bernstein, "Placing the Blame in an Infant's Death," *New York Times*, 15 May 1999; Rachel L. Swarns, "Mother Who May Have Fed Her Son Improperly Is Charged in His Death," *New York Times*, 1 October 1999.

INDEX

AAUW. *See* American Association of University Women

Abbott, John S. C., 4

Abt, Isaac, 57–58, 122–23

advertising, 71–75, 77, 78, 122, 140–41

advice (on infant care): advertising as source of, 71–75, 77, 78, 122, 140–41; for African American mothers, 39, 47, 67, 80–81; books as source of, 1–4, 7, 8, 12, 13–15, 22, 25–26, 57, 60, 76–81, 92–94, 100, 101, 107–9, 116–28, 130–31, 139–40, 146, 150–58, 160–61; contradictory, 28–30, 59, 86–87, 96, 100–102, 122–23, 149–51, 154; current sources of, 1; female networks as source of, 8, 11, 23, 25–27; for immigrant mothers, 15, 38–40, 47, 61; internet as source of, 1, 140–41, 146, 153, 157, 161, 162; magazines as source of, 1, 7, 13–15, 18, 26, 27–35, 60–61, 77–79, 92, 95, 99–100, 108, 122, 123, 126, 140, 146, 153, 157, 158; for middle-class mothers, 15, 36, 48–49, 56, 59, 123; moral, 4, 26; mothers as incapable of raising healthy children without medical, 14, 16–18, 37–39, 94–95, 121–23, 166–67; newspapers as source of, 7, 77, 123, 149; nurses as source of, 24–25, 33, 52, 81–82, 105–6, 109–10, 115–16, 127, 142, 146, 158; overwhelming amount of, 150–53, 155–57, 160–62, 166, 167; pamphlets as source of, 46–47, 49, 50–52, 55, 58–60, 75, 77–81, 85–86, 94–97, 99, 101, 120, 127, 144; as *Perfect Motherhood* focus, 8–10; physical health as emphasis of nineteenth-century, 6–7, 166; physicians as source of, 1, 7, 8–10, 12–13, 21, 32–33, 37–38, 42, 43, 47, 50–53, 59, 64–67, 70–75, 86–88, 92–93, 95–96, 99, 104, 111, 116–28, 146, 155–56, 158; psychological health as emphasis of twentieth century, 7, 65, 107–8, 117–20, 126, 128, 166; radio programs as source of, 7, 140, 146; resistance to, 47–48, 90–92, 149; scientific motherhood as breaking down female networks for, 18, 19, 34–35, 71, 75, 81, 88–90, 106, 127, 139, 168, 179n. 36; television programs as source of, 7, 140, 146; for working-class women, 15, 38, 47, 56, 61, 80. *See also* education; health; infant care; infant mortality and morbidity; scientific motherhood; *specific issues, such as bathing, feeding, toilet training*

About the Author

Rima D. Apple is Professor at the University of Wisconsin–Madison with a joint appointment in the School of Human Ecology and the Women's Studies Program. She is an affiliate of the Department of Medical History and Bioethics and a member of the Science and Technology Studies Program. She has published extensively in the history of women's health, the history of motherhood, and the history of nutrition. Among her books are *Vitamania: Vitamins in American Culture* (New Brunswick, NJ: Rutgers University Press, 1996), which received the Kremers Award in 1998 from the American Institute of the History of Pharmacy; and *Mothers and Medicine: A Social History of Infant Feeding, 1890–1950* (Madison: University of Wisconsin Press, 1987).